Christianity in the Twenty-first Century

Christianity in the Twenty-first Century

Reflections on the Challenges Ahead

ROBERT WUTHNOW

New York   Oxford
OXFORD UNIVERSITY PRESS
1993

Oxford University Press

Oxford   New York   Toronto
Delhi   Bombay   Calcutta   Madras   Karachi
Kuala Lumpur   Singapore   Hong Kong   Tokyo
Nairobi   Dar es Salaam   Cape Town
Melbourne   Auckland

and associated companies in
Berlin   Ibadan

Copyright © 1993 by Robert Wuthnow

Published by Oxford University Press, Inc.
200 Madison Avenue, New York, New York 10016

Oxford is a registered trademark of Oxford University Press, Inc.

Library of Congress Cataloging-in Publication Data
Wuthnow, Robert.
Christianity in the twenty-first century : reflections
on the challenges ahead / Robert Wuthnow.
p. cm.   Includes bibliographical references and index.
ISBN 0—19—507957—4
1. Christianity—United States.
2. Twenty-first century—Forecasts.
I. Title.
BR526.W88   1993   277.3'08—dc20
92—28689

1 3 5 7 9 8 6 4 2

Printed in the United States of America
on acid-free paper

Contents

— II —

**Ethical Challenges:
Role Models, Stories, and Learning How to Care**

— III —

**Doctrinal Challenges:
Pluralism, Polarity, and the Character of Belief**

—— IV ——

**Political Challenges:
Christianity and Conflict in the Public Realm**

—— V ——

**Cultural Challenges:
The Possibilities of Faith for Constructing Personal Lives**

Christianity in the Twenty-first Century

Introduction:
The Future in
the Present

In the past few years I have had the privilege of addressing dozens of audiences composed of church leaders from virtually all denominations and faith traditions. Listening to their comments and questions, I have come to the conclusion that they are intensely concerned about the future. They are not worried, but concerned, wanting to be effective in the years ahead and wondering how best to do that.

Christianity has always taught its followers to be mindful of the future. Jesus instructed his disciples to watch the signs of the times lest the Son of Man catch them unprepared. The early Christians eagerly awaited the bodily return of their Lord as the new king of Israel. Many believers have continued to do so over the centuries. Some have identified a specific date when great tribulations marking the end times would begin. Others have expectantly hoped for the kingdom of God to appear on earth. Still others have articulated a vision of hope to sustain themselves through the dark hours of personal trauma.

History is punctuated with special times that evoke heightened interest in the future. Birthdays and anniversaries prompt us in our personal lives to think about what may come in the year ahead. National holidays, such as Independence Day, generally elicit speeches about the country's priorities for the future. There are great ceremonial occasions, too, for collective reminiscing and looking ahead: the two-hundredth anniversary of our nation's founding, the bicentennial of the U.S. Constitution, the five-hundredth anniversary of Columbus's voyage to the New World.

When I was a child I realized one day that if Providence was kind there was a good chance I would live to see the year 2000. What a thought that was! Not only was this the beginning of a new century; it was the start of a whole new millennium. My grandfather could remember when dates didn't begin with the numerals "19." But nobody could remember when dates didn't start with "1." Someday, that would all be in the past and our calendar would have dates starting with "2."

Turning points of this kind seem to bear down upon us with special gravity, forcing us to ask what kind of people we are, whether we have been good stewards in the past, and how we can prepare to meet the challenges ahead. An ending of one time period lifts our sights from the rhythms of each day, directing our attention toward longer time frames. We want to know what lies ahead.

But do we really? This question has been much debated. If we knew what was coming, couldn't we plan better, capitalizing on the opportunities and avoiding the worst pitfalls? Yet if we really knew, wouldn't that in some way diminish the very essence of our humanity? Either we would know, and lose our freedom because nothing could be changed, or else we could change things so much that our knowledge of the future would be virtually useless.

We miss the whole point of the future when we approach it as something to predict. Then we become forecasters, trying to guess tomorrow's weather so we can carry umbrellas or sunglasses. The real reason we reflect on the future, I suspect, is not to control it, but to give ourselves room in the present to think about what we are doing.

The future extends our temporal horizons much like traveling broadens our spatial perspective. Living briefly in an imaginary world of the future helps us see better what we like and dislike about our own world. Fantasizing about the person we would like to become or the career we hope to have or the grandchildren we desire is a way to take stock of where we are now. We may decide to do nothing differently. We may take some steps to redirect our course. Or we may simply come away refreshed in our thinking.

Thinking about the Christian's place in the next century should be done in this way too. The idea is not to identify a crisis in the year 2058 that the church should begin planning for. It is to place our thinking in a new temporal dimension, and to do so (don't we think this way anyway?) *consciously*. That is, we need to consider the challenges ahead, asking about the direction of present trends, looking at what we have and what we want, and then by considering the future, assess better where our present energies should lie.

The challenges ahead, even as we can envision them now, are almost too numerous to mention. At this moment, it appears that the AIDS epidemic may well challenge the resources and imagination not only of the church, not only of the United States, but of the entire world. This epidemic could prove, as some predict, to be as catastrophic for modern civilization as the plagues that spread across Europe at the end of the Middle Ages were for that era. Medical science, however, may yield results that will forestall that grim possibility. Environmental pollution, including such devastating phenomena as acid rain, global warming, and the depletion of the ozone layer, surely is a problem of such great magnitude at the present that church leaders must become even more actively engaged in the struggle against it. International treaties and the development of environmentally sound technologies may, however, reduce the seriousness of this threat in the future. The dangers posed by capabilities for the production of nuclear weapons, especially as these capabilities spread throughout the world, constitute a challenge of enormous gravity. Predictions for the next century that focus on population dynamics alone point toward another set of wrenching life issues: poverty, starvation, land use, employment, to name only a few.

Problems of this kind merit careful, foresighted, predictive, and evaluative inquiries. None of them may be solved (or even effectively addressed) primarily by the church, and yet they raise fundamental questions about ethics, social justice, morality, and spirituality that people of faith cannot ignore. For all their importance, the social, political, economic, medical, and technological challenges that newscasters and scientists are projecting for the twenty-first century may, however, be secondary to the questions with which people of faith should be concerned. They may be secondary, not because they are any less important in terms of the human needs they present, but because the ability to meet these (and other) needs will depend on people of faith knowing the strengths and limitations of the church itself and their place in the world as Christians. Or, put differently, Christianity in the United States will face challenges of its own that will have to be addressed, both for its own sake and for the sake of its role in society.

What are these challenges? One set of issues that warrant attention perhaps more urgently than any others arises from the fact that the Christian's place has always been linked historically with the church as an institution. This connection has become greatly attenuated for a large number of people during the course of the past century. Perhaps at no time in history have individuals been more insistent that they can be spiritual without the church, that they can follow their own conscience and develop their "personal faith" in a way that is uniquely theirs. For those who, in consequence, have severed all ties with institutional religion, it may seem strange to suggest that the challenges facing the church *as an institution* deserve top billing. And yet most of us know that life never proceeds without institutions.[1] People do not expect to govern themselves without political institutions; they cannot earn their livelihoods without economic institutions; they even cannot participate in their "private" leisure activities, such as reading books, playing golf, or watching television without the benefit of social institutions. Religious life should be no different. Those who pursue spirituality apart from involvement in specific churches or synagogues nevertheless depend heavily on the fact that these institutions exist.

For clergy and other church leaders, mention of the importance of institutional challenges facing the church will undoubtedly strike a resonant chord. Questions about church finances, whether the membership of certain denominations is rising or declining, how to start new churches, and how to operate effective programs will immediately come to mind. Church planners have had a good deal to say on these subjects in recent years. Their advice will have to be tailored in the years ahead to particular faith communities faced with such immediate challenges as turnover in leadership, constructing new facilities, or meeting the needs of an aging clientele. Behind all these specific issues, however, the problem of *community* itself will remain fundamental. If the church is unable to provide community, none of these other programmatic concerns will make very much difference, for the community above all, as Karl Rahner has observed, "is the visible sign of salvation that God has established in this seemingly godless world."[2]

Community is one of those buzz words (like "meaning" or "relevance") that we should be wary of using. Study after study suggests that people in our society are searching for community. The need for "belonging" has come to be identified as one of the primary functions that religious institutions can fulfill. Members of the clergy preach sermon upon sermon, admonishing believers to find community within the church. But what does all this mean? What will it mean in the years ahead?

The church has evolved over the past century to the point that it actually provides (or tries to provide) community in several distinct ways. We need to understand the church in terms of these different kinds of community. We also need to understand how community is being reshaped by the diversity, the individualism, and the voluntarism that has become so prominent in American culture.[3] In the years ahead, diversity and the possibilities for individual choice that it presents will be even greater than it is today. African-American churches, Latino churches, Asian churches, megachurches, and whole new denominations will all be part of the religious landscape.[4] The question of community cuts across all these various denominational, ethnic, and doctrinal forms.[5]

Understanding community, therefore, is one of the challenges deserving careful attention. It is important in part because community is the way in which the church gets things done. In the most instrumental terms, involving people in warm, caring communities is a good way to enlist them in the activities of the church and to motivate them to give generously to the church. Most religious leaders, however, would deny that community is important for instrumental reasons alone. They would argue correctly that community itself is important. It embodies the relational character of the divine, providing a tangible vehicle for the manifestation of divine love.

There is one other reason why community is fundamental, however: it is the basis even of the individual's identity. We discover our identity as we interact with other people. Most communities exist prior to us, and in this sense are already there as potential sources from which we can derive our identity. If religious identity is to be significant to the individual, it must be developed in relation to some community. To be able to speak of the "Christian" as having any place at all in the twenty-first century is thus to raise fundamental questions about the source—and continuing possibilities—of this identity.

A second set of challenges that deserve serious consideration focuses on what might be termed the "ethical" dimension of faith. As much as it may be about belief, and as much as it may be about experience, Christianity is also about how to live. For the individual, the question of how to live imposes itself forcefully on a continuing basis. For the church as institution, the question is equally important, if only because individuals look to it for ethical guidance. Like the institutional challenges just considered, ethical challenges can immediately be translated into all sorts of specific questions: what to think about birth control, whether abortion is morally wrong or morally neutral, how Christians should comport themselves in the workplace, what the best curriculum would be for instructing young people how to think ethically, and so on. But again, there is an even more fundamental question that cuts across all these specific issues: How is ethical behavior of any kind cultivated?

This question poses a challenge to people of faith for the following reasons. First, it seems clear that the ability to make informed ethical decisions and to live out these decisions is a more pressing need now than ever before. Second, it is equally clear that simple, straightforward rules for deciding how to live have for the most part fallen into question; even those who insist there are such rules admit difficulty in convincing others of their correctness. And third, the whole question of how best to transmit values or to cultivate habits of moral reasoning has been opened up anew in recent years.

There is much wisdom in the Christian tradition itself about how to nurture the ethical life. Special significance, for example, has always been attached to the role of parents in teaching and setting a pattern for their children. But it is also evident that for many people parents no longer can be counted on to serve in these ways. It has also been emphasized, at least implicitly, that people learned best by listening to stories and by relating these stories to their personal experience. But how can this be done in a "multicultured" society? How can stories communicate effectively when shared experience has become fragmented, like so many shards of a broken urn? These are among the questions that pose a special challenge for the future transmission of ethical values.

A third set of issues raises a challenge in the area of doctrine. Some might prefer to call it the problem of belief. But to cast it in those terms is to capitulate to the privatized, subjective orientation that has been so

roundly criticized in recent decades. Doctrine connotes a body of systematic religious insight, rather than a purely eclectic assemblage of personal
opinions. It also suggests (again) the importance of the church as an
institution, for doctrine is generally regarded as a set of "teachings" associated with a religious community. To speak of doctrine is even to
imply some standard of truth, and some obligation to abide by this truth,
whereas belief is entirely relative. The point of talking about doctrine in
the present instance, however, is primarily to suggest—by use of this
problematic term—that the challenges ahead will include fundamental
definitional questions themselves. The challenge of doctrine will, of course,
include deep debates over certain contested truths, but it will also focus
on what we mean by such terms as doctrine, truth, and belief in the first
place.

To face this challenge it will be necessary to build on some of the
insights produced over the past century about the relationships between
religious doctrine and social conditions. It might seem to some readers
that this is a peculiar suggestion to make. Surely the insights that have
emerged in social theory since the late nineteenth century have been concerned mainly with "explaining away" the tenets of religious faith, rather
than shoring up our understanding of those tenets. But to make that
assumption is to accept an outdated conception of Marx and other social
theorists of his era. Recent work in the social sciences—say, that occurring since the middle 1960s—has been much more positive in its overall
stance toward religion. While assuming, perhaps more so than some believers would wish to, that religious orientations are always to some degree shaped by their social environments, this work has also moved beyond earlier reductionist approaches that saw religion as *nothing but* a
reflection of its environment. Leading social theorists such as Robert N.
Bellah, Peter L. Berger, Andrew M. Greeley, Paul Ricoeur, Clifford Geertz,
Jürgen Habermas, and Niklas Luhmann, to mention only a few, have
adopted a hermeneutic epistemology that relativizes earlier "positivist"
assumptions and gives greater weight to the force of truth itself.

Working largely from the outside (that is, not taking a particular
confessional tradition for granted at the start), social theorists have contributed importantly to our understanding of religious doctrine by demonstrating its *functional importance* in the lives of individuals and for entire societies. One of their most valuable insights has been to recognize
the human need for meaning. This commonplace observation, it turns
out, has opened up an important place for arguments about religion,
chiefly because the quest for meaning can easily be shown to raise questions requiring some conception of the transcendent or holistic dimension of existence. Preserving and building on this insight will be an important step toward meeting the doctrinal challenges of the future,
especially because these will increasingly be forged in the context of pluralistic and privatized cultural assumptions.

What is perhaps most puzzling about the trajectory of religious doctrine at the popular level in the United States during the past century is the continuing vitality of *fundamentalism*. The spread of modernity through higher education, science and technology, urbanization, mass communications, and international awareness was assumed to be a force against which fundamentalist religious orientations could not long survive.[6] If anything, though, fundamentalism has become more prominent in recent decades. It is by no means the religious orientation of a majority of the American population. And yet it raises two questions that are central to any consideration of the place of the Christian in the twenty-first century. First, what will the future of fundamentalism itself be? Whether one is a fundamentalist or an enemy of fundamentalism, this question deserves serious attention. It does so chiefly because fundamentalism at present appears to embody exceptional energy, or power, to shape the future. Insofar as fundamentalism is a strong carrier of the language of Christianity, of the public identity of what it means to be "Christian," understanding its future is also necessary in any attempt to reckon with the public perceptions of Christianity. Second, what does fundamentalism tell us about the broader social forces shaping religion in the United States? Viewed this way, fundamentalism can be taken as a case study, less of interest in its own right than as a way of teasing out the complex effects of social, economic, and political developments in American society. Fundamentalists themselves would need to understand these effects in trying to meet the challenges their churches will face in the years ahead. But other religious groups—moderate and liberal Protestants, Roman Catholics, pentecostalists, African-American churches, among others—can also be understood better by extrapolating from the relationships that are becoming evident in our society between fundamentalism and its social environment.

These questions may appear overly abstract, but they also bear directly on an important practical matter: will fundamentalists set the agenda for American Christianity in the twenty-first century? If that seems a remote possibility to some readers, it might be well to remember that the fundamentalist-modernist controversy arose only in the waning years of the nineteenth century and yet managed to set the tone of much of the debate that has characterized American Protestantism ever since. Among Roman Catholics, the conservative posture that emerged in papal pronouncements in the same period has also continued to be a shaping force during much of the intervening period. Those facts alone raise serious questions about the future of religious liberalism in our society. What will its role in the next century be? How strong a role, for better or worse, can it play?

The main challenge facing religious liberals is whether they will continue to let fundamentalists set their agenda for them. Will they continue to serve mainly as a countervoice, offering a haven for those who do *not* wish to be considered fundamentalists? Will they posture themselves mainly in opposition to the evils of dogmatism and rigidity that they envision in fundamentalism? Or will they in some way be able to rise above the challenge presented from fundamentalists, charting an orthogonal course based on an independent vision of who they are and what they can be? Some signs point in a hopeful direction, and yet the declining memberships of many liberal denominations, the fiscal problems that have accompanied this decline, and the seeming failure of many of their favored programs continue to suggest caution.

A fourth set of distinct challenges arises when the public role of Christianity is considered. These might be called political challenges because they emerge primarily from the efforts by people of faith to influence government policies. These efforts, in turn, tend to be shaped considerably by government's response and by the "rules of the game" that must be followed in attempting to relate to government. It has become widely accepted in recent years that the contours of American religion are increasingly characterized in the public realm along a continuum from religious liberalism to religious conservatism. Often, moreover, this continuum has become polarized to the extent that only those on the extreme left or the extreme right have prevailed in the public arena. Thus, it has appeared to many observers that the basic lines of division, the lines identifying fellow believers as friends or foes, were increasingly being determined by the rift between liberals and conservatives. This rift, indeed, has risen in importance to the point that it often overshadows the traditional membership categories that have placed people in communities identified by denominational labels.

Some observers have gone so far as to suggest that denominations themselves are a thing of the past. Nothing could be further from the truth. The evidence collected in study after study over the past several decades shows that people continue to use denominational labels when asked to state their religious preference, the vast majority of Americans still hold membership in particular denominational or confessional bodies, and these organizations remain the primary credentialing agencies for clergy, conduct the official business of associated clergy and members, take in vast sums of money, and operate programs ranging from primary schools and day-care centers to retirement homes and cemeteries. Denominational and confessional bodies are likely to remain influential in the religious politics of the future. And yet their influence must also be considered in the context of the divide that has emerged between liberals and conservatives.

The current conflict between religious liberals and religious conservatives is itself a challenge for the future. Will Christians increasingly embarrass themselves by fighting with each other in public? In their efforts to influence the public arena will they increasingly give over authority to secular institutions because they themselves can reach no agreement? Will core teachings about love, forgiveness, fellowship, and redemption be the main casualties of the battles being waged over particular public policies?

This conflict also poses a more immediate challenge: who is likely to win? What resources can be mobilized on each side to ensure its own victory and the defeat of its enemies? Will the result be passage of certain legislative bills, changes in Supreme Court rulings, the election of a new breed of officials? Moreover, what if one side wins and the other loses? What then? Will the war be over? Or will other issues emerge to perpetuate it?

Definitive answers can seldom be found for any of these questions. But asking them remains important because it forces us to think more carefully about the nature of religion in American politics. Lessons can be learned, even from events in the recent past, about the strengths and weaknesses that people of faith bring with them as they try to influence public affairs. In part, these have to do with circumstances beyond the control of any particular religious organization. There are processes at work in the wider society that make opportunities, but also limit what religious groups can do. In part, people of faith must also be aware of what the public realm itself entails. There are perhaps ways of winning in the public arena that have been little recognized to date. If Christianity is to have a continuing place in American society, it will surely have to become more aware of its possibilities for influencing the public arena.

A final set of challenges that warrants special attention concerns the personal lives of believers themselves. Despite the accusations that are frequently heard about Americans being greedy, shallow, and focused only on themselves, much evidence suggests that people for the most part still want to be good. They want to do what is right, they want to contribute positively toward the good of the world, they want to raise their children to lead happy and productive lives. The impact of the Judeo-Christian heritage is evident well beyond religious institutions themselves in many of these concerns. Ideas about caring for others, about responsibilities toward one's family and one's community, about ethics and personal morality reflect the fact that American society is still very much a product of its religious past. For people of faith, it is often as difficult to decide these matters as it is for people who claim no interest in religion or spirituality. But the issues are often more pressing, if only because religious communities provide a means for attending to them consciously.

These personal challenges occur primarily in the relationships between individual behavior and the *cultural* contexts shaping it. There are, it seems to me, three issues in particular that will increasingly be faced by people of faith in our society, whether they are black or white, Hispanic or Anglo, Catholic or Protestant, female or male. Each of these issues reflects one of the dominant cultural trends in our society, and each in turn raises special questions about what it means to be a Christian in the contemporary world.

If there is one feature of contemporary culture that we can be sure will become even more pronounced in the future, that feature is its diversity. In the past, immigration has added ethnic diversity, regional migration has created geographic subcultures, racial divisions have reinforced their own kind of diversity, and religious traditions have fostered another layer of cultural variety. In the future, many of these historic forms of diversity will continue, but their importance will have to be understood in relation to a host of new factors as well. The Spanish-speaking population of the United States will increase significantly. Immigrants from Asia will also become more numerous. Subcultures forged along lines of gender or sexual preference have emerged and are likely to continue to be important. New religious cults and sects have proliferated in recent decades. These and other sources of cultural diversity will greatly increase the significance of questions about personal identity. What am I? Of what community am I a member? How am I unique? How am I different? These questions will increasingly be asked by children and teenagers, and they will probably be asked repeatedly as adults move through the life cycle. For those interested in religious faith, these questions will also provoke quandaries for the future of faith itself. With all religious communities in flux, can religion provide a significant source of identity? Is it possible that people will simply derive their identity from the mass media and from the marketplace? Will that forge a new, perhaps stronger sense of national identity? Or will something important be lost?

Besides diversity, American culture appears likely to be characterized increasingly by materialism. The consumer culture is already evident in nearly every corner of our lives. People are working harder just to keep up, partly because they feel they need the material amenities of a comfortable life. During most of the past century the American Dream has defined the meaning of work and of material success. Many middle-class Americans have done reasonably well in realizing this dream. In the future it may become increasingly difficult for young people to attain the material prosperity they desire. But that may cause them only to try all the harder. At the same time, the problems of the needy and disadvantaged are likely to become even more severe. The old questions about God and mammon, about wealth and injustice, therefore, will appear even more forcefully. What should the responsibilities of middle-class Christians be? Can the churches challenge them to take these responsibilities seriously?

The other feature of American culture that will continue to be of special importance in the future is its emphasis on educational attainment. In the past, education has been one of the primary ways of moving up the ladder of prestige, power, and income. As more and more people have attained higher education, the tensions between the culture of colleges and universities and the culture of the churches have often become more acute. Is it possible at all, some have asked, for knowledge and faith to coexist? In the future, this question must be taken seriously. Despite widespread criticisms at present of the American higher-education system, this system will continue to exercise vast influence in the culture at large. Will it be possible for individuals to play an active part in this system, as students, professors, or as informed alumni, and still retain their identity as Christians? Are there answers, truths, dogmas that Christians must defend against the onslaught of relativism and skepticism that seems to be so much a part of the educational system? Or must the relationship between faith and knowledge become even more complex than it is now?

These are the challenges—institutional, ethical, doctrinal, political, and cultural—with which the present book is concerned. They cut across different faith traditions, denominations, ethnic groups, and sectors of the population. They comprise the foundational issues that must be considered even before more specific forecasts can be made and before attention can be turned by religious bodies to the formulation of specific programs and plans.

The basic argument of this book is that the challenges ahead can be met most effectively by understanding the underlying frameworks guiding the ways in which we think about these challenges. Certain paradigms shape our thinking all the time. They grow out of our experiences of the past. They become implicit models, assumptions about how the world works, that we project into the future. They limit both our grasp of the problems ahead and our vision of how to respond to these problems. We can never fully escape these paradigms. But we can become more conscious of them and, in doing so, gain the ability to criticize them and, when necessary, to move beyond them.

The idea of an underlying paradigm or framework of assumptions is actually less mysterious than it may seem at first glance. It is true that we make many assumptions about the world and that we are seldom conscious of these assumptions. But it is also true that many of these assumptions take shape within a kind of *space* that is available to us by virtue of the language we use and the categories in which we think. By becoming more aware of even a few of these categories, we can begin to free ourselves to think more creatively and critically about them.[7] When I suggested earlier, for example, that the future opens up a space in which to think about the present, I was pointing to precisely this kind of self-consciousness. Present and future are indeed categories in which to frame our thinking. By contrasting the present and some vision of the future, we open up a space in which to think reflectively about our lives.

In the chapters that follow, it will become evident that there are, in my view, four sets of opposing categories that currently frame much of our thinking about the nature of the world and of the role of faith: individual and community, diversity and uniformity, liberalism and conservatism, and public and private. Each of these pairs creates a kind of space in which we can think about the present. Each one also provides a framework that, for better or worse, raises certain questions as we think about the future. For example, "community" suggests that we need to think about the ways in which religious people will band together, what the nature of community will actually be, how strong it will be, and what it implies about equally strong forces such as the individual's quest for personal identity and the need for self-reliance. "Diversity" is a category that suggests a tension with people needing or wanting to be the same, searching for agreement and common ground; it also raises questions about the scope, nature, and functioning of a plurality of groups and cultural styles. "Liberalism" and "conservatism" (or related concepts such as "fundamentalism") suggest another polarity. Much of our thinking about religion at present can be organized in terms of this polarity. But with what consequences? What exists in the middle? How will this polarity be defined in the future? How will it interact with other categories, such as "diversity" or "community"? The same is true of "public" and "private." Religion exists in the public life of our society and in the private lives of individuals. At each extreme, certain problems arise, such as the relative salience of faith in comparison with secular influences. Together, the two also raise questions about how the one relates to the other.

A point that requires particular clarity, therefore, is that these categories are not merely binary opposites, mutually exclusive concepts, like "yes" and "no" or "good" and "bad." Instead, they function in our thinking to anchor the ends of a continuum, to point in opposing directions (like "north" and "south"), but, in so doing, to provide a wide conceptual space in between. My argument is that our thinking is framed by these concepts, but remains free to roam over a rather wide territory made possible by their existence.

But what constitutes this territory? My argument is that it is constituted primarily by stories. Everyone knows that we make sense of the past by telling stories. I suspect we make sense of the future by telling those stories as well. They suggest certain connections, perhaps a temporal sequence, even an unfolding of events that we believe will occur in the same way again in the future. It may seem that these stories fundamentally defy any categorization or analysis. We simply describe our past and draw implications for the future. That, however, is too simplistic a view. Stories themselves are highly structured. They take place within certain frameworks. They reveal the outer boundaries of our thinking by taking for granted, for example, that individuals stand in tension with communities or that liberals and conservatives are locked in battle. In other words, stories are told from within the space defined by opposing categories such as the ones I have just enumerated. But then stories also show how specific people or groups in specific situations carved out a clearing in the wilderness, helping those individuals or groups to construct a habitat, and guiding them in relating to their surroundings.

It is for this reason that I emphasize stories repeatedly in the following chapters. I try to show how people tell stories, for example, to guide their ethical behavior, and that they also tell stories about their stories; in other words, narratives often contain second-order narratives that tell us how to understand them. Some of the stories are ones that people have told me, and I repeat them here to give a more concrete flavor to the arguments, but also to add nuance and to illustrate how a particular individual might apply them. Some of the stories also come from my own experience. I tell them to sensitize the reader to my own frameworks and assumptions. In the end, though, the present book is not primarily a book of stories, but an analysis of the present contours of American religion and the implications of these for the future. The analysis, the stories, and the reflections raised by these analyses about the way we think are interwoven.

What do I have to contribute to this process? It should be evident from what I have already said that I make no pretensions to having a crystal ball with which to predict the future. The human sciences have advanced considerably during the past century, but they seldom predict accurately whether the stock market will rise or fall, let alone when a revolution is going to take place or what the timing of the next religious revival will be. Since their inception in the nineteenth century, though, the human sciences have been at the very center of thought about the character of social change. There has been much winnowing in this process. Most of the great scenarios once envisioned for the grand ballroom of history have been set aside by serious students of social theory. Attention has shifted to more modest questions that can be addressed with real information collected from real people.

In the past few decades a great deal of such information has been gathered about virtually all aspects of American religion. Opinion polls, reporting how many people believe in God or attend religious services or pray before meals, can be found in nearly any day's newspaper. With the accumulation of such polls, trend lines can be charted, helping to suggest what the character of religion in the future may be. Studies have also examined the inner workings of new religious movements, old established religious organizations, and all the variations in between. These studies help us understand what aspects of these entities may endure into the next century.

It would take a book much longer than the present one to serve up everything that might be helpful for considering the future of American religion. Besides, there are textbooks and well-documented reference volumes that can be consulted for that purpose.[8] My intention here is different. Having spent the past quarter century reading this literature, teaching it, and producing my share of it, I am still frequently discontent with the reflection available on what it all means. As an individual participant in the great experiment we call Christianity, I also find myself engaged in my own process of interpretation, wanting to understand better the changes it is experiencing and the challenges it is facing.

Some readers will probably find it strange for a book to be written by a social scientist with a particular confessional tradition as its primary concern and the members of that tradition as its primary audience. Certainly it has been common for scholarship to be framed in the widest possible terms. Looking toward the future, would it not then make more sense to talk about faith in the abstract, rather than focus on Christianity? Some of my argument can perhaps be extended well beyond Christianity in the United States. But it does seem to me that confessional traditions also make continuing sense: they will remain important considerations to the definition of religious institutions and to the lives of individuals of faith, and they will inform the perspectives of academicians as well.

The opportunity to begin turning these personal ruminations into more systematic reflections came when I was asked to present the Stone Lectures at Princeton Theological Seminary. I decided at that time to begin devoting serious attention to the question of what Christianity and the church might be like in the next century. Through various research projects in which I have been engaged, I have also been able to secure information to help in these reflections, especially from interviews with individual church members and pastors, from opinion surveys, and from conferences and symposia. Much of this work was assisted by grants from the Lilly Endowment and the Pew Charitable Trusts and was nurtured in interaction with colleagues and students associated with the Center for the Study of American Religion at Princeton University.

Had the next millennium started a century or two earlier, we would have likely felt more confident in making broad pronouncements about the nature of the future. If the twentieth century has taught us one thing, it is to be skeptical of such pronouncements. The future is now something, like ourselves, that we think about in nuanced and multifaceted terms. It takes stories for us to conceive of it at all, and these stories cast light from a variety of angles, often through the mirror of our own experience.

I

Institutional Challenges:
Community, Identity,
and
the Role of the Church

1

Church
and
Culture

In the early years of the twentieth century, a prominent French scholar penned the concluding lines to a book he had worked on for nearly fifteen years and sent the manuscript off to be published. That same year, a small group of German immigrants laid the final brick in a large two-story structure that rose magnificently against the prairie sky of a lonely Kansas town. Different as they were, both efforts sprang from a common source.[1]

The French scholar was Emile Durkheim, one of the founders of modern sociology; his book, *The Elementary Forms of the Religious Life*.[2] The German immigrants were a community of farmers, uprooted a generation before by the conscription laws in their homeland, now relocated after several intermediate stops along the rail arteries that linked Kansas wheat fields with world markets. Their new brick structure: a Baptist church. In both, a central question was at issue: the church and its changing cultural location.

Momentous change has altered the world dramatically in the intervening decades. As we contemplate the church today and try to think about its location in the culture of tomorrow, there is much to be learned from these distant events. Both grew from roots planted at the end of the nineteenth century and both matured in the uncertain sunlight of a new era. The Christian's place in the world today depends deeply on the succor provided by the church, as it has developed in the soil of the late twentieth century. The Christian's place in the world of tomorrow will depend equally on how well that ancient institution can adapt to the challenges that lie ahead in the twenty-first century.

Congregations and Culture

Sociologists have always been particularly fond of Emile Durkheim's classic treatment of religion, for he alone among theorists of the time did not focus primarily on matters of belief. In the work of his German contemporary Max Weber, for example, religion evokes questions chiefly about variations in ethics and values. Especially in his famous treatise on the Protestant ethic and the spirit of capitalism, Weber asks whether certain assumptions about predestination, evil, salvation, the calling, and other theological tenets inspire an ethical orientation favorable to an acquisitive life-style.[3] And even in other works, where questions of religious leadership and organization are clearly at issue, Weber remains predominantly interested in the sorts of belief that may arise from, or in turn legitimate, these institutional structures.[4] Not so with Durkheim. Although the beliefs and practices of individuals and of entire societies are also of interest to him, the central question that pervades all his work is the question of moral community: whence it arises, how it can be sustained, and in what degree it can temper the desires and instincts of the individual. The church is thus of primary concern in his treatment of religion. Indeed, it appears within the very definition he gives of religion: "a unified system of beliefs and practices relative to sacred things . . . which unite into one single moral community called a Church, all those who adhere to them."[5]

For Durkheim, then, the church lies at the core of religion and thus provides the pivotal nexus between religion and its host environment. The church, in fact, does more than merely adapt to its cultural circumstances; instead, it provides the womb in which culture itself is conceived and readied for birth. The church is a moral community that unites individuals in collective practices of worship, and these rituals give concrete meaning both to the beliefs they express and to the individuals who express them.

The Congregation

In the United States, and throughout the Christian world, the congregation has been the primary embodiment of the church.[6] In the four decades prior to 1911, the number of such congregations in the United States increased from 70,000 to approximately 225,000, with 90 percent of them housed in their own buildings.[7] The German farmers who constructed the Baptist church at Frederick, Kansas, were merely doing what people everywhere were doing. They were making a home in which a distinctively religious community with its own special cultural ethos could come alive.

Growing up in that church, as I did in the 1950s, I could readily observe how much Christianity depended on the local congregation. To be sure, this was where sermons were preached, Bible stories taught, and the Lord's Supper observed. Children learned Bible verses by the hundreds, and adults discussed their theological implications. The church, however, did more than merely pass on the timeless truths of its larger tradition. It also embedded those truths in the tangible realities of its own unique circumstances.

Sacred Places

Frederick Baptist was not so much an idea or a set of beliefs as a place.[8] People drove there on Sunday mornings and evenings, parked on the sanded roads that ran along two sides of the red brick building, climbed the eleven steps leading to the front door, hung their coats in the vestibule, and went into the sanctuary. Inside, the church was like a second home. Name plates at the bottoms of the stained glass windows reminded people of the departed. People sat in familiar pews. Downstairs was where classes and Vacation Bible School and church suppers were held. Up front, behind the pulpit, was the baptistery—which everyone had helped paint at one time or another.

Not long ago, in an exceedingly pious gathering of lay theologians, someone asked for a definition of the church, hoping for a creedally correct answer about the universal body of Christ. Before anyone else could answer, I blurted out that the church usually conjured up a picture in my mind of a building. I did not add that the building was made of red brick and had eleven steps leading to the front door.

What I would also add, having invoked Durkheim, is that the place and the beliefs taught in that place are inextricably interwoven in my imagination. When I was four or five, after listening to a long Sunday evening sermon about the wiles of the devil, the boys my age used to dare each other to run all the way around the church building in the dark by ourselves. I suspect I was not the only one, running hard by myself along the back side of the church, to hear the devil's hot breath panting close behind me.

The Moral Dimension

I am trying to suggest that the church is a powerful institution in our society because it encapsulates the individual in a community that becomes an essential part of the individual's own identity. This is what Durkheim meant when he referred to the "moral" dimension of the church.[9] The community can become, in Dietrich Bonhoeffer's memorable words, "a source of incomparable joy and strength to the believer."[10] It also shapes how we think about ourselves and becomes a part of our past, our memory, our being. Well after the community itself ceases to exist, it continues on as a community of memory.[11] At Freder-

ick Baptist, nearly all the deacons who administered the Lord's Supper
and held the church together have died. The congregation itself dissolved
more than a decade ago. The building was torn down. And yet the congregation, as a community of memory, lives on.

The church is, in this sense, a cultural force. It is also subject to the
cultural forces surrounding it. From Weber and Marx and others, we
know about the influences of rationality and science and capitalism and
bureaucracy on the church. But from Durkheim we understand the importance of geography. If the church is literally a place, then the cultural
forces that shape its geography cannot be emphasized too much.[12]

Geography

Frederick Baptist was, as I have already hinted, a product of geography.
Its founding members had fled Bismarck's conscription laws in the 1870s
and then come to Kansas as homesteaders, achieving enough of a community to form a church in 1883. The railroad, coupled with rising demand for wheat on the world market, brought more people and encouraged large families. Still dependent on the horse and buggy, families
clustered around churches in their immediate communities.

These were years of sweeping cultural change in the society at large.
In the universities Social Darwinism was spreading like wildfire. Modernism was sweeping through theological seminaries on the East Coast.
Industrialization was creating a vast new work force in the cities. And,
while shielded from these remote developments, Frederick Baptist showed
the church's power to adapt to other cultural upheavals. The transition
from Germany to the United States was one. Learning a new language
and becoming Americans were part of the process. Even before World
War I made it imperative to do so, many of these German-speaking immigrants abandoned the mother tongue and began conducting church
services in English.

But the geographic factors that facilitated its rise were also the factors that contributed to the eventual demise of the Frederick congregation. The Great Depression forced the bank, the grocery store, and the
service station to close and the population began to dwindle. After World
War II, new vitality came with the baby boom. And then a few years
later, the automobile undid the community completely.

To be precise, I should note that it was not so much the automobile
itself as it was the invention of the automobile heater that led to the
church's demise. For a generation, families had bundled themselves under lap blankets and driven the shortest possible distance to the nearest
church. But the heated sedan made it possible to drive unheard of dis-
tances. And so, within a few years more and more of the congregation
slipped away, driving the twelve miles to a flourishing Baptist church in
the county seat.

Geography was also a critical part of the mass exodus that took place throughout the rural United States during the two decades after World War II. With mechanization and uncertain agricultural price support programs pushing them, and college educations pulling them, thousands of young people fled the farms and small towns to seek new opportunities on distant campuses and in distant cities. Those who stayed behind worried about the secularism, the immorality, and even the communism in these remote places, but they knew it was basically geography that was undermining the church.

Growth and Decline

In thinking about what the church will undergo in the future, therefore, we would do well to remember the importance of geography. Many of the powerful changes that are currently shaping congregations—both negatively and positively—are geographic. Certainly it is possible to see the negative effects on congregations that have been decimated by their young people moving away to seek educations and jobs. The positive effects can be seen in those areas where populations have grown.

We can understand the recent growth of many congregations—and the growth of some whole denominations—better by reviewing what I have been saying about the mix of congregational cultures and geography. A congregational culture that provides a community of memory is something an individual can take along to a new geographic location. That is, the memory at least can be taken along. And that memory can be a very valuable source of security when everything else in one's world has changed, especially if some of the memory can be relived.

Some of the growth experienced in recent years by the Southern Baptist Convention, for example, can probably be understood in this fashion. Throughout much of the southern United States, Baptist churches are almost synonymous with the region's identity—as Gaelic Presbyterianism is in the Scottish highlands. But the South has also experienced dramatic geographic change as a result of its economic circumstances. Stagnation in the cotton and tobacco industries has jeopardized the lifestyles of many on farms and in the small towns, but "high-tech" industries, tourism, government projects, and government transfer payments have all promoted rapid growth in southern cities and suburbs. For the thousands who have migrated to these cities and suburbs, an entire way of life has had to be left behind—except the Baptist church. In the burgeoning congregations that surround Atlanta, Dallas, Houston, Memphis, and other southern cities, at least some of that familiar religious culture can still be found.[13] The same could probably be said for Assemblies of God congregations in these cities or, for that matter, the many evangelical churches in the Northeast and on the West Coast in which southern accents seem to abound. Certainly the numerous black churches that populate Chicago, Detroit, Cleveland, and other northern industrial

cities attest to the importance of congregations for those who migrated
to these areas from the South a generation or two ago.[14]

What these examples suggest is that the church's capacity to survive
in a changing culture is very high indeed. This is because the church not
only adapts to changing conditions but also creates its own communities,
which give individuals part of their identity. Being geographically local,
these communities can be disrupted by spatial, economic, and demographic change. But they can also be rebuilt in new locations. Church
leaders, denominational officials, and all who care need to be aware of
the constant need to relocate and rebuild. In the coming decades, geography is likely to continue shifting the locations where congregations are
most needed. Large-scale agribusiness is likely to deplete the population
of areas like Frederick, Kansas, even further. Immigrants from Korea and
Singapore will increase the demand for Asian Protestant churches in places
like Los Angeles and Chicago. Population flows from Mexico and Latin
America will alter the face of the Catholic church in Texas and California.
Aging baby boomers retiring in Florida and South Carolina will neces-
sitate new churches in those areas. Increasingly, the nation's byways are
also likely to be dotted with mosques and temples as immigrants arrive
from other parts of the world.

The Challenge of Diversity

In many respects the cultural environment of Frederick, Kansas, seems
simple compared with Durkheim's France. Frederick Baptist, however,
faced one challenge that Durkheim's analysis never quite envisioned. France,
for all its regional and occupational diversity, had long been subject to
the unifying influence of a single religious tradition and, after Napoleon,
to a single—and increasingly centralized—system of government, language, and public education. The wheat-farming communities of central
Kansas were subject to some of the same processes in government and
public schooling. But uniformity in religion was entirely lacking. A vibrant denominational pluralism was the raison d'être of these communities.[15]

Denominations

When United States census officials counted churches—which they did
regularly in these years—they were able to list about two hundred separate denominations and faiths in the nation at large. In the environs of
central Kansas no more than twenty-five or thirty such groupings could
have been found. But denominationalism was, as H. Richard Niebuhr
was to argue a few years later for other parts of the country, tightly
woven into the warp and woof of the social fabric itself.[16] The German
Baptists at Frederick knew clearly how different they were from the Swedish
Lutherans in nearby Lindsborg, the Catholics in Ellsworth, the Scottish

Presbyterians in Sterling, and the Mennonites in Hutchinson. They could also distinguish themselves socially and economically from the railroad workers who populated Geneseo three miles in one direction, the Methodists five miles in another direction, and even a different group of German Baptists a few miles in a third direction. Religious differences were reinforced by nationality, location, kin networks, tastes in food, and, among the older people, language.

A generation later many of these earlier sources of denominationalism had visibly eroded. Like the windstorms of the thirties that blew down fence rows and let the rains wash new gullies through the fields, a quarter century of social change altered the denominational boundaries as well. People moved around in search of new land; some moved to the larger towns; many married across denominational lines. But for all this, the importance of denominationalism was only partly diminished.

In the 1950s the religious identity of Frederick Baptists was still very much defined in denominational terms. Wider communication at one level—through the automobile, newspapers, and radio—merely created greater awareness, at another level, of the differences among religious communities. The churches in one town still looked different from the churches in another town. Children who paid visits for athletic and music competitions saw these differences—and interscholastic rivalries reinforced the lingering religious and ethnic distinctions.

For the devout, the differences were also rooted in more than the cultural past. Divine truth itself was often at stake. Indeed, it sometimes appears in retrospect that the erosion of older differences in language, ethnicity, and national background led simply to clergy and lay leaders paying more attention to the scriptural truths that legitimated their distinctive identities. What denominations taught about heaven and hell, the Bible, church government, and alcohol was enormously important.

Hailing as I did from denominationally mixed parentage, I was keenly aware of the gravity with which all these truths could be taken. To my Scottish Presbyterian mother who could never bring herself to join them, the Baptists were unforgivably devoted to dispensationalism and the other heresies of Dr. Scofield. And if my father ceased early trying to convince her, many of the stalwarts at the Baptist church grew convinced that it was nothing more than educational snobbery to follow Dr. Calvin instead of Dr. Scofield.

Cultural Change

Such controversies illustrate how much less significant denominational boundaries are today than they were even a few decades ago.[17] Some of the leaders who draw their paychecks from denominational hierarchies will perhaps defend the divine inspiration of their particular tradition.[18] But live-and-let-live is more the order of the day. People switch from denomination to denomination with alacrity. Pastors seldom refer in sermons to any distinctives of their tradition. Tolerance is the watchword. Cooperation has come to replace even ecumenism because the latter implies more awareness of formal traditions than we seem to feel in our bones. And congregations try to promote community—or at least church growth—without making denominationalism an issue.

As we contemplate the future of the church, therefore, we must ask ourselves whether denominationalism will play any role at all in shaping this future. I have not been unhappy to see denominational animosities subside, and yet I would not propose their eradication. Nor do I regard what remains of them as unimportant.

Religious Switching

One has only to look at Durkheim's France—or Sweden or Great Britain—to imagine how American religion would be impoverished by the elimination of denominational diversity. In the United States, someone who grows weary of the sermons at First Baptist can simply switch to First Methodist or First Presbyterian. Nothing, in my view, would diminish religious involvement as much as some rule requiring Baptists to be Baptists all their lives, or Presbyterians to be Presbyterians all of theirs.

Such switching of course has its down side. Denominations with declining memberships may wish it were harder for their parishioners to switch out. Even the growing denominations may be forced, as Peter Berger observed some years ago, to adopt a marketing orientation that reduces spiritual life to glitzy products and programs.[19] And the typical person in the pew may become so oriented toward local programs and personalities that denominational bureaucrats have trouble stirring interest in national projects.

Faced with these difficulties, some religious leaders have adopted the view that denominationalism is simply an anachronism that might best be forgotten. Despite their best efforts to mount new programs, people simply seem confused about the role played by the denominational identity of their church. But that view seems to me to be overly cynical.

Fostering Community

It is, perhaps ironically, from Durkheim that we gain one of the best clues for understanding the continuing role of denominationalism in American religion. Durkheim, as I said, spent his life searching for an effective basis of moral community in modern life. He was not faced with denominational diversity—or the breakup of denominational loyalties—as a particular problem. But he was acutely aware of the implications of occupational and geographic diversity. For a time, he pondered the possibilities of people finding community through their diverse occupational attachments—guilds, unions, professional societies. These could, we might suppose, function somewhat like the local church, providing fellowship with like-minded people. But what would make people loyal to these organizations? And, more troubling, how could a sense of community be fostered across an entire nation? The problem was clearly similar to the one now facing denominational leaders.

Durkheim's answer, which came only much later as he wrote his book on religion, was to pay closer attention to the role of symbolism in creating community. In a primitive society the symbolism of common ancestry, amulets, folklore, and collective ritual, he observed, plays a vital role in reinforcing community. The individual not only feels loyal to the community but feels its power and gains moral strength from participating in it. The community and the sacred become one. In a modern society individuals may no longer feel theirs is uniquely sacred, but symbolism still evokes the moral power of the collectivity.

Denominational Symbols

Turning the same analysis to the question of denominationalism, we can argue that the symbols of particular denominations still play an important role in promoting community, even if these symbols are no longer regarded as divine truth. They function more like brand names—indeed, one is reminded of Garrison Keillor's quip about how all the Lutherans in Lake Wobegon drove Chevys and all the Catholics drove Fords.[20] Most of us would not claim absolute truth for our choice of Chevy or Ford. But we would still feel a certain loyalty to our favorite brand.

That analogy may suggest a cynical interpretation of American denominationalism. I do not wish to conjure up such cynicism but rather suggest that denominational symbols do continue to be an important part of the subculture that attaches us to particular church communities. I am reminded, for example, of a conversation overheard recently between two women about hymns. One said she loved the old Methodist hymns. The other said she loved the old Baptist hymns. Before long, it became evident that both were talking about hymns like "Power in the Blood" and "Amazing Grace." To an outsider, the denominational labels might have seemed trivial. And yet, to both women they were terribly important.

In other cases, denominationalism also helps mainly to give a shorthand way of referring to certain common assumptions. Episcopalians tell jokes about Henry VIII; Baptists tell jokes about drownings during river baptisms. Other traditions and insignia—from the way clergy dress in the pulpit to the color of hymn books to the names given leadership boards—may seem equally trivial. But they help make a place seem home. For, as Durkheim observed, it is the common experience of the group that attaches itself to these symbols. Were such symbols not present, therefore, they would have to be invented.

And does it in any way diminish the importance of these symbols even to suggest that they could be invented? Not in the least. Surely nobody would suggest that the Princeton Tigers or the Louisville Cardinals could not have been called something else. But to change those mascots now would also show how importantly they are held.

Denominationalism in the contemporary church, it seems to me, is very much like the symbolism that marks the athletic teams from various universities or from various cities. Deep sentiments attach themselves to these symbols. It is important that such symbolism exists and that it differs in substance. But it is also important to recognize that it is compelled—by its cultural location—to play a correspondingly similar role in each community. The symbolism, in short, becomes isomorphic. Each team has a mascot, each team has its colors. Moreover, each team has a coach and some prominent players of whom it is proud and a tradition of win-loss records and great feats.[21]

For the future, we can expect the same of denominationalism. It will not diminish in importance; it may even become more prominent. Each denomination will be characterized by its distinctive name, publications, mode of worship, and national headquarters. But each denomination will feel compelled to have all these things—a name, publications, mode of worship, and national headquarters. Each will also make public pronouncements about key social issues. Each will organize special interest groups for its clergy around topics of the day. Some of these groups will herald the future, others will hale the past. And thus, each will host internal conflicts between self-styled liberals and self-styled conservatives.[22] We will recognize them as denominations, and think no less of them, as long as they have all these trappings of distinctive religious communities.

The Future of the Church

The curious thing about Durkheim's discussion of religion, given the emphasis he places on the church in his definition, is that he focuses hardly any attention at all on the church as we know it. Following a somewhat arcane variety of reasoning long since abandoned by social scientists of the twentieth century, he sought to discover what was basic ("elementary") in religion by going backward in the evolutionary cycle, he supposed, to its most primitive forms. Thus he devoted his analysis to the religious rites and myths of Australian aborigines. And when he turned again to modern societies, he applied his insights more to the rituals and myths of the nation-state than to the church.

There is, however, something to be learned from Durkheim's curious approach. Because he was interested in the social role played by religion and other kinds of sacred symbols under such a wide variety of circumstances, he was forced to pay more attention to the *functions* of these symbols than to their specific content or even the organizational forms they took. That can be a useful insight for us as well, especially if we want to consider how broad cultural changes may affect the church in the future.

New Organizational Forms

Thus far I have assumed that the congregation as we know it could be regarded pretty much as a synonym for the church. But that assumption needs to be bracketed. Even if the congregation as we know it continues on as the main manifestation of the church, we can already see that the congregation itself has been changing and that many new forms of religious community have arisen alongside it.

Historically, there is of course wide precedent for recognizing the variety of organizational forms the church may take. Though modeled in many respects after the synagogue, the churches that met in the homes of the first Christians also departed from the way in which the synagogue was administered and initiated new forms of worship.[23] After the establishment of the Catholic church, the appearance of religious orders represented another important organizational innovation. In our own history we have witnessed a proliferation of denominational styles as well as such variants as the circuit rider, the camp meeting, the revival meeting, the Bible society, and the urban mission. More recently, this diversity has been enlarged by religious and quasi-religious communities such as campus ministries, meditation centers, centers for spiritual direction, the so-called twelve-step groups (such as AA, ACOA, and CODA), and a host of special interest groups oriented toward particular religiomoral or religiopolitical causes.

Separating Form and Function

Understanding how these newer groups fit into the future of the church requires us to follow Durkheim in separating form from function. The various functions that religion in its several forms may fulfill include instilling a sense of transcendence or sacredness in its followers, giving them personal meaning, providing them with a community to which they can belong, communicating religious knowledge, coping with the frailties of human life, and exercising a prophetic voice to the prevailing society. While the local congregation may continue to perform all or most of these functions, it is also conceivable that some of them may be increasingly performed by other kinds of religious organization.

This possibility gains plausibility when we consider some of the specific functions of religion. The communication of religious knowledge, for example, has traditionally been accomplished by the local church. But growth over the past several centuries in higher education also resulted in more and more of this function being transferred to religiously sponsored day schools, colleges, and seminaries. In more recent decades, however, these have diminished in relation to the rapid rise of secular institutions of higher education. At present, a considerably larger share of religious knowledge than ever before is thus transmitted through courses taught at secular universities.

A similar process can be seen in religion's role in coping with human frailty. Although the local church still performs the bulk of the nation's funerals and supplies support during times of grief and illness, more specialized ministries have also emerged to deal with some of these concerns. Larger congregations may hire specially trained clergy for visitation, chaplaincy, and counseling programs. Other congregations may refer members to counseling centers run by larger churches or host lay ministries aimed at meeting these needs. Increasingly, these functions have also been taken over by professional therapists and by twelve-step groups.

Instead of having to fulfill all his or her religious needs within a single congregation like Frederick Baptist, the Christian of the twenty-first century is thus faced with a variety of options. Religious knowledge can be sought in the college classroom or, if not there, in the pages of any of the hundreds of religious magazines and books available through the mail or at a local religious bookstore. Emotional support can be sought at the counseling center and through twelve-step groups. For inspiration, put some religious music on the compact disk player. For an angry prophetic voice, turn on religious television.

Searching for Community

But where does the twenty-first century Christian turn for community? This, after all, Durkheim would argue, is more basic than all the rest. Surely this remains the function of the local congregation. And yet even this certainty needs to be questioned.

Many local churches talk a lot about community. But community in the typical church of 350 members, let alone the megachurch of 3,000 members, is quite different from community in a church like Frederick Baptist.[24] The church roll there listed only about 100 members and the whole township had a population of less than 3,000. The modern church operates on a much larger scale because pastors' salaries and desired programs demand it. For a core of active laity, the church itself may be the community. But for others, it should be likened to a referral system. You come wanting the worship experience; it is open to all. You come wanting help or information or community; the clergy can assist mainly by directing you to one of the dozen groups and ministries available, either at that church or in the wider community.

The intense support of which Durkheim wrote is more likely to come from these smaller, more intimate, but also more transient groups. Singles group this year, young marrieds next year, maybe choir at some other time, maybe the peace concerns fellowship after that. You become involved with like-minded people, develop some of the rituals and local symbolism that has always been part of the congregation, and perhaps find support and religious nurturance.

The church as a whole has been strengthened by these groups and, thus far, managed fairly well to serve as a kind of clearinghouse for them.

But there is no reason to suppose that the church will be able to retain this monopoly indefinitely. Increasingly, people start house churches that have no official denominational connection, seek spiritual direction at centers operated separately from local churches, and pray the Lord's Prayer at twelve-step groups to their "higher power." For a geographically mobile people, these are the sorts of groups most likely to flourish. They require little overhead, few construction costs, and perhaps little even in the way of paid salaries. If the local population expands, they grow; if the local population ages, they change in focus; if the population declines, they cease to exist.

The greatest gap that will be left by these alternative forms of religious community, though, is the training of the young. Communities of memory require participation during early childhood. It is little wonder, therefore, that those concerned most about the survival of the church have turned much of their attention toward the family and toward other agencies of socialization such as the schools and television. Should the congregation be replaced by the shopping mall and the soap opera, we might well fear for the survival of both the church and our culture itself.

The likelihood that Christians will have a place in the twenty-first century, therefore, depends to a large extent on the ways in which the church meets the cultural challenges it presently faces. Geographic mobility and the declining significance of denominational identities raise serious questions about the church's ability to sustain community in a way that attracts people to it.

2

Can the Church
Sustain Community?

The church of the twenty-first century, like that of previous centuries, will probably remain vibrant as long as it can provide people with a strong sense of community. The congregation, therefore, remains at the heart of the church and, in turn, at the heart of Christianity. But can the congregation continue adequately to sustain community? What exactly will it be able to do? Will it continue to function much as it does at present? Or will corrosive forces in the wider society undermine its ability to function at all? These, as I suggested broadly in the last chapter, are among the most pressing questions facing the church. To probe them more deeply, we must now ask specifically what we mean by the need for community and how the church, among other institutions, may fulfill that need.

Historical analysis shows clearly that for centuries the Christian church has been the mainstay of community life in Western society.[1] In the Middle Ages people lived within walking distance of the church, woke to its bells, took their animals to it to be blessed, and followed its calendar.[2] After the Reformation people formed their own churches and called pastors who lived as they did.[3] In our own history the church was first an integral part of the colony, then of towns (like Frederick, Kansas), and later of the urban and suburban neighborhood.[4]

But now our society seems to be at a loss for community. Critics say we have become a nation of individualists, obsessed with our jobs, our bank accounts, our feelings—our selves. We live in anonymous places, jealously protecting our personal privacy, and whatever hopes we entertain of finding a warm, supportive community are threatened by our incessant moving about and the pressures that impinge upon our time.

The question that faces us, then, is whether the church can still be a vital source of community, or whether it too is beginning to succumb to the impersonal forces that fragment our society. Students of American religion have begun to debate this question with increasing interest but as yet remain divided. Some see continuity with the past and even a rebirth of interest in the communal values of religion; others envision a declining role for the church. The evidence that can be pieced together from surveys and from talking with people in greater depth provides many indications of the vitality of American religion as a facilitator of community, but also points toward some worrisome signs for the future.

The Varieties of Community

The church's role in sustaining community can be understood in several different respects. Within the Christian tradition itself the word *koinonia* has always received special attention. It connotes the group of believers themselves who constitute a community of support—support both of one another's commitments to the faith and of each other's physical and emotional needs. In addition to this theological meaning, the concept of community has also held historical connotations in relation to the church. Because the fellowship of believers exists in space and time, it is of necessity related to its broader surroundings, particularly the village, town, neighborhood, suburb, or city in which its members reside. Finally, there is also an ethical meaning to the relation between church and community. The fellowship of believers is expected to be of service, not only to one another within its own group, but to the needs of others, whether this be the immediate neighborhood or the wider community of humankind. Each of these meanings of community—support, residence, service—is vital to any discussion of the church's role, now and in the future.

Communities of Support

Evidence from recent studies indicates that for many people the church does in fact function as a community of support. Church members, particularly those who actively participate, feel they can count on one another for various kinds of help. For example, when asked, "If you or someone in your family became seriously ill, do you think you could count on any of the following for help?", 64 percent of the public in one national survey said they would be able to count on members of a church or synagogue, and among weekly churchgoers, this proportion was 86 percent. By comparison, only 50 percent of the public thought they could count on people at work, and a mere 35 percent said they could expect help from public agencies.[5]

Other studies have routinely documented that churchgoers often select their friends among people who share the same faith tradition and
usually count some of the people within their own church among their
very closest friends. One study of church members in California, for example, found that 61 percent listed at least one of their five closest friends
as being a member of their congregation, and about 30 percent said at
least three belonged to their congregation.[6] Increasingly, these informal
bases of support are also being supplemented by church programs that
formally encourage the expression of needs among small groups of members. In addition to the ladies' auxiliaries, men's retreats, and youth clubs
that have been prominent for decades, churches are now likely to sponsor
Alcoholics Anonymous groups, singles' fellowships, job seekers meetings,
gatherings for divorced parents, and a variety of other support groups.

Communities of Residence

Much evidence also suggests that participation in churches reinforces ties
to the physical community in which a person resides. The caring that
churches teach spills over to the wider community. As I shall indicate,
studies usually find church members more actively involved in volunteering and helping behavior than nonmembers. Sometimes this compassion
results in efforts to care for total strangers or for people in remote cor-
ners of the world. But it is more likely to spill over to the immediate
community—to friends and neighbors. For example, the Gallup Poll,
summarizing a survey on patterns of charitable giving, found an interesting geographic factor in the helping behavior of church members. When
asked if they had helped strangers, such as a homeless person or someone
on the street, church members were no more likely than nonmembers to
say they had. But when asked if they had helped a neighbor, 53 percent
of the church members said yes, compared with only 42 percent of the
nonmembers.[7]

The most comprehensive study to date of the relationship between
religious involvement and communities of residence is *The Connecticut
Mutual Life Report on American Values.*[8] Although the study was not
designed to focus primarily on religion, its authors discovered that religious involvement was one of the strongest predictors of community
attachments of any of the factors they examined. Compared with the
least intensely religious, the study showed that:

- The most religiously committed Americans are far more likely to
  vote in local elections (77 percent versus 49 percent).
- They are far more likely to attend community or neighborhood
  meetings (34 percent versus 5 percent).
- They are more likely to discuss local issues with friends and neighbors (54 percent versus 33 percent).

• They are far more likely to visit with neighbors (45 percent versus 30 percent).

In addition to these findings, the study also showed that the religiously committed were more likely than the nonreligious to feel they had a voice in how their community was run, to feel they could rely on their neighbors, and to say they would like to remain living in their present community.

Communities of Service

Churches not only cultivate loyalties to their members' neighborhoods; they also promote an ethic of service that forges chains of caring through various sectors of the community. According to a Gallup survey, for instance, church members outstripped nonmembers in several major forms of charitable giving. By a margin of 78 percent to 66 percent, they were more likely to have contributed food, clothing, or other property to the needy. Seventy-three percent of members had given monetary contributions to charities (other than their church or denomination), compared with 64 percent of nonmembers. And 46 percent had done unpaid volunteer work during the past year, compared with 32 percent of nonmembers.[9]

The role of churches as communities of service is also evident in comparisons between frequent churchgoers and infrequent churchgoers. These differences were clearly in evidence in a research study I conducted on patterns of altruistic behavior in the United States. Among persons who attended church every week, 43 percent said they were currently involved in some kind of charitable or social service activity, such as helping the sick or the needy, compared with 36 percent of those who attended church several times a month, and only 24 percent of those who attended less than once a month.[10]

In this study, the role of community was also evident in relationships between churchgoing and *attitudes* toward caring for other people. Among weekly churchgoers, 70 percent said it was absolutely essential or very important to them to "give time to help others," whereas only 57 percent said this among those who seldom attended church. The former were also more likely than the latter to say they received a great deal of fulfillment from "doing things for people" (62 percent versus 42 percent).

These attitudes, moreover, are reinforced specifically by what people see and hear when they participate in church services. For example, 86 percent of weekly church attenders said they had heard a sermon within the past year that specifically talked about loving your neighbor. Sixty-nine percent said they could tell the story of the Good Samaritan if they were asked to do so.

Other research, based on direct information from a representative sample of churches in the United States, estimates that 90 percent of these congregations sponsor some kind of community service activity. Approximately half of the volunteer work donated to churches goes to programs that extend beyond the religious purposes of the congregation itself. In addition to this volunteer labor, churches supply an estimated $6.3 billion in contributions for community services each year.[11]

In each of these ways, then, the results of statistical studies point to the continuing importance of churches in sustaining community. Those who participate actively in churches reveal that this involvement provides individuals with communities of support, links them with their communities of residence, and encourages them to engage in communities of service. What the statistical studies do not indicate, but which is enormously important as well, is the *human* dimension in these types of community.

Miriam Waters

Miriam Waters says the church is her life. It instructs her, nurtures her, helps her to be more caring. She feels comfortable there. The people share her values. When they need help, she helps them. When she needs help, they help her. The church Miriam Waters belongs to is not in some sleepy little town where elderly ladies gather on Thursday afternoons to make quilts. It is located in an affluent suburb of Knoxville, Tennessee. The people who go there are busy professionals. Miriam's husband is a middle-level executive in a large electronics firm. She herself is the director of a prospering day-care center.

For Miriam Waters, the church gives her a sense of community in all three of the ways I have just described. As a community of support, the church has been her mainstay. Indeed, support was the reason why she and her husband joined in the first place. "My daddy had cancer at the time," she explained, "and it was really important to our family to all get back in the same church while he was sick." Her sister and brother-in-law had joined the church, so Miriam and her husband quit the church they were attending and switched to the present one. "We're really glad we did," she says. Then, reflecting about what the church has meant to her, she adds: "Y'know we are a family group—when we're sick we all bring food, y'know—that's just what we're about."

The way the church gives support was especially evident when Miriam's husband had to have eye surgery. "My husband had five eye surgeries, and it was when I was just a mess, and he really wasn't making a lot of money. Our insurance paid all but 20 percent, but when you're talking about thousands and thousands and thousands of dollars of hospital and doctor's bills, 20 percent adds up to be a lot of money. And at that time his Sunday School class took up money, and I'll never forget the day they brought the money in. We always said, my husband and I, that for the rest of our married life we would try to help other people anytime we saw a need."

Through the church, and because of the values it teaches, Miriam Waters also feels more a part of her community of residence. She does volunteer work for the local PTA. But mostly she just tries to be interested in her neighbors and show them little acts of kindness. For example? "Well, y'know, taking food is something we do real often—when someone's sick. Helping someone move is something my husband recently did. That's the kind of thing we do. Neighbor type things, y'know, helping with yard work when a neighbor had surgery and couldn't do it, that's the kinds of things we do."

Last year, after her husband received a big promotion, they seriously considered moving to a different neighborhood. But community eventually won out. "I decided we were going to buy a new house. We've lived here for fifteen years, and I wanted a nicer, bigger house. But the kids didn't want to move. My husband didn't either. And I figured it'd be a lot of trouble, you know, moving alone! So we stayed. I'm glad we did."

The community of service in which Miriam participates also centers directly around the church. Much of the informal helping she does is directed at needs she learns about through the church. Besides the money she gives directly to the church, she tries to give informally to people who may be in financial need. "I've always done it anonymously through another person," she comments. Even if the financial need is not severe, she tries to help. Not long ago, for instance, she learned about a family that was struggling because the father had lost his job, so she bought a Nintendo video game and sent it anonymously for the children.

Sometimes she becomes more directly involved in trying to be of service to the community—still in small ways, but occasionally with greater cost than she expected. With a laugh that anticipated what was to come, she recalled keeping the fourteen-year-old son of a couple who had to be out of town because the husband was having cancer surgery. One night, she remembers, "he shot a hole through our TV with a gun! A direct hit—right in the middle of the screen! Oh gosh! It was a long night that night. It was a very tense visit from then on, but—that's the kind of thing we do."

In a broader sense, the church also animates Miriam's thinking about the worth of everything she does. The old doctrine of the "calling" to which the Protestant reformers of the sixteenth and seventeenth centuries gave so much attention is still central to her worldview. And for her it means service. "I believe we are called by God—you people at Princeton won't understand this—but I feel personally that I'm where I'm supposed to be. I'm part of the church here, and that's important to me, because I can minister to all sorts of families. And you never know what seed may be planted."

The Church and Individualism

As mentioned earlier, though, critics of our society believe these forms of community, and the caring and personal attachments that go with them, may be breaking down. In their book *Habits of the Heart,* for example, sociologist Robert Bellah and his associates suggest that an obsession with our personal interests, our feelings, and whether things are going to advance our own ambitions is undermining the vital bonds of community that have sustained our society in the past.[12] Despite public appeals for people to reach out to their neighbors and rediscover the community values that could again make us a kinder and gentler nation, many observers fear we are simply becoming more selfish and inward with each successive decade. Rather than the "Me Generation" becoming the "We Generation," it has only become the "Mine Generation."

The relation between the church and individualism has a long and variegated history.[13] Martin Luther tried to reinvigorate the church's role in the community by conducting services in the vernacular, writing hymns that common people could understand, and encouraging town magistrates to be more responsive to the welfare needs of the poor. But he has also been accused of setting modern individualism into motion by emphasizing the believer's need for faith and individual salvation. The role of John Calvin is similarly ambiguous. One could hardly imagine a more community-oriented religion than the teachings that Calvin put into practice in sixteenth-century Geneva. And yet, as Max Weber revealed in his classic study, *The Protestant Ethic and the Spirit of Capitalism,* the teachings of Calvin also contributed to the rise of an individualistic ethos conducive to the acquisition of material goods.[14]

The church in contemporary America also displays this curious mixture of community and individualistic values. Rather than simply standing in the way of the fragmenting trends in our society—rather than simply pitting Christ against culture, as theologian H. Richard Niebuhr once expressed it—the church also accommodates these dominant trends.[15] Indeed, observers of contemporary religion have often diagnosed the same tendencies within the church that critics point to in the wider society. They see a growing emphasis on private spirituality, on personal needs, on taking care of oneself—all occurring within the church itself.[16]

Some of the studies I have already cited provide evidence on the extent to which churchgoers in the United States buy into the individualistic values that prevail in our society. Despite their involvement in community service and caring, churchgoers differ little from nonattenders on many of the commonly understood traits of American individualism. In my study, for example, 76 percent of the weekly churchgoers said "being successful in your work" was absolutely essential or very important to them, compared with 79 percent of those who seldom attended church. On another question that asked about the importance of "taking care of yourself," the two groups were also virtually indistinguishable (88 percent and 86 percent, respectively, said this was absolutely essential or very important). A majority of churchgoers (59 percent) also agreed with the statement "You have to take care of yourself first, and if you have any energy left over, then help others"—almost as many as said this among the unchurched (67 percent).

The utilitarianism in our culture that assesses everything in terms of the question, What's in it for me? is also present among American churchgoers. Blatant expressions of this idea sometimes occur in sermons and in church publications themselves—for example, in calling on people to serve others because it will make them feel good. When asked in surveys about such motives, most people feel uncomfortable admitting they actually think this way. But a minority do admit such thoughts, and this minority is as common within the churches as it is outside of them. For example, 27 percent of weekly churchgoers said "being kind and considerate helps me get what I want in life" was a major reason why they tried to be a caring person, and this was larger than the comparable proportion (19 percent) among the unchurched.

The New Voluntarism

In addition to the corrosive effects of individualism and utilitarianism, the church's role in sustaining community also appears to be endangered by social forces that impinge on the lives of church members. Despite the fact that four in ten Americans still attend church on any given Sunday, for example, some evidence is beginning to show that the increasing involvement of women in the labor force is reducing the time and energy they may have to devote to church work and church-related volunteer activities.[17] The involvement of churchgoers in their communities of residence is also being affected by the high levels of geographic mobility in the American population. Church attendance itself appears to be substantially lower among people who have moved within the past five years than among more stable members of the community.

In their book *American Mainline Religion,* sociologists Wade Clark Roof and William McKinney identify a "new voluntarism" that seems to be the American way of adapting our faith to the breakup of traditional community loyalties.[18] Instead of remaining loyal to one congregation, or even to a single denomination, we flit from one church to another, depending on where our jobs take us, what happens to be most convenient, and how we happen to feel at the moment. Roof and McKinney believe all this flitting about is yet another indication that the church's ability to sustain community may be weakening.

My book *The Restructuring of American Religion* showed that denominational loyalties are indeed becoming increasingly fragile. Substantial minorities of the members of nearly all denominations and faiths were raised in some other religious tradition than their present one. Many are married to someone of a different faith. Many have switched denominations several times during their adult lives. And many more choose their friends outside their churches, attend a variety of churches, and see little reason why they should become members of a particular denomination— especially when the denominations themselves no longer draw sharp distinctions between members and nonmembers.[19]

The evidence on attitudes is often even stronger than the data on behavior. If roughly half of church members stay in the same denominations in which they were raised, this does not mean that their loyalties run very deep. For example, a survey of eleven hundred Presbyterian members nationwide showed that only 30 percent agreed with the statement "While they may have disagreements from time to time, Christians should remain loyal to one denomination throughout their adult lives." By comparison, 73 percent agreed with the statement, "There are several other denominations where I could serve and be just as satisfied."[20] The same study showed that only about half of all Presbyterian members discuss their personal religious beliefs with people in their congregation. Only a third said it was important that their close friends share their religious beliefs.

What of the Future?

There is always the possibility that voluntarism, individualism, utilitarianism, and the social circumstances reinforcing these trends will greatly diminish the church's ability to sustain community in the future. There is also the possibility that the inherent desire for community that seems to pervade so many of our lives, together with the enormous resources the church still has at its disposal, will continue to give the church an important community-sustaining role in our society. At present, the best available evidence suggests that churchgoers are indeed community-oriented, but they are individualistic at the same time.

The vital tension between community and individualism within the churches, as in the broader society, will not be decided from on high by church leaders or from below by the blind forces of societal change. It will be determined where it is experienced most acutely—in the individual life experiences of the average churchgoer. If people want to have community and be individualists as well, they will have to be creative in reconciling the two.

To see how that tension and reconciliation may be experienced, let us return again in concluding to the example of Miriam Waters. Despite her commitment to her church and to her neighbors, she is scarcely immune to the tensions inherent in trying to be community-oriented in an individualistic society. She worries, for example, about the values she sees portrayed on television. "The value system in the United States is very money-oriented," she laments. "People are placing importance on the wrong things in life." She points to the drug problem as a symptom of the breakup of family and community. She also points out how impersonal the business world has become: when her husband had his eye operations, nobody from his workplace even bothered to call.

Sometimes Miriam Waters also feels like she is alone culturally. So many people seem not to share her faith. She doubts that people elsewhere understand her idea of service—as her comment about Princeton not sharing her notion of the calling indicates. She finds it increasingly difficult, because of her own job and the schedules of her neighbors, to feel really a part of a close circle of friends. She admits, for example, that she has only one close female friend and that it takes an extraordinary amount of effort to be available even to that one friend.

And yet, more than anything else, it is Miriam Waters's faith that gives her the courage to go on trying and the hope that things in our society are not as bad as they sometimes seem. "Y' know," she says, "if people would practice Christian principles, it would really help." Then, recognizing that this is her personal view, and that others might not share it, she rephrases it: "Maybe what would help most is when people are really cared for by someone else. Maybe that would make people stop and think."

3

A Place for
the Christian

At the beginning of the twentieth century, religious leaders in the United States confidently declared the coming period a "Christian century." Now at the end of that century, despite the continuing role of the church, it would seem more appropriate to ask whether the next one will hold a place for the Christian at all. I do not mean that values long associated with the Christian tradition, such as love and peace, will disappear from the North American continent. But will it be likely, or possible, for people to call themselves "Christians?" Even if the church were able to sustain community, it would be necessary to ask if that would be sufficient to carry forward the label of Christian. Would it be a distinctively "Christian" community? Would it be sufficient to encourage people to call themselves "Christians"? Or is it more likely that people in the next century will identify themselves increasingly by other labels, such as their profession or their nation of citizenship? And if they did, would anything important be lost?

The fact that it is already awkward to ask these questions reveals how close we are to the next century and how urgent it may be to consider it. It seems doubtful whether many people at the end of the nineteenth century, other than a few academics with European training, would have questioned the value of people calling themselves Christians. But now we have to be mindful that spirituality is frequently distinguished from religiosity and that religious commitment is often described in generic, rather than confessional, terms. Some observers lament the development of invisible religion and religionless Christianity. Others, however, regard it as parochial to be concerned with labels. What matters, they argue, is the depth of people's faith, not whether they adopt one label or another.

An initial task, therefore, must be to indicate why the identity "Christian" may be important. I want to withhold giving a normative answer to this question for the moment, and stay at least temporarily within the bounds generally imposed by the social sciences. It is important to ask whether the identity "Christian" will remain significant in the next century because this identity has played such a prominent cultural role in the past, not only in this century but in the two millennia preceding it. If this identity should cease to exist, or be modified greatly in the coming century, it would surely imply many other changes in how we think of ourselves religiously and culturally as well.

There is also a more specific reason for being interested in this question. The term "Christian" is, as already stated, an identity—something we attach to ourselves to define who we are, individually and collectively, just as we do when we say we are Americans, residents of Princeton, a professor, a pastor, or stamp collector. Although we can think of identity in the collective sense (as we do, for example, when we speak of "the Russians" or "the Third World"), usually the question of identity comes up in the context of giving a suitable definition of who we are individually. Three characteristics of modern culture press this question upon us at this level: first, we live in a society, as suggested in the last chapter, that is highly individualistic, meaning that we attach high value to the dignity and freedom of the individual, and regard the individual as the primary unit of moral responsibility; second, living as we do in a society of strangers, and moving into and out of multiple roles, we are constantly asked by others to define ourselves ("Who is this?" is a repeated query); and third, because we attach high importance to the interior life, viewing it as a frontier needing to be explored, we ourselves are often the source of the question, "Who am I?"[1] Each of these reasons suggests to us that identity is a question arising chiefly in the context of the self.

But modern social theory suggests a different perspective. Even if identity pertains to the self, and even if it is something we must work at to develop, it is generally *conferred* upon us.[2] Most of us were born Americans; this identity was conferred upon us at birth, or perhaps later by a federal judge, if we immigrated. Most of us may not have been born in the place in which we currently reside; our choice to live here, we tell ourselves, was our own decision. But the identity was still conferred; most of us did not invent the town in which we live, but an address was conferred on us when we moved into our house. Becoming a professor, pastor, or stamp collector seems even more like having an identity we have worked for, created, or chosen for ourselves. But it is again significant that most of us talk about "choosing" a career, rather than inventing one. You invent something from scratch; you choose something that already exists. You become, say, a professor by entering an institution you know in advance has the authority to confer this identy on you at some point. In social theory identities then are understood to be conferred on individuals by social institutions.

To ask about the future of the identity "Christian," therefore, is to raise questions not so much about individuals but about social institutions. In the past, the identity of Christian could be conferred by the state; indeed, from the fourth century till the nineteenth century, the state was the primary institution from which the Christian identity derived. The religious identity of the individual was given by the religion of the territory, and in most cases the religion of the territory was that of its ruler. As religious pluralism gradually came to be recognized, starting with the religious wars of the seventeenth century but not reaching full bloom until the nineteenth century, religious identity could also be conferred by the family. A person became a Christian and a member of a particular Christian tradition by being born into a family that adhered to that tradition. But over the past two centuries religious identity has increasingly, as we know, become a matter of voluntary association, of willful identification with a particular religious institution.

At the risk of belaboring the point, let me emphasize that even in an era of religious voluntarism, it is the institution that confers the identity of "Christian" on the individual. We encourage individuals to seek the truth, to read the Bible, to grow in their faith, and in some traditions to make a personal decision for Christ. These teachings are so readily available in the West at least that an isolated individual might, as testimonials sometimes indicate, become a believer simply through private reading and reflection. But with few exceptions it is the church that confers the identity of "Christian." In some traditions this occurs through baptism and confirmation; in others, through people making a public profession of their faith to the assembled members of a congregation; and in others still, through joining or attending a particular church.

Recognizing the role of the church in conferring a religious identity on individuals is important because it reverses a common assumption about the history of the church over the past two centuries. Voluntarism has, in the social sciences at least, been regarded as a sign of the weakening influence of the church: presumably the balance between institutions and individuals was shifting toward the latter. Quite the contrary. The more individuals were expected to adopt a religious identity, the more important the church became as the social institution responsible for conferring that identity. Indeed, we have ample evidence of this relationship from comparisons with countries where religious identity is still ascribed at birth by territorial residence and countries where religious identity is voluntary.

What we must also recognize, though, is that identity is not the only thing churches confer on the individual. Over the past two centuries, at the time this role was increasing, churches also retained much of their authority to confer certified biblical knowledge and doctrine, assurance about individuals' eternal destiny and perhaps that of their ancestors and children as well, the sanctity of the marriage vow, respectability and social standing in the community, and many other things. Indeed, we might say that the great age of the church corresponded with the period in which it conferred not only individual identity but goods and services of a wide variety as well.

The identity-conferring function of the church looms all the more important now at the end of the twentieth century because so many of these other functions have eroded. In many cases, it seems, churches no longer confer much of anything else, other than identity. They do not certify people as being wise. That capacity has fallen largely to the colleges and universities, to science, and to professional associations. Even when a distinction is drawn between wisdom and knowledge, the wise are seldom any longer theologians and clergy. The expressivist orientation in modern culture attaches wisdom to the artist and the activist. They are the ones who create, who invent by experiencing life and probing its boundaries. Nor do the churches necessarily have the authority any longer to certify what it means to be spiritual. Public opinion polls reveal that most Americans think you should come up with your own definition of spirituality, rather than following the dictates of any religious institutions.[3] Indeed, many of the people I have interviewed in various research projects describe a negative trade-off between spirituality and religious institutions. The latter, they say, are too formal and bureaucratic, even hypocritical, always raising money and running programs; spirituality, they say, cannot be forced into a mold, for it is too ephemeral, emotional, intuitive, impulsive. Who defines spirituality—the institutions that certify what it means—are independent writers, again the artists and activists, but also mystics, secular saints, and just ordinary people in our neighborhoods, or the people we know from Alcoholics Amonymous. We regard them as spiritual because we know more of their private lives; these lives are shielded from view by the formality of most religious institutions. Perhaps the churches do still play a role in certifying that we are good citizens and responsible parents. In the world of suburban America, these are certifications well worth having, of course. We want the respect of our neighbors, whether we actually know them or not, and so being involved in community organizations is the thing to do. With fewer children, sky-rocketing educational costs, and inflated expectations, we make everything revolve around parenting. And with all the uncertainty now associated with this role, many churches play a useful role in helping us believe we are good parents when we take our children to a youth group or in telling us it really isn't our fault when our children fall short of our expectations.

But mostly, what churches can still do is give people identities as Christians. They still do this for most of the population by baptizing infants and confirming teenagers. Surprisingly high proportions of the population claim to have had born-again experiences, which are probably described that way because religious institutions still help to define them. Other people may only be cultural Christians, but genuinely so, because the churches have in the past taught them, and evoked a deep, primordial identification with, distinctively Christian stories. In nominal ways, others may identify themselves as Christians because their parents belonged to a church, because they still attend on Christmas and Easter, and because they know they are not Muslims or Hindus.

The thesis I want to consider in this chapter, then, is that the likelihood of "Christian" having any place in the next century depends on the continuing power of the church to confer this as a meaningful identity. I want to consider three ways in which the church confers a Christian identity, focusing on the challenges that beset it in each of these areas: the church as a community of memory, the church as denomination, and the church as a supportive community. Each of these has already been mentioned in previous chapters. Now we must inquire more specifically about the likelihood that the church, in these ways, will carry on the very identity of the Christian.

The Church as Community of Memory

In *Habits of the Heart,* Bellah and his colleagues suggest that part of the genuine, sustaining community, which in their view we so desperately need in our otherwise individualistic society, must be a strong conception of the past, a community of memory:

> Communities . . . have a history—in an important sense they are constituted by their past—and for this reason we can speak of a real community as a "community of memory," one that does not forget its past. In order not to forget that past, a community is involved in retelling its story, its constitutive narrative, and in so doing, it offers examples of the men and women who have embodied and exemplified the meaning of the community. These stories of collective history and exemplary individuals are an important part of the tradition that is so central to a community of memory.[4]

Their emphasis on stories, it is worth noting, points to an idea so fundamental that it deserves consideration in its own right.[5] But in the present context I want only to observe that Bellah and his associates draw a connection between communities of memory and both the topics on which this chapter focuses: the church and identity. That the church, along with neighborhoods and kin groups, is an important community of memory goes without saying. That communities of memory are essential to the formation of an individual's identity is also a commonplace, although part of what is implied here is the importance of tradition, as opposed to detached rationality, a theme that philosophers Hans-Georg Gadamer and Alasdair MacIntyre, among others, have asserted with particular force.

MacIntyre, for example, underscores the point already made about identity being conferred by social institutions, stating that any conception of moral action must therefore be accompanied by a sociology of the same. His treatment of tradition, moreover, explicates perhaps more clearly the mechanisms by which communities of memory and individual identities are linked. He writes:

> A living tradition . . . is an historically extended, socially embodied argument, and an argument precisely in part about the goods which constitute that tradition. Within a tradition the pursuit of goods extends through generations, sometimes through many generations. Hence the individual's search for his or her good is generally and characteristically conducted within a context defined by those traditions of which the individual's life is a part.[6]

I have included this statement from MacIntyre also because it points to the fact that communities of memory must be considered in evaluative terms. Unlike the authors of *Habits of the Heart,* who give the impression that American individualism simply leaves people without communities of memory, MacIntyre correctly perceives that everyone lives within these communities, if only because our personal narratives always depend on a sense of history and tradition. The variation comes when we consider what he refers to as the "goods" constituting different traditions. In considering churches as communities of memory, therefore, we must ask how strong this tradition will be and what goods it will convey.

The Loss of Tradition

A useful starting point for trying to answer these questions is to observe that the church's role as a community of memory is being emphasized by MacIntyre, Bellah, and indeed many church leaders precisely at a time when an increasing percentage of the American population includes those not being born and raised in churches; even if they are, such people are not being reared in the churches of their ancestors, and are probably not attending churches that their children will also attend. In other words, memory is being emphasized because memory is now increasingly problematic. We can raise questions about tradition with greater urgency now than we could have had we lived in the thirteenth century.

It is also instructive that the church is increasingly regarded as an important community of memory in our society. This is because the other sources of rich narrative tradition, namely ethnic groups, residential communities, and families, are also subject to the growing pressures of change, while many of our more recent institutions, such as business firms and the mass media, are believed to have only shallow ties to the past. As many of the other functions of the church to which reference has already been made erode, the memory-preserving function may also gain in relative importance. But what does it mean to say that the church functions as a community of memory, especially at a time when so many of its actual historic links are being weakened?

Telling Stories of the Past

As a community of memory, the church must, among other things, be backward looking; it has a special mission to preserve the past, to carry on a tradition. The church must be a community of memory by perpetuating the narratives of the past, by telling stories that bring the past into the present. And, while the idea of church-as-storyteller may seem to diminish its importance, this function must actually be seen as having the utmost significance.[7] For the very likelihood of anyone in the future retaining the identity of "Christian" depends on it.

At first glance, telling stories may also seem easy; this, after all, is what the church does: preaching relates stories, and the liturgy reenacts them. But modern literary theory also demonstrates the complexity of storytelling. Decisions must be made about which past to memorialize, how to make it contemporary, and how to evoke identification between the listener and the characters in the text. These tasks are made all the more difficult by the institutional settings in which the stories are told.

Challenges

One institutional challenge facing the church is that it has often robbed itself of the authority to tell its stories. In the interest of demonstrating its scientific, historical, and theological sophistication, it has talked in these terms instead of telling its stories. People who go to the theater, we must remember, want to see a play; they do not come to hear theories of the play. A second institutional challenge comes from the fact that increasing numbers of people, as I have mentioned, are transient and infrequent participants in religious communities. At one time, churches could probably do more than tell and enact stories; they could also embody these stories. The past was not the universal past of Christians everywhere, but of Christians in this place: our forebears, our ancestors, our elders. Now churches shy away from such stories because they know newcomers will not understand. A third institutional challenge comes from the fact that the church faces increasing competition in modern societies as purveyor of stories about the past. If one does not think so, consider the extensive indoctrination children receive in school about the past; or perhaps more important, consider how powerful the motion picture industry has become as a source of stories about the past. And a fourth challenge involves the continuing emphasis our society places on progress, novelty, innovation. Stories about the past are desperately needed, but we also want them to help us fantasize about the future, and we want them related in innovative ways.

At best, then, the church may be able to create temporary pasts, modular traditions, in which people can participate for short periods of time, as they do when they see a movie based on a historical novel. Some churches may be able to present their stories as "The Story," as the story around which all of history revolves, the "greatest story ever told." But even that kind of story will not instill a deep Christian identity unless it is told and retold, related in innovative ways, and intertwined with the other individual and collective pasts that are part of every person's tradition. Paradoxically, the church must also diminish the particularism of its various local, regional, and national histories, but at the same time include itself in the stories it tells, reinforcing its own authority as it does so. This does not mean a return to triumphalism, but it does mean facing squarely the history of the church and redeeming what is unique about its past. It also means that the church must be a place where discourse, whether about the past, present, or future, is actively encouraged. Memory may connote an element of individual biography, tucked away in the recesses of the mind. But memory comes alive and is renewed only when it is discussed. Stanley Hauerwas expresses this idea eloquently when he writes: "The church not only is but must be a 'community of moral discourse'—that is, a community that sustains the ongoing implications of its commitments across generations as it necessarily faces new challenges and situations."[8]

The Church as Denomination

In the past century denominationalism was of course a very large part of what it meant to be Christian. People were Baptists or Presbyterians as much as they were Christians. They were Catholics or Orthodox, and their Christian identity was inseparable from these traditions. But denominationalism has, as we know, declined in many ways.[9] Fewer people remain in the denominations in which they were raised, fewer people think their own denomination has a better grasp on the truth than other denominations, and fewer denominations themselves impose creedal tests that people must meet in order to become members or participate in church services. Growing numbers of churches might be characterized as open systems, attempting to embrace everyone, while imposing little on anyone.

Tom Haskens

At times, it is hearing someone like yourself express these orientations that makes you most aware of them, even more than having statistics or theories that demonstrate them. Listen to what Tom Haskens, a devout Christian in his early forties, has to say about his denominational affiliation: "I don't care whether it's called a Methodist or a Presbyterian church or Community Bible church. I don't care what the name is on the front. . . . I don't think I have to be a member of any particular religion to be a Christian. I don't look at a name on the front of the church. I look for a fellowship that is committed to serving Christ. That's where I am now." Tom Haskens identifies himself as a Christian; he is not like Bellah's character, Sheila, who had her own private religion named after herself. Tom Haskens is deeply involved in his local church, but it is also clear that denominations don't mean much to him. He is happy now because the preaching and the fellowship appeal to him. In a few years, he may pick up his family and switch to a different church.

There are probably lots of people, like Tom Haskens, who think of themselves simply as Christians, rather than Baptists, Presbyterians, or Catholics. But a vital element is lost in the process. Imagine what it would be like if everybody in the United States thought of themselves as Americans, but had no sense of themselves as New Yorkers, San Franciscans, Virginians, Midwesterners, or Italian-Americans. The result seems an awful lot like the specter of mass society that was so much discussed in the 1950s.[10] No identity stands between the atomized individual and the nation-state. Everyone sinks into boring sameness.

The Retention of Local Identity

Is such a mass society the destiny of the church as well? I think not. Mass society is not an apt description of our identity in the secular sphere. I suspect Christians will also retain more than some vague, universal identity as well. The slogan "think globally, act locally" is what comes to mind. The Christian identity will, on the one hand, become more global as denominational boundaries erode, and also as Christians realize their kinship with fellow Christians around the world.[11] This global identity will be significantly enriched and strengthened, though, if it is accompanied by a local identity.[12] And this local identity will still come about chiefly in churches associated with various denominations.[13]

The key point, though, is that denominational identity will in practice mean a *local* identity. We see virtually the same thing in every other sphere of social life. People identify themselves as New Yorkers because this helps to locate them in a local geographic space. When they identify themselves as Italian-Americans, they also evoke a local neighborhood and kin network, not an affinity with an organization in Washington. Truly national organizations, such as political parties, are eroding in their ability to retain people's loyalties, just as denominations are. But local civic clubs and community organizations are flourishing. We know that the same thing is happening in the religious sphere. People belong to the Presbyterian church, not because of deep loyalty to the denomination at large, but because they like the pastor, they feel comfortable with the people, the building fits their architectural tastes, the church is not too far away, and it provides activities for their family.

Challenges

The challenges here are all too familiar. When the church functions mainly as a source of local identity, it must then compete with all the other civic associations that provide identity at this level. School programs and athletic teams serve the same function for children, and are often far more attractive than the local youth group at church. Voluntary associations, neighbors, and the workplace constitute the local identities of adults. Church leaders are simply deluded if they think people "out there" are desperately seeking a "community" with which to associate and will attend church in hopes of finding it there. Despite the individualism of our society, most people have all the community associations they can stand. If they attend church, it will have to be for other reasons than that.

But I want to emphasize a different challenge that also arises from the church's increasingly local identity. If laity cares less and less about the denomination as a larger entity, this means that the guardians of denominationalism will increasingly be the clergy. Perhaps it has always been so, but now the clergy must take on the additional responsibility of caring for bureaucratic structures built up over the past century that are presently in serious decline. Were there a way to cover the financial costs of these structures, they might well serve as an outlet for the surplus numbers of clergy currently being trained in many denominations. A more likely outcome, though, is an increasing separation between clergy and laity. Members of the clergy will sit on denominational committees, read denominational publications, worry about the policies and public pronouncements of their denominations, and look to denominational networks for new jobs and promotions; laity will register extreme disinterest in any of these activities.

The negative result may well be an increase in the levels of anticlericalism that are already beginning to show up in studies of lay attitudes.[14] Despite the relatively high respect in which members of the clergy are still held, compared with politicians and business leaders, they are nevertheless revered most as care givers, and least as petty bureaucrats concerned with their denominations. Lacking the divine authority that once derived from conceptions of the priestly calling, they are often criticized for paying too much attention to finances, their own prestige, and other quests commonly associated with the mentality of the bureaucrat.

A more positive result may be opportunities for lay leaders to play a more active role in shaping their local churches. Members of the clergy may also find it valuable to retrieve their ancient authority, leaving denominational work to professional administrators, and paying more attention to becoming spiritual guides or personal witnesses of what it means to be Christian. Giving care and support is likely to become an increasingly significant role for laity and clergy alike.

The Church as Support Group

This brings us, then, to a final way in which the church can function as a source of Christian identity. Personal identity is always shaped most formatively through firsthand interaction in intimate reference groups, the family of origin of course being the most significant of all. The family, though, is currently undergoing enormous changes of the kind that probably will not lead, as some argue, to its breakdown or demise, but are creating many uncertainties about desirable role relationships among parents and children. With the heightened responsibility we now accept as individuals for our own personal growth and self realization, we are also much more oriented than ever before toward the continuing resocialization of ourselves beyond our families of origin. Concepts of midlife crisis and slogans such as "It's never too late to have a happy childhood" attest to these heightened responsibilities. And, while these quests are intensely personal, they too require institutional support—support in the form of a language that confers legitimacy on the outcome, and support for the deep emotional work involved in any process of identity reformation.

In the past churches typically served as intimate reference groups, augmenting the family with adult role models and social support. Even until fairly recently, age-graded classes, gender-based groups for men and women, and special programs for young married people, families with small children, and the like, probably functioned to reinforce conventional understandings of family roles. Probably many people can also point to particular elders, deacons, and Sunday school teachers as adult role models who fulfilled the vital function, emphasized recently in Robert Bly's book about men, of initiating the young and helping them differentiate their own identity from that of their parents.[15] Two developments, though, have eroded the churches' capacity to perform these identity-shaping tasks: the changing conceptions of family and self to which I have already referred, and the growing size and impersonality of many churches. Megachurches of several thousand members cannot by themselves provide such intimate socialization, but neither can the leftover neighborhood church of twenty people, all of whom are in their retirement years. And yet the church still has a mission to fulfill in this area, because the athletic teams, civic organizations, and workplaces I mentioned previously provide association but not intimacy and deep personal support.

Evidence on Small Groups

The hunger for such support is perhaps best evidenced by the explosion in recent years of twelve-step groups, self-help groups, and support groups of all kinds. In a national survey conducted in November 1990, for example, 29 percent of the American public said they were "currently involved in a small group that meets regularly and provides support or caring for those who participate in it." Another 12 percent said they had been involved in such a group in the past, but were not currently involved.[16]

The connection between these groups and spirituality has often been noted, particularly because twelve-step groups generally acknowledge dependence on a higher power, but also because many such groups are in fact sponsored by churches. Founding small groups has been one way in which megachurches have been able to meet the need for intimacy among their members, and in some cases these groups appear to have generated further growth in their sponsoring organizations. In the survey, the spiritual dimension was also clearly in evidence. Among those currently involved in small support groups, 73 percent said their faith or spirituality had been influenced as a result of their involvement, and of this number, 70 percent said their faith had been deepened a lot. In more specific ways, the spiritual influence of group involvement was also apparent: of the people currently involved, 90 percent claimed they were better able to forgive others, 79 percent said they had been enabled to share their faith with others outside the group, 78 percent felt closer to God, and 66 percent had experienced answers to prayer.[17]

If spirituality in its generic sense is reinforced by these groups, the evidence that a specifically Christian identity is being nurtured is, however, less compelling. On the one hand, more of those who were involved, than of those who were not involved, said their church had become more important to them during the past five years. We don't know, of course, whether group involvement was the source of their increasing interest in the church or whether they were already becoming more interested in the church and this was the source of their group involvement. On the other hand, 40 percent of the people involved in small support groups said these groups were not part of the activities of any church or religious organization. In other words, many of these groups may be cultivating spirituality that is not associated with anything specifically Christian or linked to any specific religious tradition. If so, that is certainly a challenge the churches will need to confront. Either they will need to incorporate these groups more closely into their traditional structures or see the new structures themselves become functional alternatives to the church.

The Transmission of Identity

There is, however, another challenge that these groups pose, particularly in connection with the question of identity that I raised at the beginning of this chapter. The most serious task that the churches have always faced has been the transmission of identity to new generations, and the maintenance of that identity across the life cycle. Support groups are vulnerable in both these respects. They do not for the most part provide anything for children or for parents and children, and they are often deliberately conceived for adults experiencing crises at particular transitions in their lives, rather than being part of a larger congregation or community that encompasses the individual in the way the church typically has in the past from cradle to grave.

These limitations do not mean that small support groups fail to be of any effect in either of these areas. Certainly they provide support and sustenance for parents, thereby raising the chances that parents will be able to perform their own socializing functions more effectively. By enhancing the self-awareness of parents, they may increase the ability of parents to deal with their children in better ways than if they were still struggling to recover from their own dysfunctional childhoods. Furthermore, in helping adults through particularly difficult life transitions, they may provide the role models that are often lacking in modern society, and even build bridges from one life stage to the next in a way that allows people to retain their Christian identity.

In conclusion, then, let me suggest that the identity of "Christian" is very well likely to continue in the twenty-first century, but its vitality will depend on the ability of churches and other religious institutions to perpetuate it. Whether churches serve primarily as communities of memory, as denominations that help people to act locally while thinking globally, or as support groups that nurture the in-depth work required to reshape one's identity, they will need to provide role models and turn these role models into characters in the stories we all tell ourselves. It is in these stories that we find our true identity and, as I shall discuss in the next section, these stories also become the means by which we are challenged to live ethically and morally.

II

Ethical Challenges: Role Models, Stories, and Learning How to Care

4

Stories to
Live By

Frankie lies on a hill now. Toward the north is the hill where Central High
School looms, and where her principal used to talk about heroes. Maybe
three miles away to the southeast is the house where she spent the first nine
years of her life—and that is on a hill also. And away off beyond the environs of Fountain City and Knoxville, bigger ridges stand purple. You might
imagine that Frankie was up there somewhere, waltzing; she'd always loved
to dance.

   She could be, too. Could have been dancing with her darling, and snug-
gling delightedly with him in bed, running through life with all the verve,
perplexity, heartbreak and exultation of any young wife during 5000 nights
and days of these past 15 years.

   "Except that something made her go back into that airplane cabin 11
times, and 11 times was just one time too many.

   "A crashed airplane is strictly for the stalwart men in asbestos suits and
masks. It is not for the petite little Miss Pretty—not unless she is a Mary
Frances Housley. Then she has such love in her heart that no high-octane
explosion can ever blast it out.[1]

So concludes the heartrending account of a young stewardess who gave
her life that others might live. Five short pages in a magazine purchased
at the supermarket, tossed in between the tomatoes and canned soup.
On the next page, as if to relieve the reader of these weighty reflections,
are humorous quips about neighbors and police, haberdashers and traveling salesmen. But one would have to be calloused to the quick not to
be moved by the story of Mary Frances Housley.

The Ethical Challenge

As we reflect on life in the twenty-first century, we surely must hope that goodness and mercy, even of the extreme kind demonstrated by Mary Frances Housely, will be preserved. Traditionally, it has fallen to the church to pass on such ethical ideals. In the future, the social role of the Christian will hopefully include the ethical life, a life of caring and compassion for those in need.

But how can the ethical ideals of the past be transmitted effectively to the coming generation? In science fiction, the future will be one in which chemicals, computers, hypnosis, and other means of brainwashing are used to transmit the society's ideals. Will the church be replaced by these means?

Philosophical Views

Ethicists would, of course, say no. But ethicists pose a different, and perhaps equally debatable, scenario of the future. University of Chicago philosopher Russell Hardin, for example, suggests in his book *Morality within the Limits of Reason* that we cannot transmit our ethical standards to the next generation with effectiveness until we have grounded these standards more clearly in the detached logic of rational utilitarianism. In his view, we must weigh the goodness of various outcomes by applying the principles of probability calculations and game theory, and make our ethical decisions according to those considerations.[2] Others have taken a similar approach. German social philosopher Jürgen Habermas, for example, pins his hopes for the future of ethics on the ability of dispassionate people to thematize their interests and communicate about these underlying themes in rational terms.[3]

The Role of Narrative

I have the greatest respect for these philosophers and their efforts to save a place in the intellectual domain for ethical deliberation. But I doubt whether this is the domain in which hard ethical choices will actually be hammered out in the future. I do not mean that we must opt for emotivism in favor of the intellect. How we think about ethical questions is of enormous importance. But our thinking is less likely to be shaped by the abstract claims of the philosopher than by the concrete tutelage of the storyteller. Indeed, if we turn to other philosophers, we find a growing recognition of the importance of stories. Alasdair MacIntyre, as we have seen, emphasizes the role of narrative in creating communities of memory. Stanley Hauerwas extends this idea specifically to questions of ethical commitment. He observes: "We rightly discover that to which we are deeply committed only by having our lives challenged by others. That challenge does not come only from without but rather is entailed by narrative that has captured our lives."[4]

Others, also writing with a particular interest in the relationship between religion and ethics, have arrived at similar conclusions.[5] But whether their claims are correct, and if so, in what manner, questions remain that must be addressed in real-life situations. I shall attempt to demonstrate the power of stories as vehicles of ethical transmission, not through a theoretical argument about their nature but by recounting from the lives of real people with whom I have talked how they learned the great biblical truth of loving one's neighbor as oneself.[6] In this and the following two chapters I shall report further on what I learned from the research I did for my book *Acts of Compassion*. In that book I examined the ways in which caring people in our society make sense of their efforts to help others. Some of the information came from a national survey, but often people found it necessary to tell personal stories to deal adequately with their understandings of their lives. Here, I wish to consider the role of stories themselves more fully. How do these stories encapsulate our experiences of ethical behavior? Who are the contemporary saints that supply our stories with models of caring and compassion? What does it take for us to draw ethical lessons from the stories of these saints? Can we learn from these stories ways in which we might do a better job of balancing our need for individuality and our need for community in the years ahead?

Stories of Love

Stories of brave people like Mary Frances Housely are a very important feature of American culture. They are simply more extreme, more vivid, more heroic versions of the stories that are a part of everyone's autobiography. In talking with people who had learned the value of caring, I discovered that everyone has stories to tell about the compassionate people they have known, heard of, read about, or admired from afar. They had read stories and seen films about famous men and women of compassion, such as Mother Teresa of Calcutta, Gandhi, and Martin Luther King, Jr. They also had moving stories to tell about friends, relatives, and other personal acquaintances who had shown them what it means to be compassionate. They had learned how to care by being cared for themselves and they had encoded these lessons in vivid personal narratives.

Mothers as Role Models

For many of us, stories of being cared for take us back to our childhoods, especially to our mothers. In the vestiges of our memories lie images of goodness that can become powerful models later on. Our mothers embody compassion. We remember how they cared for us, how they cared for others. Their example makes us think caring is primordial.

I remember vividly one elderly man who recounted the following story from his childhood: "When I was eight years old I got typhoid fever. I was in the hospital for five weeks. And, you know, my mother only missed one night during all that time spending the night with me in the hospital. That really stands out." He said he had always thought of his mother as a caring person, but it was really that event that he always recalled most clearly.

Similarly, a young man who spent many of his odd hours volunteering with the handicapped remembered the example his mother (and sister) had set for him through a business she operated: "Back in the sixties my mother opened an ice cream store right across from the city hall. She had a spare room in the back, so she turned it into a teen center where kids could come and hang out. My sister ran that. My mother was the authority figure and my sister was the friend people could relate to. Kids would come to my mother with questions like, 'I'm pregnant, what should I do?' And they'd come to my sister with questions like, 'I'm having trouble with my boyfriend, can I tell you about it?' Between the two of them, they really modeled what caring should be about."

Another young man described the caring he had experienced from his mother metaphorically: "Her whole life was a smile."

For many of us, the compassion we saw in our mothers is the inspiration for our own caring, as parents, volunteers, or friends. Our mothers provide us, as it were, with role models. But these models become operative for us—they shape our ethical conduct—because we have encoded their behavior in stories. The future of such conduct will undoubtedly depend on the continuing power of these stories about our mothers.

"She is the most caring and the most compassionate person I have ever known," is how one woman, a leader in the Mothers Against Drunk Driving (MADD) movement, described her mother. "She cares about people, she cares about children, she loves children, she makes sure you feel good about yourself." At that moment her train of thought was interrupted by a loud cry of "Mommy!" from the next room. After dealing gently with her son's pleading, she resumed, describing how much her mother's example had influenced her own attitudes toward childrearing. "I hope I love my own kids the way she loved us. She just spent lots of time holding us, loving us. She always said the housework could wait, but kids wouldn't, they just grow up on you. I really believe that. What you do for your children when they're little is so important when they're grown. So, you know, I just kiss my kids a lot and love them and, you know, spend time with them and tell them lots of stories."

Fathers as Role Models

Fathers are often the subjects of stories illustrating an ethic of compassion, too, although not as frequently, it seems, as mothers. A young businessman who had followed closely in his father's footsteps recalled that his father had always tried to be scrupulously ethical, but also compassionate, in the way he conducted business. One specific story that stood out in his memory involved a man whose business had failed. " 'What do you do?' my father asked, 'Let him starve or help him get back on his feet?' So my father found a way to get him back in business. And the guy was overcome. He said, 'Nat, how can I help you? I'll give you some of my best produce.' But my father said, 'Wait a minute. You don't have to do that. Just be a good guy, you know, like you've always been. You actually gave me the opportunity to do something good.' "

Other men and women recalled how their fathers had stopped to help strangers having car trouble or had helped with community-improvement projects sponsored by Rotary or Kiwanis clubs. Often the deeds were small, but held lasting significance in children's memories. They showed that Dad had a caring heart within his tough exterior.

Some people—the fortunate among us—are able to describe both their fathers and mothers in glowing terms as models of caring and compassion. A retired woman who spent time each week doing volunteer work at the local library remembered the sacrifices her parents had made for their children and the hard work that still reminded her of how much they cared for her. They had been immigrants and did not have much education, she said. "But one thing they taught us as children was the importance of giving of yourself. They always said the country has given you a lot, and you have to give something in return. I think I've carried that since childhood." Another woman said simply that she felt very lucky because her parents had showered her with warmth and affection.

Beyond our Parents

But many of us are not so lucky. The caring we received as children provides no model of compassion. It is something we would rather forget, something we hesitate to mention. Our mothers did not show us how to care. Neither did our fathers. We cannot turn to their example to find stories of compassion or of other ethical ideals. And, as we look to the future, we must recognize, sad as it may be, that this will be the experience of a growing number of children in our society. Divorce will leave its scars. Child abuse will leave its scars, too, literally.

Dysfunctional Families

This was the experience of a woman now in her late forties, divorced, who runs her own printing business. She is a deeply caring person who does volunteer work, helps people with drug abuse and alcoholism problems, and tries hard to be a witness to the unconditional love she believes is embodied in God. But she can think of nobody who exemplified caring and compassion while she was growing up. Her father committed suicide when she was a year and a half old. She describes both her mother and her grandfather, who lived with her mother, as drinking alcoholics. "Since that was the only thing I knew, I thought it was typical. I found out later, no, that it's not." She says there was no physical violence, but she was subjected to a great deal of "emotional battering." Mostly, she just grew up being confused about love and how to behave in order to receive it. She remarks, "It was just hard to figure out why you were told one time if you do it this way you'll get loved, and then the next time that wasn't right." Sometimes her mother tried to show love by buying her something. But this woman never experienced that as genuine caring. Instead, she found herself struggling to take care of others' needs without really knowing how to. She says, "Both my mother and my grandfather were very needy people and since I was the oldest child they did a lot of depending on me to meet their needs, which was really dumb. No wonder I was confused. No thirteen-year-old can meet an adult's needs." It was not until years later, when she became involved in Alcoholics Anonymous, that she found the unconditional love she had always wanted. Only then was she able to begin showing compassion to others.

Emotional Distance

Here is another example. Janet is a tough, outspoken woman who spends time each week as a volunteer at a shelter for abused women. She admits that she has mixed feelings about her mother. The caring her mother exemplified was not tender or warm or emotionally involved. Caring for others mostly meant being strong, independent, and responsible. She recalls, "Mom didn't let anybody else do anything. She was sort of a perfectionist who just thought she could do things better and more efficiently." At a time when most women did not work outside the home, Janet's mother was a busy career woman. As a result, Janet remembers feeling more distant from her mother than close. "There were many times growing up when I felt lonely and not cared for," she says. And when pressed to recall if there were any times growing up when she especially felt cared for, Janet admits, "I guess I'm a little sensitive in that area." As she looks back on her childhood, she believes she got so little care that she simply decided she did not like being pampered and quit seeking the warmth and affection most children experience.

If having warm, loving parents we feel close to and who cared for us and made us happy as children is the recipe for learning compassion, then people like these two women are the exceptions. They violate the psychologists' dictum that warm, loving people come from warm, loving homes.[7] So do lots of other people.

Other Examples

Jack is a remarkable young man who has risked his own life to save people and who spends many hours as a volunteer fireman and rescue squad worker. He says his father was an alcoholic and his mother sued for a divorce when Jack was a teenager. "All my father ever taught me," Jack says, "is that I didn't want to grow up to be like him." Elmer, a retired broadcaster who works with Recording for the Blind, describes his upbringing in similarly negative terms. His parents were divorced when he was seven years old. For the next several years he lived with foster parents and then was sent away to boarding school. When he was fourteen, his parents remarried—each other. But Elmer stayed on at boarding school. As soon as he was old enough, he ran away and joined the Navy. "It was a funny sort of existence," he observes. "I don't know how I managed to turn out as normal as I did, considering how fragmented and unconventional my upbringing was."

In talking with other volunteers about the kind of caring they experienced as children, I found that many denied closeness and warmth as being part of their family experience. A middle-aged man who spent much of his spare time doing church work asserted that his family background was "a mixed bag with a lot of anger and frustration; a lot of feelings of neglect and judgment." A woman in her late seventies recounted that she had never experienced much caring as a child because, as she observed, "my father was about fifty when I was born and wasn't in very good health and my mother was just one notch below a professional musician, so she had a very busy life too." Another older woman remembered taking her dolls around to other poor children during the Depression in the 1930s, but denied that her sense of caring had anything to do with the way she was raised. Her mother died when she was nine and she was shunted from one foster home to another. "I can't remember any particular time when I was really cared for," she said. "Sometimes it was just the opposite. There were times in foster homes when I was abused. In fact, I remember a bloomer boy saying to me one time, 'How come you didn't go wrong?' because of all the things I had experienced."

Survey Evidence

As it turns out, evidence from large surveys also fails to support the idea that parental role models necessarily reinforce caring behavior. In one national study, for example, respondents who said they felt very close to their mothers and fathers were no more likely than respondents who said they felt less close to their parents to have donated money to charitable causes, to have given a donation to be used for a relief program, to have donated time to helping disadvantaged or needy people, to describe themselves as generous, or to say their efforts to help other people were very important or very satisfying. The study did not include more direct questions about parents' caring behavior, but closeness provides a reasonable enough proxy that some relationships might have been expected.[8]

The effect of parental role models is also cast into some doubt by the relationship between involvement in charitable activity and perceived happiness as a child. Present happiness and involvement in caring behavior are positively associated with each other. When perceived happiness as a child is introduced into the equation as well, this relation persists. However, the relationship between childhood happiness and charitable involvement is statistically insignificant.[9]

Other Role Models

But people can learn how to be caring even if they do not have warm, loving parents who provide role models. They learn it from other people and by telling stories. Some experience sticks in their memories. It is a vivid event that can be told and retold. In the telling it becomes a symbol, a turning point. It shows that caring is possible.

The first woman mentioned above is able to tell a story of becoming involved in AA. It is the event she recounts to tell how she became able to care. It was a genuine turning point in her life. Janet's memory of her mother as a distant, independent individual is tempered by her memory of being in the hospital as a teenager to have her tonsils removed. She was very frightened and alone. But she remembers a nurse who was especially kind to her. For a long time afterward, she was moved by this woman's compassion. It was she who provided the inspiration for Janet to enter nursing herself. And even though she eventually gave up nursing, Janet feels she began to recognize her interest in caring for others at this time.

The rescue squad worker experienced a lot of care from the various scout leaders he modeled himself after as a child—they filled some of the gap he experienced with his parents. The story he feels most moved by, though, involves the care he received from his friends when his parents announced their divorce. It was during midterm exam week the fall semester of his freshman year. He remembers, "My father came up to see me. I had no idea he was coming. My sister called to tell me he was coming, but my stupid roommate didn't give me the message. So all of a sudden my father just walks into the room, and I could tell something was wrong. He said, 'Let's go for a walk.' And he told me about it, and we were both in tears, and it was really a pretty big blow. I had no preparation for it. Wham! It was right in the middle of midterms and I was taking a bunch of killer courses. I had just gone through an emotional blowout with a girl I'd been in love with for a year. I was already in a situation that would stress out a lot of people I know. Well, anyway, I had a big problem set due the next day. Right! There was no way I was going to be able to concentrate enough to do it. So this guy in my class who found out about it told me just not to worry about it. He'd cover for me. And another friend dragged me off to play pinball and tried to help me relax. He had no idea what to do. He had no experience with this type of thing. We're just not good at this kind of stuff—helping people who are having deep emotional crises. He was basically a light-hearted person, but when the chips were down, he was there. Any time in my life, if I was really, really, really in a jam, he's someone I'd call. I was touched by the fact that he knew the chips were down and that I really needed him."

For Elmer, the retired broadcaster, the caring he did not receive as a child came later from his wife. Her example helped him become more caring too. In his case the story that best captured her caring was also a time of crisis, although one that he experienced vicariously through the pain of a friend. He recounts, "Some years ago a dear friend of ours, Patty, lost her husband to cancer and then, not much later, she developed cancer herself. My wife, Mildred, was always the first person to help out anytime she needed something. Like, she'd say, 'Let me drive you to the doctor.' It didn't make any difference that she had plans to do something else. She immediately jumped in to help our friend wherever she could. And when Patty realized she was running out of time and wanted to go back to England to visit her family before she died, Mildred told her we would drive her to New York to the airport. With anyone, Mildred is immediately there to help if somebody needs an errand run or just a friend to talk to. She's great. She's the perfect example of a caring, willing, self-sacrificing, drive-you-crazy soul!"

Another person, a very interesting woman who worked for a number of years with international women in her community and is now in Africa with her husband serving as a medical missionary, had been most impressed by the caring she received from her best friend. She described her relationship with her parents while she was growing up in qualified terms. She says, "My mother was always there and I always knew she cared. She took us to the zoo a lot and on picnics. But she wasn't super-involved with us. She let us be independent and go out to play in the neighborhood. It was just knowing she was there and if we got hurt we could come and she'd be there. Nobody showered me with great amounts of compassion, but it was just nice as a child to be secure." Her father, in contrast, was more detached. She admits her relationship with him was not a very positive experience. "I feel a lot of pain from the fact that my father wasn't there. He traveled a lot, but it was also just obvious that he really didn't enjoy children. He was the kind of person for whom work was everything and children were just in the way. So he'd come home on the weekend and just shoo us away. There just wasn't any caring at all. If I ever had any emotional needs, he just couldn't relate to them." More reflectively then, she added: "I guess I've kind of blocked a lot of that out. It's been more in recent years that I've realized it would have been nice to have had a father who cared."

It was the friend, more than her mother or any other relative, who showed this woman compassion at its best. "Although I've had friends all my life who cared," she explained, "I've never really known anyone like her who could just sense my needs and do little things for me. With my second baby I was kind of ill and she was in the hospital just down the hall having her second baby too, and that's when our friendship really became close." She described some of the things her friend had done for her. "Here she was in bed, healing, and she was thinking of someone else. She made this little handmade cutout with my daughter's name on it. Right after that, she wanted to keep my oldest for me, and all through the last six years, raising these little kids, she's been there. She's always willing to help. I've just never had a friend like that. She really has an ability to care for people. As one of the guys said once, with her around, who needs a mother!"

She paused momentarily to explain that she and her husband had been living in Alabama when she met this friend. One of the very special times she remembers that vividly demonstrated her friend's ability to care was when she and her husband moved away, leaving her friend behind in Alabama. As we drove off, she recalls, "we saw her standing in the driveway crying her eyes out. It was the hardest thing. We knew she loved us so much that it would be hard for her to see us go. She was willing to make herself vulnerable." And at this point, her story broke off. There were tears in her eyes and a catch in her throat as she remembered her friend.

Moments of Vulnerability

We need to pause here for a moment to reflect on something important about the relationship between stories and the moral lessons we derive from them. In these examples the stories are about moments of special need. They situate the story—and usually the story teller—in a time of crisis. There is, as this woman says of her friend, vulnerability. One experiences the pain of loss, the sorrow of need. Someone else helps you through your time of need. From them you learn what it means to be cared for. The story becomes an object lesson, an experience you recount to encourage yourself to pass the kindness along.

A young mother—whose children kept her busy enough that the only formal volunteer work she had been able to do for several years was helping with Vacation Bible School at her church—explained the relation between experiencing a personal crisis and wanting to care for others this way: "I went through a really hard personal crisis that lasted for a long time. I had a friend who was willing to sit and listen to me every single day. I was able to sit down and talk to her for, you know, a couple of hours at a time. As I look back on it, I was probably saying the same thing day after day after day. But she was willing to listen anyway and helped me work through that particular crisis. In return, as I've known people going through some crisis themselves, I've tried to be there for them. Because of that experience in my own life, I've been trying to be a better listener."

Experiences of Crisis

In the American population at large, having experienced a personal crisis yourself does appear to be associated with being a more caring and compassionate person. Thirty-eight percent of those in a national survey who said they had experienced a personal crisis, for example, were currently involved in charitable or social service activities, compared with only 28 percent of those who said they had never experienced a personal crisis. The former were also more likely than the latter to have loaned money in the past year, donated time to a volunteer organization, stopped to help someone with car trouble, cared for someone who was very sick, given money to a beggar, contributed money to a charitable organization, tried to stop someone from using alcohol or drugs, visited someone in the hospital, helped a relative or friend through a personal crisis, and taken care of an elderly relative in their home.[10]

Importantly, those who had experienced personal crises did *not* differ from those who had never experienced a personal crisis in terms of the *value* they placed on helping the needy or giving time to help others. Thus it appears that the effect of being able to recall a time when one was in need is not so much to convince one of the importance of helping others but to transform that conviction into action. Having a story to tell about a time when one received caring, it would seem, provides a lesson in the importance of actually taking action. It kicks one in the seat of the pants, as it were, turning the vague thought that "I should help" into an actual donation of time, energy, or money.

The other effect of having experienced a personal crisis is to realize more clearly that helping others is a way of helping yourself. Those who had experienced a crisis, for example, were 12 percentage points more likely than those who had not had a crisis experience to agree strongly with the statement "By helping others, you discover things about yourself that allow you to be a better helper in the future." They were also more likely to say that good feelings and personal growth were important reasons for trying to be a caring person.[11] Receiving fulfillment from helping others, it appears, necessitates identifying some type of deficit in one's own life that can be filled. Having experienced a personal crisis is one such deficit. It forces you to admit being vulnerable. You recall being in need of help. As a result, you have a space in which to put the gifts you receive from helping others. You have room to grow. The experience of receiving care shows you that you can also learn and grow stronger by caring. The stories you can tell about your crises and about those who cared for you help you remember the deficit so you can fill it up again.

Our personal crises, therefore, loom in our memories, providing occasions for the telling of stories. They become a part of our repertoire, like packaged goods that can be pulled off the shelf when company comes. We remember them because they stand out from the daily routine. They are containers of emotions gone by. With the retelling, we experience the feelings again. But we also gain closure. Amid the crisis itself, the conclusion remains uncertain. In the narrative of crisis, the ending is under our control. It can become a message of hope and inspiration, a directive, a connective tissue linking action and outcome.

From Stories to Action

Researchers who have tried to capture the essential role of personal stories in our lives suggest that stories help us encapsulate experience so we can remember it.[12] As we remember these experiences, our stories also become part of our subsequent life events, shaping them, and molding our interpretations of what is good and right. Psychologist Jerome Bruner puts it this way: "Narrative imitates life, life imitates narrative." Adding: "In the end, [life] is a narrative achievement. There is no such thing psychologically as 'life itself.' At very least, it is a selective achievement of memory recall; beyond that, recounting one's life is an interpretive feat."[13]

If we are concerned about transmitting ethical ideals to the future, for ourselves and for our children, we would be wise then to embed these ideals in stories. As the stories recounted here suggest, people remember the caring they have experienced, and recall these experiences, by telling stories. But stories do more than keep our memories alive.

Acting Out Stories

Sometimes these stories become so implanted in our minds that they act back upon us, directly and powerfully. We find ourselves acting them out. The characters in our stories show us how to behave. They may even speak the words that we now utter from our own mouths. Jerome Bruner again: "I believe that the ways of telling and the ways of conceptualizing that go with them become so habitual that they finally become recipes for structuring experience itself, for laying down routes into memory, for not only guiding the life narrative up to the present but directing it into the future."[14] Bruner has in mind a primordial, all-encompassing, life-shaping influence. My research shows that *specific* stories can also have a powerful effect on our ethical behavior.

Jack, the rescue squad worker, believes you cannot learn compassion from books. You have to see it lived out in front of you. He talks at length about the things he has learned by watching his boss on the rescue squad. But without realizing it, the most vivid illustration of his argument about the importance of modeling was embedded in a story he told about a particular accident to which he had been called. His narrative, however, began some years earlier: "Once when I was a child I had to have five teeth pulled under general anesthetic. I remember the nurse standing there and just saying, 'Don't worry, I'll be here right beside you no matter what happens.' And when I woke up again, she was still there.

That came back to me a few weeks ago when we had a man who was pinned upside down in his pickup truck. I was inside trying to get him out and gasoline was dripping down on both of us. They were using power tools to cut the metal, so one spark might have caused us to go up in smoke. The whole time he was saying how scared of dying he was. And I kept saying, 'Look, don't worry, I'm right here with you, I'm not going anywhere.' When I said that, I was reminded of how that nurse said the same thing and she never left me. Now, they always tell you never to get yourself into a situation where you are risking your life, not unless there's a very good chance of both you and the patient being okay. So I weighed the risks and I told the man I was going to stay right there with him, and I did. And later he told me, 'You were an idiot, you know that the thing could have exploded and we'd have both been burned up!' And I told him I felt I just couldn't leave him."

Nearly two decades had passed between the time Jack's nurse held his hand, promising she would not leave him, and the time he stayed with the man in the pickup truck. But the memory was so powerful it helped him legitimate risking his life. The memory was powerful, not just as a vague recollection of having been cared for, but because the story provided a script, the exact words, for Jack to use when he became the caregiver. Usually the circumstances are not as dramatic as this. And yet the caring we receive may touch us so deeply that we feel especially gratified when we are able to pass it on to someone else.

An elderly man who died only a few weeks after the interview he granted from his hospital bed told of the impact having a stroke had made on his life. Shortly after he retired from a long career in government service, he suffered a massive stroke that left him partially paralyzed and seriously affected his speech. He had never before done volunteer work, but when he recovered enough to become ambulatory again he decided to try to repay some of the kindness he had received by visiting other stroke patients. "You know," he reflected, "having a stroke does a lot of funny things to you, things you don't expect. For the first year after I had mine, I couldn't laugh. Something would seem funny to me, but instead of being able to laugh, all I could do was cry. It was just a physical thing—since my muscles wouldn't laugh, the emotions came out as tears instead. Well, I used to just hate that. And finally I got so I could laugh again. Well, when I started working as a volunteer here at the Red Cross, I met another guy who had had a stroke and he had the same problem I'd had. He couldn't talk for more than five minutes without having tears come out. So I told him about it and told him he'd probably get over it like I did. And, you know, about six months later he called me up and he talked for half an hour and never cried once. It was just a little thing I did to assist him, but I think it probably helped."

Stories like this show the diversity of ways in which caring can be shown. They define it, package it, so that others can recognize it and emulate it. Here, it was possible to give compassion because the giver had experienced exactly the same problem as the person for whom he cared. The story shows the special, peculiar bond that may form between the giver and the recipient. It defines the character of empathy. The act of giving is itself quite modest, but it shows that even little things matter. Indeed, the triviality of the deed helps the listener to identify with the speaker. It becomes possible to imagine that our small deeds too can be acts of compassion.

Stories of Care Received

In other cases it may not be a specific episode that we reenact, but a powerful experience that becomes a part of our larger story of ourselves. A narrative about care received becomes part of our autobiography. It supplies a way of accounting for our behavior. Care received becomes a debt owed. A subsequent encounter with need then becomes a time of reckoning. The individual who reaches out to us touches our conscience.

The head of pediatric cardiology at a large university medical center explained that her decision to help parents of dying children bear their grief owes its origin to the director of pediatric cardiology under whose supervision she worked as a young resident. It was he who reached out to her when her own child died, showing her compassion, but also touching her conscience in the process. "He came over to me the day my baby died and put his arms around me, and I remember thinking, he's the only person who did that."

The Role of Christianity

What then is the role of Christianity in all this? An ethic of love and compassion is of course central to the Christian gospel. The stories of caring that we experience in our own lives are an epiphany. They become part of the gospel message. When they are related to the biblical tradition, they take on a larger meaning, an added historical and sacred significance. When they are told in community, their power is amplified. Other people hear them and are encouraged to love by identifying with the characters in the story. The parable of the Good Samaritan is a vivid example. Stories in our own lives and the lives of those we have known often make real the message of the Good Samaritan.

Let me conclude with one final story. Freddie Jackson Taylor, now in his late fifties, is one of those remarkable individuals who seems to be able to give and give and give without ever thinking of himself. He remembers feeling loved as a child, but his family was very poor and there were several younger brothers and sisters who needed more care than he did. When he was in ninth grade, he quit school to help the family make ends meet. Over the years he worked at more odd jobs than he can remember. But he always had a soft spot for those less fortunate than himself. At present he holds a job paid for by United Way that puts him in daily contact with the poorest homeless men and women in Los Angeles. Although he is nearing retirement age, he has managed to save less than five hundred dollars. Most of the rest he has given away.

What inspired Freddie Jackson Taylor to a life of service like this? It was the example of a man he met many years ago, he says. "I never met such a selfless man as Michael," Freddie recalls. "I mean he literally would give people the shirt off his back. I remember one incident when he had been saving up money to buy this motorcycle that he had wanted for a long time. He bought the motorcycle, but then the Eastside neighborhood center got into financial trouble, so he sold the motorcycle in order to give them the eight hundred dollars they needed. I can tell you hundreds and hundreds of stories about Michael, I mean, how he took a vow of poverty and how he chose to live in a skid-row hotel for ten years, and how, when I visited him in his room, his room was always bare. He'd open his closet door and there might be a jacket hanging there; he had nothing, just absolutely nothing, and he didn't want anything. I really admired him. He, he's one of my heroes, Michael is."

These are the heroes that should inspire us all. Their stories encourage us to live lives of compassion and, more generally, lives guided by ethical conduct. Let us hope their stories remain a vital part of our culture in the century to come.

5

The Saints in
Our World

If one of the serious ethical challenges facing Christians in the twenty-first century is having personal stories that tell them how to be caring and compassionate, then a similar challenge exists as Americans think about themselves collectively. For believers and nonbelievers alike, there need to be heroes, public figures, role models at the collective level who can exemplify the nation's highest ethical ideals. These "saints" are likely to be different in the twenty-first century than the ones we admire today. But how we relate to them may well not change. Thus, we can ask not only about the personalities who currently embody ethical ideals but also what we learn from these figures. Why do they impress us? How closely do we identify with them? What does "our world" do to domesticate these unnerving exemplars of a higher calling?

Men and women of compassion have always been included among the heroes and public figures we most admire. Mother Teresa of Calcutta, for example, was among the top ten most admired women in national surveys every year between 1979 and 1990. Albert Schweitzer was among the top ten most admired men every year between 1954 and 1964. Other humanitarians and leaders of charitable movements who have frequently been listed include Martin Luther King, Jr., Coretta King, Pope John Paul II, Archbishop Desmond Tutu, Sister Kenny, and Pearl Buck.[1]

In this chapter I want to consider the meaning of these people of compassion. How widely are they known and admired? What ethical ideals do they exemplify? To what extent do we turn them into dime-store illustrations of our own shortcomings and limited life-styles? How significant are these figures for perpetuating good behavior into the future?

Who Embodies Compassion?

When asked if they could think of anyone who illustrates what it means to be a caring and compassionate person, 62 percent of the American public in a national survey could identify someone specifically. Of this number, about a third mentioned someone they knew personally—a friend, relative, or neighbor. Another 6 percent mentioned their minister or pastor. The remainder—more than six in ten—identified public figures. Mother Teresa was the most frequently mentioned (by approximately a quarter of the respondents). Pope John Paul II, Jesse Jackson, and President George Bush and his wife, Barbara, all received a number of mentions. Others named included evangelist Billy Graham, former president Ronald Reagan and Nancy Reagan, and television personalities such as Bob Hope, Jerry Lewis, Sally Strothers, and Elizabeth Taylor.[2]

By a margin of 79 percent to 55 percent, individuals who were themselves involved in charitable activities were more likely than uninvolved individuals to be able to think of someone who exemplified caring and compassion. Those with higher levels of education were also more likely to mention someone they thought of as a model of compassion, such as Mother Teresa, whereas those with lower levels of education mentioned people they knew personally. Seventy-six percent of the respondents with college degrees identified someone and 40 percent of these mentioned Mother Teresa. Among those with only grade school educations, only 45 percent mentioned someone and of these 60 percent gave the name of a relative, friend, neighbor, or minister. Women and men were equally likely to give the name of someone they thought illustrated compassion. Among both, Mother Teresa and other women were mentioned more often than men. But there was also a tendency for women to mention women and for men to mention men.

Impressions of the Saints

The impressions people had of these public figures were not as personal, rich in detail, or emotionally intense as the stories about relatives and friends who illustrated compassion that we considered in the last chapter. Some individuals observed that they were familiar with names such as Mother Teresa and Gandhi, but otherwise had little knowledge of their lives or what they did. Jack, the rescue squad volunteer we met in the last chapter, for instance, mentioned Mother Teresa as an example of a compassionate person, but then remarked: "Not that I really know what she's done with her life, but I understand she's famous." Jumping to Albert Schweitzer, in hopes of finding himself on more familiar territory, he was again forced to backtrack almost immediately: "I'm sure I sound profoundly ignorant, but I don't even know what Albert Schweitzer did."

Several people noted that they had little time to read, watch television, or go to movies and were generally less impressed by the personalities depicted in the media than the people they met in person. A few others scanned their memories, thinking they had surely been influenced by reading about famous people who were compassionate, but were unable to recall specific names. For many, though, encounters with famous men and women of compassion through reading, the visual media, and (on occasion) even in person were vivid and powerful.

In the case of Freddie Jackson Taylor, it was the time he participated in one of the civil rights marches organized by Martin Luther King, Jr., that would always make Dr. King one of his special heroes. "It was that march, and then I got involved in a lot of other rallies for the Southern Christian Leadership Conference," he recalled. "Martin was such a beautiful person." Ralph Abernathy, Rosa Parks, and Malcolm X were also among the people with whom Freddie, himself a black man, identified. But he had always held Dr. King in special favor. "It was his understanding of the world and the world's problems. It went beyond just an understanding of the plight of the black and the poor. It was broader than that. I often wish I was that broad. Sometimes I'm more narrow than I should be."

A middle-aged woman who spent much of her spare time working with AIDS patients referred immediately to Eleanor Roosevelt when asked who she thought best exemplified caring and compassion. "My model really was Eleanor Roosevelt, whose picture I have there on the wall. I was a teenager when she was doing her work across the country with people who were out of work and on the verge of starvation. I admired her and felt a kinship with her. Later, I had a chance to meet her when I was in college and I thought that was just the culmination of everything in the world!"

Another person I interviewed, the head of a volunteer organization that arranged for business leaders to spend time working with the poor in Third World countries, identified Mother Teresa as the person he admired most for her compassion. After discussing her work in considerable detail for about ten minutes, he started to turn to another topic, so I interrupted him to make some observation about how inspiring it was just to hear about the things Mother Teresa was accomplishing. "Thanks," he said, "I'll tell her you said that next time I see her." This humble man, I learned later, had worked closely with Mother Teresa for more than a decade.

Stories of the Saints

When personal encounters are absent, as is usually the case, great leaders of compassion become known through the stories we read and hear about them. Freddie Jackson Taylor had never met Gandhi, as he had Dr. King, but the stories he had heard about Gandhi as a child made a lasting impression on him. "When I was a little kid I was a movie freak, and in those days, back in the 1940s, in addition to having double features, they showed newsreels, and I remember, from time to time they would show newsreels about India and about this man in a loin cloth. I was too young to understand what he was doing, but I just got this feeling about him. This man is a saint, I thought, he has to be a saint. And then one day I remember going to the movie theater and they were showing his funeral. Somebody had assassinated him and that affected me for the longest time. And then when I was older, I started reading his works and I just felt that peaceful nonviolence was the way to go. I admire just about everything about him."

Sometimes we associate so completely with the stories we read or hear about famous men and women of compassion that the persons and the stories become one and the same. Indeed, individuals sometimes talked more as if they were referring to a story, a speech, or a text than if they were actually talking about a person. Mentioning Gandhi, for example, Elmer (the retired broadcaster) remarked, "It's a terrific story. I was very influenced by the movie, how he marched all the way over to the ocean to get salt." Also referring to Gandhi, a woman who worked as a therapist recalled having read his autobiography in high school. "I was very impressed with it," she said. Another person spoke of Martin Luther King, Jr., as a figure that seemed to be almost synonymous with a film he had seen.

A young woman who was learning to be a psychiatric social worker said Jane Addams came to mind as an example of a compassionate person because of studying about her in classes on social work. "We learn all about her philosophy," she commented. Another person selected Martin Luther King, Jr., as her model of compassion, but had nothing to say about his life, only: "I've gone back and read his speech, it's a great message." Another woman picked Mother Teresa as the woman of compassion she most admired and then, without prompting, launched into a description of a recent documentary she had seen. "I read a book about her once, and then recently I saw this two-hour video about her life. I'm really impressed with her ability to have such compassion on people. She's able to just give, give, give, and still have more to give. The video was interesting. It kind of brought out that she wasn't anything particularly special in her younger years. But she felt a calling to take care of people in India who were dying, and I guess that's how she started."

Saints as Role Models

These examples demonstrate that heroes of compassion, like Gandhi and Mother Teresa, do serve as role models for individuals who try to lead ethical lives in more ordinary ways. People aspire to be like them. And even if they realize the impossibility of showing kindness in the same ways, they hold these figures up as objective examples of the desirability of being compassionate.

The pediatric cardiologist we met in the last chapter lamented that one of the problems she struggles with "is that I always feel like I should be a Mother Teresa." A businessman did not see it as a problem; he just admired everything about Mother Teresa and hoped his Meals on Wheels program was expressing the same kind of values. "She's making the ultimate sacrifice, living in extreme poverty herself, giving her whole life to doing good deeds for these people who are very much in need. That's where it's at. And I'd like to think of us as being the Mother Teresas of our community here. We need more individuals like that." Another person, a man in his seventies who had only a grade school education and had done manual labor all his life, brimmed with enthusiasm: "Mother Theresa evidently is quite a gal. There's no question about it, someday she'll be a saint."

Gandhi's admirers focused on his selflessness and courage. "Just incredible selflessness and dedication," were the words one man used to describe him. Another man emphasized "the steadfastness that's necessary to change the world." Another, an elderly woman, said she had always thought of Gandhi as an example of what an ordinary person can do if he really wants to improve things. "With so very little, he changed the world." She felt his example had often encouraged her to try to do her part to make things better too. "There's a lot that needs to be done, and it could be done if each one of us chipped in." A young woman who was training to become a social worker observed that just seeing the movie about Gandhi had been a kind of conversion experience for her: "When I saw the movie, I came away from there feeling like I just needed to dedicate my life to something more than what I had done before."

Eleanor Roosevelt was the most compassionate person many people, especially those among the older individuals with whom we spoke, could think of. One older woman described her as "an indefatigable machine helping people." Another woman marveled at "her enormous humanitarian caring and unstinting activities on behalf of many different causes." Others spoke of the huge heart she had for the downtrodden. They held her up as an example to follow. As one put it, "I don't spend a lot of time thinking about her, but when I do, it's like, God, I would like to be more like her, to be more compassionate and caring." Some of the other models of compassion that individuals mentioned were selected because they had in fact provided a model of a very specific sort. A young woman who hoped to become a doctor some day, for example, singled out Albert Schweitzer as her special hero. "He gave up the chance to lead a comfortable life in the United States and went to Africa to help people. He felt like he could help people better there. And that's what I want to do. I want to go to Turkey and help people there."

Identifying with the Saints

These comments point to an important feature of our public heroes. Even though they are remote, idolized, they are still people with whom we can identify. Why? Famous people of compassion are able to serve as role models because we can identify with at least some of their own personal characteristics. Despite their exceptional capacity to endure hardship, or the accolades and awards heaped upon them, they are similar to ordinary mortals in some respects. Some are women, some are men. Some are old, some are young. Some are large-boned, others are small. Some have overcome physical handicaps, others share a particular religious or political perspective. We can find points of similarity between ourselves and them. As a result it becomes possible for us to say, in effect, yes, I can understand them and behave in some of the same ways.

One elderly woman who worked with blind people in her spare time talked fondly of Eleanor Roosevelt as a model of compassion. She had admired Mrs. Roosevelt because they were about the same age and were from the same part of the country. "One of my champions when I was a young woman, I remember, was Eleanor Roosevelt. She was a wonderful woman. I admired everything about her. In the days when a woman especially didn't speak out the way she did, she was a true champion for the underdog." Another person, the woman I quoted who had Eleanor Roosevelt's picture hanging on her wall, said one of the reasons she had admired Mrs. Roosevelt as a teenager was that she thought of her as a large, gangly woman like herself.

The similarities between yourself and the person you admire do not have to be strong. There simply has to be something about them that strikes a resonant chord, perhaps a hobby, even some offhand remark. A retired school teacher, for example, said that she had read a lot about Eleanor Roosevelt back in the 1930s and 1940s and could still remember lots of little things about her. "Like I remember her talking about how her mother always kept the house dark in order to preserve the furniture. I remember that because I always used to do the same thing. I was always very rigid. And then when my son was born, I remember my mother telling me to let the housework go and just enjoy him because he wouldn't be around all that long. And I thought about Eleanor Roosevelt in that context."

In other cases people were sometimes able to identify closely with a famous person because of some personal acquaintance who, in a sense, served as a mediating link—someone who resembled the famous person but was more approachable because he or she was a relative or friend. One older woman, for example, said she had always admired Mother Teresa, but in trying to explain why began talking about her own sister instead. The sister had been a missionary in India for thirty years. When the woman thought of personal dedication and compassion, therefore, she often thought of Mother Teresa and her sister at the same time. The head of a community services organization in a large city on the West Coast had a similar affinity for Jane Addams because of an aunt who had been an early leader in the social work movement. Although her aunt had done work primarily in the Hispanic community in Los Angeles, she resembled Jane Addams in her concern for the poor. The woman also admired both for the leadership they had shown at a time when it was difficult for women to play such roles.

When a link of this kind was lacking, it was sometimes hard for people to identify closely with public figures unless something about a particular leader had resonated with their personal situation. The pediatric cardiologist said it was hard for her to identify with Mother Teresa or Gandhi because they were distant, from another culture, and never seemed to lose their tempers as she did. But she had always identified with Martin Luther King, Jr. Even though he was black and she was white, she thought of him as a volunteer like herself, someone who went around making speeches as she did. She had in fact identified with him even as a teenager growing up in the rural Midwest. Where she was raised happened to be a very poor red-clay farming area populated almost equally by blacks and whites. The black children she saw at school were even poorer than she was. And so, with childish goodwill, she entertained thoughts of trying to help them.

"Most of the whites were pretty poor, but they weren't as poor as the blacks. There were blacks just living in hovels with the roofs caving in. Most of them couldn't speak intelligible English. They had a one-room school with one teacher to teach grades one through seven. It was easy even as a child to see that they were never going to get themselves out of that kind of situation unless there was some big change."

Pausing briefly to chuckle at her childhood innocence, she continued. "I remember when I was about ten or twelve thinking that if I grew up and made a lot of money I was going to give it to these people. Of course when I got older I realized that's not the solution. It was about that time that Martin Luther King came along. And I realized that handing them money is not going to cure their problems. They need better education. They needed more opportunities to help themselves." For her, then, Martin Luther King was not only someone with whom she could identify, but a person whose vision of change was one she could share.

The Symbolic Value of Contemporary Saints

Great men and women of compassion, though, do more than simply challenge us to be more caring. Their lives have symbolic value. They are the contemporary Christs. They symbolize goodness, hope for the goodness of the future, just as public villains—persons of ruthlessness and greed—symbolize evil, despair.

Symbols of Hope

The pediatric cardiologist commented: "They make me feel hopeful about humanity in general, just the fact that there are still people like this who are willing to be thoughtful about people instead of so materialistic." A young volunteer for an environmental group put it this way: "I hear about people like Mother Teresa and it's nice. It tells me that the Ivan Boesky's of the world are not the only ones out there." Another man remarked: "I feel like maybe the salvation of the world lies in these people."

It is like the old saying about one rotten apple spoiling the barrel, but in reverse. One good apple makes the whole barrel more appealing. It is like the story of God's encounter with Abraham before the destruction of Sodom. If Abraham could have identified a handful of righteous people in the city, God had promised to spare it. Being able to identify a handful of compassionate people in our world gives us hope too that the city will be spared. It does not make us sanguine about the selfishness that prevails in our society. For example, people in the survey who could think of a particularly compassionate person were no less likely than anyone else to assert that most people in our society look out for themselves rather than being concerned about the needy.[3] There was a significant difference, though, in the belief that people are gradually becoming more compassionate. Those who could identify at least one compassionate person were significantly more likely to say people in our society are becoming more interested in helping the needy than those who could not think of anyone who was compassionate.[4]

Being able to identify a person who exemplifies compassion also makes us more hopeful about our own prospects of receiving care if we need it. We are more likely to believe we can count on our neighbors for help. We are also more likely to think our associates at work would help us out if we were in need. Knowing about someone who is compassionate is especially likely to make us feel we could rely on community volunteers for help. It even makes us somewhat more likely to think we could depend on the help of social welfare agencies if we had to.[5] In short, there is a kind of security that comes from having compassionate role models in our lives. We may be rugged individualists, but we recognize that we do not have to be rugged individualists all the time. If we really find ourselves in a bad spot, we believe we can turn to others in a variety of contexts and receive the help we need. We believe this because we can think of specific individuals who in fact lead compassionate lives.

Saints in Our Own Image

But, like all heroes, champions of compassion do not simply symbolize goodness and hope because they are compassionate. We transform them in subtle ways. They become symbols of our other values as well. A villain in the movies always stands for other things besides some abstract conception of evil. He conjures up our fears of the dark, the unknown, perhaps our fears of big cities, or the unknown dangers of science and technology. The same is true with heroes of compassion. Their compassion evokes our admiration, indeed, makes them heroes rather than villains. But after that it may well be their courage that inspires us most. Or it may be their drive and determination. We can transform them into a symbol of almost any value we hold dear. Mother Teresa can become an entrepreneur; Ronald Reagan, a patron of the arts. Collectively, they become a pantheon of saints. Each one dramatizes some specific quality or feat or virtue we admire: one illustrates the capacity to triumph over stigma, another the importance of standing up for what we think, still another the possibility of combining compassion with worldly success.

A young man who was studying to become a rabbi saw Gandhi not simply as a man of compassion, but as a deeply religious man, even a man of the Torah, and a champion of religious freedom. "He said we shouldn't try to convert people to our religion, but that we should make Christians better Christians, Jews better Jews, and Buddhists better Buddhists. His steadfast devotion to nonviolence created a homeland for the people of India. He was a man of the Torah, even though he didn't realize it."

A woman in her late thirties who was a deeply religious Christian condensed a whole sermon about meekness, sacrifice, and the ability of faith to move mountains into a brief commentary on what she admired about Mother Teresa. "She just started doing what she thought needed to be done, and this whole big thing was just an outgrowth of that. She just felt like something needed to be done and she was the one to do it, so she started doing it. She has nothing materially, not even a normal life; all she's done is just be faithful to what she thought she should do, and yet she's been called the most powerful woman in the world."

One person who saw compassion mainly as a question of willpower returned to the same theme when he described what he admired about Mother Teresa. "She's overcome so many things. In working with such destitute people, she's certainly shown a lot of intestinal fortitude, so to speak. I figure if she did what she did, maybe I can jump over a few hurdles too." She inspired him because she illustrated the possibility of gaining one's objectives in life by being persistent and struggling hard. Another individual said he had always tried not to let other people's opinions influence his decisions. Later, in describing Eleanor Roosevelt, he characterized her the same way. "She always truly seemed to care. It wasn't something she did for the press. It came from within. She did things because they were right, not because it would play well in Peoria."

Exemplars of Our Individualism

What I am pointing to should now be evident. In an individualistic culture such as ours, we transform our heroes of compassion into rugged individualists. This is one of the ways we resolve the problem of how to be compassionate and individualistic at the same time. We simply look to our heroes. And what we see—more correctly, what we impute to them—is that they are not only compassionate but individualistic. We see their goodness and try to draw lessons from it. We also see their individualism, emphasizing it above many of their other qualities, and take comfort from it.

The Stouthearted and Strong Minded

One person said he admired Martin Luther King, Jr., because "he had strong beliefs and he was not afraid to articulate them." Another commented, "I admire him for his stoutheartedness; he wasn't afraid of the outcome." Of Gandhi and Christ, similar statements were made: "The most compassionate people are those who've been able to go against the tide and stand up and do it. Gandhi went through a lot of prisons and Christ had to endure all kinds of things in his life." Many of the comments made about Eleanor Roosevelt also emphasized persistence, determination, and nonconformity in the face of adversity. In one man's words: "She was a strong-minded woman who took stands on things that were not popular at the time." And a therapist echoed: "She was a strong woman who overcame some early hard times to become caring. She wasn't saintly; she was just motivated by some very strong ideals."

Occasionally the link between individualism and compassion was made directly, as the social worker did in commenting about Mother Teresa and Gandhi: "They were very individualistic, even single-minded in what they set out to do; they were very strong; they knew what they wanted; they didn't let other people pick them apart and tell them this isn't possible."

These are the same sentiments that are evident when people talk about their own individuality. The individualism we admire consists of strong convictions, nonconformity, independence, taking responsibility for yourself, finding your special niche, and doing what you feel is right. We read these characteristics into our heroes. We would probably see them in the sports heroes, movie stars, and business leaders we admire as well. We might even find them in some of our villains. The fact that we can observe them in our heroes of compassion tells us that these traits are not altogether bad. Individualism may even be a necessary component of compassion.

The Lone Ranger

It is this capacity to be individualistic as well as compassionate, self-possessed as well as giving, that inspires the accounts we read in newspapers and magazines. Mary Frances Housely, the airline stewardess who gave her life, is the girl next door—with the exception that her compassion and her individualism both become, in death, larger than life. The fictional characters we love to admire also bring together an imaginative mixture of compassionate decency and individualistic determination. The Lone Ranger is thus a person we can admire, despite his unusual ways, because he shows the possibility of being a genuine nonconformist, an independent creature to the end, but a warmhearted caregiver as well. He stands in for everyone, everywhere who combines the same virtues. As one person remarked, "There's gotta be lone rangers, even if they work in the back of a bank somewhere. He's compassionate, always looking out for the little guy, and he's adventurous. He's better than Robin Hood. He doesn't just stay in the woods. He's a man on the move."

This perhaps is the signal limitation of public heroes as sources of ethical depth for American culture in the next century. We need them because they inspire us to higher ideals, such as self-sacrifice and compassion. The stories that tell us what it means to be an ethical person become concrete in the biographies of contemporary saints. Even though they stand high above us in terms of their commitment, we are able to identify with them because we see something similar about their lives and ours. And yet we also need structured ways to think about these saints—lessons, concrete role models in our personal lives, the tutelage provided by our churches, our schools, our volunteer organizations. We need more than mere storytelling. We need people in our own experience to answer our questions about these saints, to interpret the implications of their lives, to tell us, No, Mother Teresa is not just a strong-minded entrepreneur, she cares for the poorest of the poor because she sees embodied in them Christ's love. Otherwise, the individualism in our culture is so strong that we can easily turn them into mirrors of ourselves, seeing only what we like as we peer into the looking glass.

6

Ethical Ambivalence

If Mother Teresa, the Lone Ranger, and Mary Frances Housely all embody the individualistic ethos prevalent in our culture, they still outshine what any of us are ever likely to accomplish, or even aspire to, in bravery and devotion. In an era of so-called lite heroes, whose small deeds of virtue are overplayed in the media one day and are gone from view the next, these giants of compassion necessarily stand out as the genuine exemplars of high ethics and lasting goodness. Indeed their example is a clear step removed from the valor we associate with ordinary acts of kindness and charity. Someone who rushes into a burning house to save a child, losing his or her own life in the process, must be placed in an entirely distinct category from the proverbial Boy Scout who performs his charitable deed for the day by helping old ladies cross the street. The Boy Scout can be said to have acted charitably, but it would be a gross understatement to say the person who rescued you from the flames was charitable.[1]

It is not just to honor the courage and dedication of those who display exceptional compassion, though, that causes us to set them apart. We feel ambivalent about them, as we do with all heroes and villains.[2] It is hard for us to identify fully with their example. We may admire them in some respects and even see them as standards to which we should aspire. But they also disturb us and evoke negative reactions. The contemporary saints may serve in our society as Christ figures. But if they do, they also suggest that we are sometimes "put off" by the Christ. Stories of great courage, true love of God, and genuine devotion to the needs of others lift our sights to a higher plane. But we may say to ourselves, why can't they just be like the rest of us? It has always been this way. The biblical prophets were admired and despised. The meekest of the apostles were exonerated—and stoned to death. It is never enough just to set the saints on a pedestal. We must also find ways to deal with the mixed feelings they evoke. To understand further how ethical role models may serve American culture in the future, therefore, we must consider the nature of this ambivalence and how thoughtful people actually learn to benefit from the role models they love and hate at the same time.[3]

Uncomfortable in the Presence of Good

Many of the people we met in the last chapter were frank in expressing their ambivalence about famous models of compassion. The therapist I quoted previously admitted she simply did not understand Mother Teresa. "I think it's great she's doing what she is, but I don't understand that kind of life." She felt ambivalent about Mother Teresa's sacrificial life-style: "It's too stark for me." The therapist, who was Jewish, also found Mother Teresa hard to reconcile with some of the values she had come to appreciate in the Jewish community. "Part of being Jewish is not cutting yourself off from the community. I think Mother Teresa is a wonderful person when she goes off by herself, but somehow I think we need each other more than that."

Expressions of Ambivalence

The young mother I quoted in chapter 4 who worked as a Vacation Bible School volunteer admired Mother Teresa's selflessness, but found it hard to identify with her because of her stance on abortion. "She's adamantly opposed to abortion and, I've heard, even to birth control of any kind, and yet I look at some of the people she's helping and it just seems to me that they are often victims of having too many children." Another woman said she was ambivalent about Mother Teresa because she did not fully accept the idea that compassion should involve a giving up of yourself. "She is totally selfless, thoroughly selfless, and I admire that. But that's not the way I want to live." Her view, she said, was that you can serve better by taking care of yourself. She thought it best to fill herself up, and then serve from her abundance, rather than denying yourself. "I feel that if I am fulfilled in other areas of my life then I can be a more effective volunteer. I don't understand someone like Mother Teresa, although I do admire her very much."[4]

The same sort of ambivalence was sometimes expressed, incidentally, when people talked about Jesus or other figures from the Bible. A young man who worked in a clerical position selected Christ as the most compassionate person he could think of in history, but said he sometimes did not like Christ very much because of guilt: "There is a certain amount of inspiration when you look at his life, and the reason why he was here, and the reason for his death and resurrection—that is very inspiring. It's very comforting. The guilt comes in because I know from time to time there are things I should not do that I do."

Neutralizing Our Heroes

Finding yourself confronted with any hero who looms larger than life, you are not only likely to feel some ambivalence but also likely to seek ways to neutralize these heroes—to cool them out, or put some distance between them and you, so that you can escape the harsh challenge they plant in your imagination. You cut them down to size, as it were. You find things about them you do not admire. Or you simply push them away, telling yourself that they are too far above you to be real, too wooden to be believable, or even too pathetically peculiar to want to imitate.

Speaking about Gandhi, the therapist remarked: "He was perfectly dreadful to people who were close to him. I don't think that's a good thing." The young clerk said he admired Mother Teresa, but then quickly neutralized her example by transforming her into an abstract image rather than a model one would actually try to emulate: "I can't say that she has done one particular thing that caused me to say, hey, I want to do that too."

The social worker I quoted in the last chapter spoke admiringly of Mother Teresa, but made a point of distancing herself from Mother Teresa's example: "I sometimes get tired of the whole thing and just want a break from it. I get to thinking that maybe I don't want to do this the rest of my life. So I know I don't have the full-blown devotion of a Mother Teresa. I just don't have it. I care about the unfortunate, but I guess I have my limits." Another young woman, this one still in high school, also recognized that Mother Teresa was someone to admire, but not necessarily an example she wished to follow: "I know I don't have that in me. I wouldn't be able to give things up; I like luxuries too much. But I definitely admire her and am very impressed."

Learning to Interpret Stories

The stories that we tell about compassion, and the heroes we admire, then, are not simply role models that we try to be like. We recognize that stories and heroes are just that—stories and heroes. And so, rather than blindly molding our behavior to fit some image we see projected, we engage in an interpretive process. Not only do we selectively construct our heroes to represent the values we share; we also develop secondary narratives—accounts to tell ourselves about how to understand these heroes. We have, as it were, instruction manuals in our imaginations that tell us how to read the heroic stories we hear.

Instruction Manuals

A young man who did volunteer work as a political organizer provided a candid glimpse into the pages of his instruction manual as he talked about the ways in which he could—and could not—make use of Mother Teresa as a role model. "She's incredible," he cautioned, choosing his words deliberately. "Nobody can come close to her." And then he explained: "She goes a little overboard; she's a martyr-type person who sacrifices everything including herself for other people." In good relativistic language he went on: "That works for her, but there's a lot of people in our society who have to be careful with that because it can become workaholism. It can become martyrdom that is destructive to the individual. I don't think there are very many people who should try to imitate her. She must be an exceptional person to be able to have that kind of life work. I don't think the rest of us could really pull it off."

Having made his analysis of the limitations of Mother Teresa's lifestyle, he turned from societal observations to a more personal set of reflections. "Part of me would like to be that selfless, that caring and compassionate; but I get depressed when I'm around people who are real sad, like people who are dying. I can't handle it. I wish I could. She doesn't get depressed like I would. When she sees grief it motivates her, it inspires her. She is able to work among the sick and the dying, and be incredibly uplifted and motivated. I'm sure she has her bad days. I'm sure she gets tired, but she continues to do this work. You never hear about her going to the mountains to take the summer off, you know, she doesn't do that, she just keeps on going. And there's a part of me that wishes I could do that, but I can't."

It was the idealism of Mother Teresa, Gandhi, Schweitzer, and others that most people felt necessary to factor out in some way. They not only rejected this idealism but inserted a paragraph in their guidebooks that said, in effect, "Don't get carried away with things; you can admire these people, but remember, moderation is the better part of virtue." A man in his late forties who had done volunteer work for more community organizations than he could remember said he had always been inspired by compassionate people but was wise enough to know that most of the time you just have to muddle through. "You can read about Albert Schweitzer and get all excited and go to medical school and become a doctor in Africa. But that's not the way it really works." Even the most laudable individuals, he said, have their bad sides as well as their good sides. If we remember that, we are less likely to become overly impressed with them. "Take Gandhi for example. You can admire his policies of nonviolence. But he never really understood that those policies only worked when you were up against civilized people [the British]. If he'd have tried it in the Soviet Union, they'd have shot him. So, you look at these people with all their compassion and all their dedication to a cause, and to me they seem anything from naive to ineffective to downright dangerous at times. Sure, Gandhi got the British out of India, but he also set off a war between India and Pakistan that killed over a million people." A cautionary tale: read Gandhi, but read him with a critical eye.

Looking for Principles

And yet, despite the suspicions we share of idealism, it is the principle, more than the practice, that we tell ourselves to extract from these heroes of compassion. Our guidebooks tell us to learn the value of caring but to distinguish this value from the way any specific individual may put it into practice. We locate ourselves in our own unique situations, comparing our story to theirs, and then decide for ourselves how much we can learn. Like some preface we might find in an advice book, the formula for reading stories of compassion says, "Read, enjoy, but decide for yourself how you are going to apply this."

Applications

A young mother in Virginia provided one of the best commentaries on how to read the stories of Mother Teresa and others who demonstrate exceptional compassion. "I think you have to see someone like that and say, for you, take the principles of her life and put it in the context of your life and who you are." Just as in real life, she argues, and indeed as in the way people frame their own stories of caring and being cared for, we must engage in an act of individuation. "We kind of get outselves in a jam when we think about trying to be like another person. Just personality-wise, or circumstantially, we might be totally different." The main principle, what we can admire in someone else, and what we can always strive for ourselves, this woman believes, is to live a life of significance. "You can see the significance of what she's doing. I think that's a great thing—just to know that your life is touching other people. So many times, no matter how we live our lives, we don't see that. We can get to thinking that we're not very useful. With her life, there's just no question of how she's touched people."

Using herself as an example, this woman tried to illustrate how one can make use of a role model like Mother Teresa, even though one's circumstances and abilities may be very different. "I think about how to imitate some of her qualities, given the situation I'm in with a family and everything. I can't possibly live like she is, and I don't think she feels that everybody should be doing what she's doing. In fact, she has said she doesn't want people to be like her, but just to stay in their own situation and do what they can. She encourages people to be who they are and do things where they are. The main quality she exhibits is just selflessness, being able to give of herself. Anytime you're able to do that you just get so much back. I think of the verse that says if you lose your life, you gain it. That's really true for her."

Thus in this woman's case, at least for the time being, she tries to do little things for her friends and neighbors, for her children, and for people in the community. She takes heart from the fact that her situation is different from Mother Teresa's and from Mother Teresa's own encouragement to be different and do what one can. It is the principle of selflessness that she tries to remember to apply in day-to-day situations. And yet it is not just an abstract principle to be followed, but an orientation that Mother Teresa symbolizes in her life. From this symbol, one gains both the conviction that selflessness is possible and the confidence that it is rewarding, significant, worthwhile.

The Worth of the Individual

Stories of compassion, whether of compassion received firsthand or witnessed at a distance, are exemplary tales that tell us what it means to be a caring individual. They bear distinctly the imprint of individualism in our culture, but they demonstrate how this individualism can be combined with a concern for others. They are not tales about organizations or groups but about individuals. In every case we have considered, it was an individual who received care and an individual who gave care. People could have told stories about the care given by their neighborhood, their church, or even their family. But they did not. They told stories about their mother, their nurse, their boss, their friend. Their stories were tales of morality—about the possibilities of desirable behavior on the part of the individual.

A Personal Bond

In many of the stories a peculiar bond between the individual caregiver and the recipient of care was emphasized. In one instance it was the experience of having a baby die; in another the awful feeling of trying to laugh and being able only to cry; in others a shared stage of life, a similar illness, an emotional crisis, or a common addiction. These stories reveal the character of empathy. By locating the caregiver and the recipient in an unusual social space, they emphasize the special relationship that developed between them. They make caring, in one sense, a deviant act. But in so doing they also magnify the humanness of the encounter. Caring is not simply an ordinary relationship. Its exceptionality shows that something special was present between the giver and the receiver.

By focusing on the exceptional qualities of the relationship we are able to legitimate our caring in an otherwise no-nonsense, calculating society. We are often reluctant to say we cared for someone simply out of the goodness of our hearts. We tell stories of how a needy person sparked some impulse within us we could not resist. Stories of others' caring play a similar role. They give us an excuse for being compassionate by showing we had a debt to be repaid.

Empathy

Consider the following: "One night I stayed up late talking—listening actually—to a friend whose brother had killed himself. My friend was having a lot of problems dealing with it and needed a sympathetic ear. He had listened to many of my problems and I wanted to help if I could. Besides, I had been in a kind of similar situation before, and I remembered how I didn't have anyone to talk to and how miserable that made me. It was really special when one of my friends heard me out. You see, my brother tried to kill himself twice. He shot himself when I was a freshman in high school and last fall he took a bunch of sleeping pills. Luckily, he didn't succeed. But there was a moment when I thought he had, so I knew kind of how my friend felt."

This is clearly a story of empathy—the kind of empathy defined by the circumstances presented in the story, an emotional bond created by the sharing of unusual experiences. But it is also a story that allows the storyteller, a young man in his late teens who says he usually tries to put up a tough front, to talk about being compassionate. Because he can load the weight of his decision to listen onto the circumstances he describes, he can present himself as a caring person without having to say anything about deeper values or motivations.

Inner Qualities

Many stories of compassion, though, also reveal something about the inner qualities it takes to be a caring person. Sometimes in fact they are told with a specific hortatory purpose in mind. One man for example lamented the fact that there were not more people willing to exert themselves for the good of others. The main problem, he felt, was a lack of drive. Too many people "prefer to just sit at home in their easy chair." He recognized that he sometimes felt this way himself. But the inclination to do nothing is a temptation he tries to resist: "A lot of days I just have to tell myself I'm going to get out there and do something for somebody." And then he told a story—a cautionary tale that inspires him when he gets lazy and one he hoped would inspire others as well: "I had a broken leg once and the physical therapist got me out with a cane and told me to walk around the block. It was a big block too. She told me I had three weeks to get it done. I told her, 'Chris, I can't do it.' But I did. It took every ounce of strength I had. She played me like a violin. She told me later that she had given me a time limit because she knew I'd get it done before then."

In many of their depictions of caregivers, both of personal acquaintances and of public figures, storytellers emphasized this kind of persistence. It is the ability to go against all odds, to buck the system, to do what others are unwilling to do that we associate with compassion Fortitude, character, believing strongly in a cause are the traits we admire in those who care. We also admire sincerity, affection, and sometimes these traits are demonstrated by a display of emotion. But it is more common for stories of compassion to display sincerity by commitment in the face of adversity. Mary Frances Housely does not cry, she simply does what has to be done.

All of this fits well with the individualism in our culture. Except that the heroes we admire are more self-sacrificing and more principled than we. They give up their lives for the principles they hold dear. For that, we are unable to identify with them completely. We may aspire to compassion but not to genuine altruism. And so, we express our ambivalence about great men and women of compassion, distance ourselves from them, and articulate secondary narratives about how to relate to them.

And these secondary narratives reflect another level of individualism in our thinking. They emphasize the importance of individual differences. Mother Teresa may be a strong individual, but if so, we also need to place her in the uniqueness of her own context, recognize the differences between her context and ours. Compassion is not simply a function of determination. It is an expression of our selves. It reflects our desires and interests—indeed, our individual limitations. We find it legitimate to articulate these limitations in defense of our own life-styles, which require something less than total commitment. That is fine for Mother Teresa, we say, but it is not for me. I could not be myself and lead the life she does.

Community (Again)

Where, then, does community come into the picture? Is caring in our society merely the work of stalwart individuals, or do the stories about these individuals in some way demonstrate that community too is important? I was taught in sociology courses that the community precedes our ability to tell moral tales at all.[5] Only as a member of a moral community am I able to make judgments about right and wrong that carry weight. Only in community do particular individuals and events become symbolic. Even if a hero is a rugged individualist, it is the community that defines that rugged individualist as an important symbol of its values and its social relationships.

I still believe this view is correct—but only partially so. It is correct to the extent that one can in fact see the hand of community in the shaping of stories. It is incorrect insofar as it emphasizes only the social relationships from which storytelling emerges. Community may precede the telling of tales, but it is also created in the telling itself.

Symbols in Community

Although the stories I have reported here deal mostly with compassion-ate individuals, the important role played by community is always an implicit feature of these stories. The way our communities define our heroes of compassion is especially evident in a case where someone is an active member of a church or, for that matter, of a quasi-secular support group such as Alcoholics Anonymous. These settings encourage social interaction and provide their members with a distinct vocabulary. Com-munities like this often have their own heroes as well. One woman who was active in AA, for example, passed quickly over such figures as Mother Teresa and Gandhi in thinking about models of compassion and men-tioned a priest whose writings she had been encouraged to read in AA. His work showed her that love of others must start with love of self and helped her escape from the self-hatred that had always plagued her. "He gave me the hope that I could become lovable. I never thought that could be possible. I thought maybe I could learn to love other people, but I never thought I was worth being lovable. And he made me see that I was." By disclosing himself, he also showed her the possibility of relat-ing more openly, without fear, to other people. She had always been afraid "that if I tell you who I am and you don't like me I don't have anything left." But studying his teachings made her see that what other people think is less important than what you think about yourself. "You can help me when you tell me what you see, but I'm the only one it matters to. So he gave me the hope to find out that I'm worthwhile."

Many of the heroes of compassion people admired from their own personal experience also reflected their involvement in close interactive communities. The rescue squad member's role model was his boss on the rescue squad and, beyond him, the other members of his squad. Freddie Jackson Taylor's hero, the man who sold his motorcycle to bail out the neighborhood center, was a man he knew through the neighborhood center. The young mother in Virginia had a role model who was both a neighbor and a fellow church member. Other role models were family members, close friends, fellow volunteers.

Community through Symbols

It is harder to see the element of community in connection with individ-ualized heroes like Gandhi, Mother Teresa, or Albert Schweitzer. They stand for, as I have suggested, the stalwart nonconformists who go off among people in a different land and live remarkable lives. And yet a kind of shared community of values emerges from the collective admira-tion we bestow on these individuals. They become a part of our shared experience, models of goodness that we can talk about with one another, that we can refer to in conversations without having to explain our ref-erence in full. Mother Teresa is not only a model of hope in the abstract, but a model of hope for us, in our time, as humanity, and even as a society. She represents us by symbolizing the goodness we aspire to, just as a national leader represents the hopes and concerns that caused him to win elective office. She is an incarnation around which other expressions of caring can congeal. The mythologized image of her that we create culturally becomes our icon, an object, a focus for emulation and discussion.[6]

In these ways community is implicit in all stories of caring. It does, as sociologists have argued, precede our ability to construct tales of moral virtue. But this view of the relation between community and stories is, as I say, only partly correct. Stories not only grow out of our social relationships, they also create these relationships. Community is a result of storytelling, as well as its precondition.

I find this argument attractive, not because it highlights a weakness in the premises of my discipline, but because it suggests a better way of thinking about community. Given the circumstances of our lives, most of us do not have, as it were, "a community." We do not live, as humans did for many centuries, within an enclosed tribe or clan or village that gives us our identity, our values, our stories. We have more diffuse, scattered attachments—to friends, family, neighborhoods, places of work, places of worship, interest groups, voluntary associations. These are not part of a single community but are largely separate communities. Those we know in our neighborhoods may be an entirely different set of acquaintances than those we know at work. But it is not even correct to say, as some do, that we participate in multiple communities. We do not simply become involved in communities that are somehow there whether we participate or not. Instead, we create our communities as we go along. Our neighbors are not simply the people who live in a certain geographic area. They are people we choose to interact with and identify as neighbors. They come and go. At any given time, our sense of what we call the neighborhood is really the perception we have of the people we know best and with whom we interact.

Stories play a powerful role in defining such perceptions of community. A neighbor is to a significant degree someone we can tell a story about—often a story of caring. The community I identify with at a particular moment in my life may be symbolized by the friend who was in the hospital having a baby the same time I was. My story about her creates an immediate sense of community involving the two of us. To the extent that my story selects certain features of our collective identity as being important—maybe common beliefs about children or women's roles—it also defines us as a part of some broader community. Freddie Jackson Taylor's story about Martin Luther King, Jr., therefore, is not simply about a relationship between an admirer and a public figure but a tale of shared identities and shared affinities with other members of the black community. And the rescue squad member's story of his college friends helping him adjust to his parents' divorce is not only a tale of individual caring but a story of colleagueship among fellow students.

Please do not misunderstand me. I am not saying the shallow networks we find in suburban neighborhoods, college dormitories, and voluntary associations are all we can hope for. I am saying these networks may not be as shallow as we think. Transient they certainly are, compared with a tribal community. But they do constitute communities of memory. How? In the telling of stories. As we have seen, people construct a portion of their autobiographies around stories of caring and being cared for. These stories make communities part of their remembered past, part of their memory.

In addition, the act of telling and retelling these stories makes them a part of the shared present. We may never have cared for a stroke patient ourselves or had a baby die, but we can empathize with the caring described when such stories are told. They tell us all that caring exists, that it has existed as part of the experience of individuals like us, and that it is a feature of our lives. Because it is told, it is shared, and because it is shared, the possibility of it happening to us becomes plausible. Even if we ourselves have not experienced being cared for recently, we believe it is a feature of human experience.

Storytelling as Caring

This means that the telling of stories about caring is itself a form of caring. I do not mean it can ever substitute for a helping hand when one is actually needed, a kind word, a shoulder to cry on, or the giving of food to the hungry and shelter to the homeless. But tales told of the giving and receiving of compassion are in fact a kind of gift. They are gifts of hope and encouragement, as we have seen. They reveal something intimate about an individual's biography. They show us that the people we know are perhaps more compassionate than we might have guessed. As they tell their stories, they also frame them in a way that actually casts us in the role of one of the characters. When I hear about a friend standing in the driveway crying her eyes out because I am leaving, I become that person she cares for. I experience vicariously some of the love she showed for her friend. I can also imagine myself wanting to laugh and being able only to cry. So when I hear a story about a fellow stroke patient saying a kind word, that word is spoken to me as well. In this way too, then, community is created through the telling of stories.

Small Lessons

I said earlier that the instruction manuals people devise to interpret the stories they hear about caring emphasize principle. It is the principle of dedication we learn from Gandhi and the principle of selflessness that we learn from Mother Teresa. We are inspired by the evidence we see in their stories that dedication and selflessness are possible. Even when we remind ourselves that we cannot follow their examples completely, we gain some small lesson in the value of dedication and selflessness.

But what is this small lesson? Stories have often been thought of as the vehicles by which we learn the situational rules of social behavior— that is, the context-specific norms that should govern our actions in particular situations. From this perspective a story about mother love for a child provides a model from which one abstracts rules about how to care for one's own children. In a particular situation, say, a bruised elbow from a bicycle accident, one responds to the child's needs by following patterns one has learned from stories about similar situations. You recall a story you heard from a neighbor about a bicycle accident, so you rush your child to the hospital to see if there has been a concussion, or you keep the child quiet with an ice pack on the injury. In short, you learn what to do. The stories are encoded lessons in technical, social, and even moral competence.

I do not believe stories—at least stories of compassion—work this way. When we asked people about the rules they followed in trying to be caring and compassionate, they generally had little to say. Their stories of caring and being cared for had not resulted in a set of norms of the kind "if such and such happens, then do so and so." When we posed them with hypothetical situations and asked them to respond, they also expressed reluctance. In other words, the stories they had heard did not seem to give them the capacity to put themselves in some new situation and conjecture about how they would behave. The cues they had learned from their own stories, it appeared, came so directly from the specific situations in which they found themselves that they were unable to devise plans of action on the basis of hypothetical events. They certainly were not intrigued with the idea of playing little games devised to test their moral reasoning by being placed in hypothetical situations involving ethical dilemmas. And the stories they told gave a strong indication why not: they were about experiences in which the very nature of the response was heavily contingent on the specific circumstances of the event (such as a facial expression, what was said and not said, how one felt, or what other options were present).

The stories people told seemed not so much to be about rules of caring as about the reality and possibility of caring. They did not conclude with assertions such as "And so I learned from this experience that if you are ever faced with such and such, you should . . ." Instead, they included observations such as "I really admire her," "she has been an inspiration to me," "I could go on all day about him."

When I call these tales stories to live by, then, I do not mean that they provide rules to follow. I mean they give us hope for living. They give us encouragement. We can see ourselves as caregivers and as recipients of care. It becomes possible to say to ourselves, I am like that, I understand that, I can relate to it. As we identify with the character in the story we see the necessity of relating to others and the opportunities available for demonstrating kindness. Models of compassion provide models of hope, of the selves we think it is possible to be.

III

Doctrinal Challenges: Pluralism, Polarity, and the Character of Belief

7

Religious Orientations

A century ago, the question of religious belief would have been relatively simple to address in at least one respect: belief was indeed the salient question, and what people believed could largely be summarized in terms of assent to particular doctrines, creeds, and teachings. One of the significant developments of the twentieth century is that the role of belief in religious commitment has become problematic. In considering the doctrinal challenges that lie ahead in the next century, the necessary starting point, therefore, must be a consideration of the character of religious orientations themselves.[1]

Transcendent Meaning

Social scientists, including sociologists, anthropologists, and students of comparative religions, generally conceive of religion as a system of symbols that evokes a sense of holistic or transcendent meaning.[2] They take this seemingly oblique approach because the world's religions are so different that more specific definitions involving particular beliefs often fail to capture this diversity. A definition like this also reflects social scientists' claim that symbols are essential to the human capacity to experience and interpret reality. Symbols are acts, objects, utterances, or events that stand for something—that is, they give meaning to something by connecting it to something else. Symbols give order and meaning to life. Without them, life would be experienced as senseless and chaotic. Indeed, research suggests that individuals are able to experience and understand only those aspects of their worlds for which they have symbols.[3]

Contextual Meaning

Social scientists' emphasis on holistic or transcendent meaning as the defining feature of religion arises from their view that meaning is always contextual.[4] We can understand why this assumption makes sense if we turn momentarily from the question of religion to a problem we all confront when we have to decide how to interpret a sentence we read. The meaning of a particular word in a sentence depends on the other words that form its immediate context. For example, the word "courts" means one thing if it appears with the word "tennis," but something different when the words "justice" or "dating" are present. Similarly, in their daily lives, people give meaning to their activities by associating them with various frames of reference. Hitting a tennis ball has meaning, for example, because it is associated with the rules of the game of tennis. Each frame of reference, moreover, has meaning because it can be placed within a more encompassing symbolic context (tennis, say, within the context of physical exercise and health). But if each symbolic framework requires a broader framework to have meaning, then some form of holistic or transcendent symbol system that embraces all of life must be present. These are what social scientists call religious orientations or religious systems.

Ultimate Questions

The questions that typically invoke religious symbols involve the quest to make life itself meaningful. Such questions arise at the extremities of human existence. Where did I come from? Why am I here? What happens when I die? These questions, framed at the individual level, may also be asked about the collectivity to which one belongs or about humanity in general. How did our tribe originate? Where is humanity headed? Other questions focus on the absolutes or landmarks that make life recognizable in its most basic sense. What is beauty? What is truth? How can we know truth? What is essential about the human condition? There are also questions that arise because the events they deal with make no sense to us on the surface. Why must I die? Why is there suffering in the world? What is the reason for evil?

Transcendent symbol systems address these questions at a variety of levels. Elaborate philosophical and theological doctrines sometimes supply rational answers that satisfy canons of logic and empirical evidence. Certainly the great creeds and confessions that Christians have espoused over the centuries have often been framed in this manner. They give precise, rational answers to the perplexing questions of human existence, and these answers are said to be integrated into larger, internally logical systems. But in daily life the enduring questions of human existence are more likely to be addressed through narratives, proverbs and maxims, and iconic representations rich with experiential connotations. Religious orientations are likely to be structured less by abstract deductive reasoning than by parables that raise questions but leave open precise answers, by personal stories that link experience with wider realities, and by creeds and images that have acquired meaning through long histories of interpretation in human communities.[5] Our considerations of the role of stories in the transmission of ethical ideals in the last section are thus an example of what has increasingly come to be understood as a fundamental feature of religious truth itself.

One important implication that derives from this understanding of religious orientations is that their role in the future is, to a significant degree, secure against the onslaught of scientific and philosophical arguments of the kind that drew so much concern during the nineteenth century. This is not to suggest that religious orientations will be immune from philosophical criticism or from the naturalistic attacks of scientists. It does mean, however, that the influence of science and philosophy will be felt more at the level of story than in terms of rational argument alone.

Social Interaction

Like other symbol systems, religious orientations are also recognized increasingly by students of human behavior to depend on social interaction. Although the role of such factors as divine revelation must be considered on a different plane, social scientists emphasize the ways in which symbols come to have meaning through the interaction of individuals and groups in human communities. Sometimes these communities invent collective symbols to articulate powerful experiences they may have undergone. More commonly, communities borrow symbols available within their cultural traditions but then adapt these symbols to their own use, giving them new meanings and interpretations. Communities also underwrite the plausibility of religious belief systems.[6] They do so by providing evidence that such beliefs are not the product of individual imaginations alone, by encouraging the public expression of beliefs, and by creating occasions in which beliefs may be enacted and predictions fulfilled. Without the ongoing interaction of people in communities, it is doubtful whether belief systems could long be sustained. Research has also demonstrated that personal religious orientations are more likely to have behavioral consequences if these orientations are supported by communities of like-minded individuals.[7]

In defining religion as a symbol system that deals with ultimate questions, social scientists assume that humans have the capacity to question their experience and a desire to make sense of their worlds. Whether all people pursue this desire with equal intensity is more doubtful. It is possible, for example, to explain a plane crash by observing that a rivet came loose. It is also possible to let the incident raise questions about the meaning of pain, the frailty of human existence, or the meaning and purpose of one's own life. How much the quest for holistic meaning and transcendence enters into people's lives is, therefore, a matter of variation.

Individual Variations

Studies indicate that most people say they have thought about the meaning and purpose of life, but individuals vary in the extent to which they have been troubled by this issue. They also vary in the amount of explicit attention they have devoted to it and in their views about the possibility of arriving at definite answers.[8] Agnosticism, for example, is a religious orientation that grants the importance of ultimate questions about meaning and purpose but denies the possibility of finding answers to these questions.

Whether people will continue to be deeply concerned about questions of meaning and purpose in the future is more difficult to predict than might be supposed. On the surface, these would seem to be enduring questions that people in all times and places have to confront. The degree to which people actually think about them, however, depends on two additional considerations: whether they think it is *possible* to find answers, and whether they have already found satisfactory answers. If traditional creeds and doctrines are eroding, this trend would suggest that people might think more about meaning and purpose in the future because they would not already have ready-made answers available to them. But modern culture also teaches it may not be worthwhile asking such cosmic questions. Since the Reformation, daily life itself has been taken much more seriously, supplying as it were bits and pieces of meaning, but precluding the search for an overarching Meaning. Searching for answers that may be impossible to find, one hears people suggest, may simply be a good way to make yourself unhappy.

Varieties of Belief

The kind of symbols that come into play in relation to questions about meaning and purpose in life is also a matter of variation. While all such symbol systems may perform functionally similar roles, it is useful to distinguish them substantively. These substantive distinctions are usually the basis on which religious orientations are delineated in popular discourse.

Theism

At the broadest level, students of religion distinguish theistic meaning systems, which recognize the existence of a God or divine being, from atheistic systems, which do not acknowledge a divine being.[9] Christianity is an example of the former; Marxism, of the latter. Insofar as it addresses the same higher-order questions about the meaning of life, Marxism would be considered functionally similar to Christianity. But this does not mean that Marxism necessarily functions this way. Just as one might study Marxism to derive economic principles, so one might study Christianity simply as an example of literature. In neither case would it be appropriate to say that a religious orientation is at work. Only as they function to evoke holistic meaning and transcendence do symbol systems become religious orientations. One implication of this fact for Christianity in the next century is that higher levels of education may encourage the *study of* religion without actually nurturing religious orientations themselves.

A Trend toward Ambiguity

The distinction between theistic and atheistic meaning systems is useful when the relevant concept is the presence or absence of a divine entity. But this distinction may be less useful in other contexts. For example, contemporary discussions in theology and in science sometimes distinguish religious orientations on the basis of whether they posit a reality that is humanly knowable or ultimately mysterious, whether reality is empirical or includes a supraempirical dimension, or whether being implies something that is not being itself but the ground of being. In these debates the boundary between varieties of ultimate meaning systems is often ambiguous.

The next century is likely to produce increasing ambiguity about the distinction between theistic and atheistic (or nontheistic) meaning systems. Already, the influx of Eastern religions into the United States has made it more difficult to decide if something such as Buddhism or yoga is genuinely a kind of religion or simply a secular practice of meditation and exercise. Often the answer depends on strategic considerations, such as the right of religious groups to tax exemption or their exclusion from receiving public monies. As people in increasing numbers make up their own beliefs, rather than accepting established creeds, it will also be more difficult to determine whether their notions of God are actually oriented toward the supernatural or merely something higher than themselves.

In contemporary societies, religious orientations are often distinguished in popular belief according to the dominant force or power that people perceive as governing their lives. Some people may conceive of this force as God; others as luck or fate. Natural or human causes may also be considered dominant—for example, the force of heredity, scientific law, society, or individual willpower. Whether a part of elaborate philosophical systems or simple pieces of folk wisdom, such understandings help people to make sense of their lives by identifying the causal agents that control human events. Judging from many contemporary studies, people in the future will be increasingly eclectic in attributing events to a variety of such forces.

Consequences of Religious Outlooks

Students of the social sciences have insisted that religious orientations become important to the study of human behavior insofar as these orientations are internalized as part of the individual's worldview. A worldview can be defined as a person's guiding outlook on life. The essential aspects of a religious orientation are the person's beliefs and assumptions about the meaning of life and such matters as the existence and nature of God, goodness and evil, life beyond death, truth, and the human condition. These beliefs and assumptions help the individual make sense of life cognitively. They also have an emotional dimension, perhaps including a feeling of awe, reverence, and fear, or peace, comfort, and security. In addition, they are regarded as behavioral predispositions that lead to various actions, such as participation in worship, prayer, or ethical decisions.[10] The depth of a person's religious commitment is often indicated by the extent to which all three of these functions are present. One of the significant developments of the twentieth century that seems likely to continue into the next century, however, is the increasing emphasis that has been placed on the emotional functions of religious outlooks. Religion, it is often said, makes people feel better about themselves; it in this sense is part of the therapeutic orientation that has come to be of increasing significance in American culture.[11]

Ethical Implications

The importance of religious orientations for ethical decisions has also been of long-standing interest to students of human behavior. In the classical work of Max Weber, religious orientations were conceived of as symbolic frameworks that made sense of the world, in part, by providing explanations for the existence of evil (also known as theodicies). Some religious orientations, for example, explained evil as a struggle between God and the devil; others saw evil as part of a cycle of regeneration and renewal; still others attributed evil to the workings of an all-powerful but inscrutable deity. The implications for ethical action derive from the prescriptions for salvation implied by these different conceptions of evil. In one tradition, for example, people might be expected to pray and meditate in order to escape from the cycle of evil and regeneration; in another tradition, they might be expected to do good deeds as a way of siding with the forces of good against those of evil.

As I argued in the previous section, the implications of religious orientations for ethical action now seem more complex than they did in Max Weber's day. Among other reasons, this is because motivations are now understood to be more complicated. Rather than people simply siding with the good against forces of evil, they now juxtapose multiple concepts of the good and situationalize these concepts in a way that makes all of them relativistic. Stories have the advantage of recognizing multiple motives and giving people a way to consider their consequences in terms of the interplay among the characters in the stories they tell.

Emphasis on the Self

Much of the research by social scientists on religious orientations during the past half century has dealt with their subjective aspects, perhaps because religion in our society is so fundamentally colored by American individualism. Assuming that the important feature of symbolism is its meaning, researchers have tried to discover what religious symbols mean to individuals. Efforts have been made to tap the deeper predispositions presumed to underlie such religious expressions as prayer and worship, to say how deeply implanted the religious impulse is, and to classify varieties of religious outlooks and experiences. As our interest in the inner life of the self deepens, this approach is likely to become even more pronounced in studies of religion in the future.

The Public Dimension

Recent developments in social theory have, however, resulted in some rethinking of this emphasis on subjective religiosity. Current research is beginning to focus more on the observable manifestations of religious symbolism itself, rather than claiming to know what lies beneath the surface in the subjective consciousness of the individual. Discourse, language, gesture, and ritual have become more important in their own right.[12] The contrast between this and the earlier approach can be illustrated by comparing two statements: "I believe God exists" and "God speaks to us through the Word." A subjective approach would treat both statements as manifestations of some inner conviction on the part of the individual. The more recent approach would pay closer attention to the language itself, noting, for example, the more personalized style of the first statement and the collective reference contained in the second.

The value of the more recent approach is that it recognizes the public or social dimension of religious orientations. Observers may not know what goes on in the dark recesses of the believer's soul. But if that person tells a story, or participates in worship, the researcher can then study the observable manifestations of that person's faith. For students of religion and practitioners alike, the rediscovery of language may well be one of the developments of the late twentieth century that is most consequential for subsequent efforts to gain deeper understandings of religious orientations.

Influences on Religious Belief

To account for variations in religious orientations, students of human behavior usually look at the social conditions to which people are exposed. They assume that most people do not make up their own religions from scratch. Rather, they borrow from the various symbol systems that are available in their environment. The most significant borrowing occurs in early childhood. Family is thus an important factor and it, in turn, is influenced by broader conditions such as social class, levels of education, race and ethnicity, and exposure to regional subcultures.

Social Determination

A generation ago, social scientists often held the view that scientific generalizations could be made about the relationships between social factors and religious orientations. For example, much work was inspired by the hypothesis that theistic religious orientations were more common among persons with lower levels of education than among persons in better-educated social strata. Another common hypothesis suggested that religious orientations were likely to be associated with various kinds of social deprivation, since the deprived would presumably seek solace in other-worldly beliefs. Empirical studies have found some support for such hypotheses. But the ability to make generalizations has remained limited. Different relationships seem to be present in different communities and in different time periods.

More attention has turned in recent years, therefore, toward describing the rich and complex processes by which religious orientations and social environments intermingle. In one setting people without college educations may turn to religious views that shield them from the uncertainties of science and other modern ideas. In another setting people with high levels of education may also turn to religion, but do so in a way that combines ideas from science and scripture or that focuses on the therapeutic needs of people working in the professions. In both settings, religious orientations provide answers to ultimate questions. But the composition of these orientations reflects ideas present in the different social settings.

Reductionism

An earlier generation of social theorists also sought to explain the variations in religious orientations in ways that often reduced them to little more than the by-products of social or psychological needs. Sociologists following in the tradition of Karl Marx, for example, regarded religion merely as a reflection of class struggles, while some following Emile Durkheim viewed it as a reflection of the corporate authority of society.[13] The reductionism in these approaches consisted not only of regarding social structure as more basic than religion but also of implying that religion would gradually disappear as people became more aware of its origins. Recent work is decidedly less reductionistic in its assumptions about religion. It still assumes that religion fulfills human needs and that it is influenced by social conditions, but regards religion as a more active contributor to human experience and considers its future more viable. In the future, this shift in the dominant focus of social theory may well provide room for closer and more creative interactions between students of human society and practitioners of particular religious faiths.

In addition to the more general social conditions that may influence the religious orientations of individuals, social scientists have also been particularly interested in the institutions that devote specific energies to the promulgation of religious orientations. These institutions supply the resources needed for religious orientations to be perpetuated. Leadership, producers of religious knowledge, specialists in the dissemination of such knowledge, organizational skills, physical facilities, and financial resources are all required for religious orientations to be maintained over time. Religious institutions must compete with other institutions, such as governments, businesses, and families, for these resources. As I argued in part I, the future of Christian beliefs in the United States will depend greatly on how well these institutions respond to changing social conditions.

Aspects of Religious Pluralism

In most modern societies competition is also present among the adherents of various religious orientations. When such competition has been recognized either governmentally or culturally, we say that a condition of religious pluralism exists.[14] Pluralism often becomes a kind of religious orientation itself, imposing norms of civility and tolerance on particularistic religious traditions. When multiple religious orientations are forced to compete with one another, the plausibility of any one such tradition may be diminished as a result of believers' seeing others who hold views different from their own. At the same time, pluralism appears to contribute to the overall vitality of religious orientations in a society by encouraging competition among them for adherents and by giving believers more options from which to choose.[15]

It has been common in the past for individuals to choose one particular religious orientation with which to identify. Often these orientations have been defined by religious institutions, such as the Roman Catholic church, or by denominational organizations, such as the Presbyterian or Methodist churches. Increasingly, however, it appears that individuals in modern societies are exposed to a variety of religious institutions and orientations. As a result, they may pick and choose particular elements from several different faiths and traditions. Their religious orientation therefore takes on a more personalized character.

Although some individuals work out highly coherent religious orientations that have internal consistency and integrity, it appears that the more common result of living in religiously pluralistic settings is a form of personalized eclecticism. People become heteroglossic; that is, they gain the capacity to speak with many religious voices. Their religious orientations may not provide a guiding philosophy of life that maintains an orderly view of the world. Rather, religious orientations become tool kits, assembled from a variety of personal experiences, social contacts, books, sermons, and other cultural repertoires, from which the individual is able to draw as he or she is confronted with the challenges of life.[16]

At present, research studies indicate that large proportions of the population in societies like the United States hold theistic religious orientations. In other societies where religious institutions have had fewer resources in the past, such orientations are less common. In all societies, though, theistic orientations are confronted by the humanistic orientations promulgated by secular institutions. The outcome appears to involve a balance between pressures to adapt, on the one hand, and tendencies on the part of religious adherents to resist these pressures, on the other hand. Much of the struggle depends on the ability of religious leaders to articulate visions that grow out of particular confessional traditions in ways that appeal to the universalistic norms governing wider social audiences.

Polarization

Although religious orientations are becoming more diverse and eclectic as a result of cultural contact and mass communication, evidence also suggests that in some societies a basic polarization has emerged between those whose orientation involves traditionalistic, fundamentalistic, or conservative norms, on one side, and those whose orientation involves progressive, modernistic, or liberal norms, on the other side. Conservatives are characterized by adherence to the authority of traditional scriptural texts, whereas liberals emphasize more the relativity of these texts and the need for reason and experience in interpreting them. Liberal religious orientations have been nurtured by relativistic views in higher education, in the professions, and in the mass media in market-oriented societies, but conservative orientations have grown as well, not only in reaction to liberalism, but also as a result of conservatives gaining educational or political advantages and seizing on opportunities created by the ill effects of rapid societal change. Whereas earlier discussions predicted the demise of fundamentalist religious orientations, current studies are thus more concerned with the ongoing tensions between fundamentalist and more liberal or humanistic religious orientations. In the next two chapters I shall consider, respectively, what the prospects are for the future of fundamentalism and how liberalism and fundamentalistic beliefs interact with each other.

8

The Future of Fundamentalism

One of the most surprising features of American religion in the twentieth century has been the survival of fundamentalism. Indeed, it might almost be appropriate to say that this has been one of the defining elements of the religious mosaic in this period. Why? Why has Christian fundamentalism remained a vibrant force in American society despite advances in science, technology, higher education, and other developments once thought to have diminished its appeal? What are the social and cultural factors empowering it? Will these factors continue to perpetuate it as a significant expression of religious belief in the twenty-first century? [1]

To address these questions I am going to suggest a broad sensitizing framework that seeks to make sense of the sources of Christian fundamentalism without taking a reductionistic stance toward the phenomenon being explained. [2] In other words, I want to distance myself from much in the sociological tradition that would try to account for Christian fundamentalism by demonstrating it to be a reflection of social factors somehow more basic or foundational, such as the struggle between social classes or the authority relations of sovereign groups. [3] At the same time, I argue that an understanding of Christian fundamentalism must ultimately pay attention to its interaction with the social context in which it occurs, and that this interaction exercises an influence over the character of fundamentalism that, while scarcely causal, determinant, or unidirectional, is nevertheless real.

The Environment of Christian Fundamentalism

For historic reasons, far more of the fruits of economic growth have been channeled into religion in the U.S. than in many other societies. Particularly during the nineteenth century, when a number of societies in western Europe, as well as the United States, were experiencing rapid economic growth as a result of industrialization, governments with strong control over religion were often reluctant to allocate money to the construction of church buildings or the training of clergy, preferring instead to expend these resources on secular capital construction outlays, such as railways, or on military programs, or even on nascent social welfare policies. In contrast, the U. S. Constitution forbade such tampering with religion by government, placing exclusive responsibility for its fortunes in the hands of local citizens, who built churches with alacrity to adorn their local communities. As a result, religion entered the twentieth century in the United States with a much stronger social position than in virtually any other country. And fundamentalism grew in this context more so than in many societies where religion in general was simply weaker. In recent decades it has grown again, not so much (as its leaders might say) because of the secularity of American society but because of our society's basic wealth of religious resources.

We can see from this example that similar arguments can be presented that help to make sense of variations in the strength of fundamentalism in other societies as well. For example, the strength of militant Protestant and Catholic orthodoxies in Northern Ireland, or the recent resurgence of conservative Catholic movements in Italy, or the growth of Protestant pentecostalism in Latin America, can to some extent be understood in terms of the historic strength of religion more generally in those societies. Religion provided a richer institutional context in which reform movements could emerge in those societies than in, say, France, Germany, or Sweden, where historic relations with government inhibited the strength of established religious institutions. What this example also suggests, though, is that a number of other environmental conditions also need to be brought into consideration.

Government

One that is clearly implied in this example is the role of government. Let us consider three societies in which religion in general has remained strong, at least until fairly recently: the United States, the Netherlands, and Northern Ireland. All three have been dominated by a Protestant majority but have a significant Roman Catholic population as well. Indeed, this interfaith competition has contributed to the overall vitality of religious institutions in these societies. But the role of government has resulted in quite different opportunities for fundamentalist movements to emerge. In the United States, Protestant hegemony has been maintained by asserting a strict wall of separation between church and state, which among other things has prevented public monies from being used to support Catholic schools. Fundamentalists have been able to draw on this tradition to argue against all sorts of government interference in other realms of life, from regulations affecting their own parochial schools to the use of tax money for abortions. In the Netherlands, Protestant-Catholic relations were guided more by active government intervention. Tax monies were used to underwrite church programs, including Protestant and Catholic schools, which formed the basis of the so-called "pillarized" system of socioreligious institutions. There was always room for a free church movement as well, but less legitimacy and opportunity for fundamentalists to form large-scale institutions of their own. In Northern Ireland the relations between Protestants and Catholics have been governed more by an external force in the form of the British government. Militant fundamentalist Protestantism and Catholicism have emerged with strong antigovernment biases that nevertheless look to policy makers to implement their demands.[4]

As these examples suggest, fundamentalism is often like a third party in politics. If dominant religious institutions are tied closely to government and receive sufficient resources to carry out their work, there may be little room for a third force to develop. But if the dominant institutions are supporting a government that is disliked, or are themselves sometimes in opposition to government, third parties may be able to develop a niche of their own. The analogy should of course not be pushed too far, for religious institutions differ from political parties in many ways. There are, however, historic precedents indicating the validity of the idea. For example, historian Mary Fulbrook has shown that pietist beliefs in the eighteenth century took on quite different forms in England, Prussia, and Württemburg because of the patterns between established religious institutions and government.[5]

The irony in the United States is that liberal Protestants—those most likely to be outraged by the fundamentalists' claims—can see the results of their own earlier tensions with Catholics being replayed in fundamentalists' efforts to stay the hand of government. Liberal rhetoric notwithstanding, these efforts have in fact been much more concerned with restraining government initiatives in the moral sphere than with using government funds in some way for the benefit of fundamentalist institutions themselves.

Political Involvement

Apart from these predisposing political conditions, there also appears to be an increasing tendency for fundamentalists of all kinds to view politics as a legitimate activity. Fundamentalism in many Latin American and European countries, as it has been in the United States, is often associated with political parties or with opposition movements that seek to influence electoral, legislative, and judicial outcomes. Why?

The question is especially important in view of the fact that fundamentalism in the past—and even many contemporary varieties—largely disdained political involvement. Until the early 1970s, for example, fundamentalists in the United States had generally viewed the political domain with distrust, preferring to pray, rather than mounting public campaigns or even voting. And yet at present it appears that fundamentalism is increasingly distinguished by political militancy.

This shift in orientation can in part be accounted for by the fact that the state has simply become a more prominent feature of the social environment in which most fundamentalist movements operate. To achieve their ends, they feel they must influence the political process. Even in democratic societies that guarantee constitutional separation of church and state, the latter has grown in countless ways that intrude on the "voluntary space" in which religion has generally functioned.[6] From safety regulations governing public assemblies to the ways in which old-age insurance and funding for day-care centers are provided, the state is an actor whose claims must be taken into account. And it is precisely in these free spaces historically that the smaller sects of which contemporary fundamentalism is reminiscent were able to flourish.[7] They, unlike the established faiths that often entered into mutually beneficial arrangements with the state, depended on the state's coercive powers to be held in abeyance. Where it is not, and even when symbolic gestures are made by the state that may seem to suggest intrusions, fundamentalist groups are likely to feel especially beleaguered. Certainly, a large number of the issues around which fundamentalists in the United States have organized since the 1960s has been of this type.

But again we generalize too broadly if we assume that fundamentalist militancy emerged in the United States in recent decades simply because of state expansion. The period following World War II in fact witnessed unparalleled state expansion—in outlays for national defense and public education, in entitlement programs and transfer payments, and even in numbers of federal employees. Some of this expansion pinched the purses of individual fundamentalists, just as it did nonfundamentalists, but without generating negative responses (national defense is an example). Other forms of state expansion touched fundamentalist churches more directly—for instance, regulations requiring the marking of fire exits, ramps for the disabled, or more careful reporting of pastors' salaries. These regulations perhaps prompted greater awareness of "big brother," but resulted in few overt protests. Where fundamentalists responded is to situations they believed involved moral issues—abortion, homosexuality, the right to pray in public schools, among others. Thus, it was not so much government expansion in general but penetration specifically into the moral sphere that prompted fundamentalist reactions.

The World Economy

In discussing the political environment in which contemporary fundamentalism reappeared, we also need to be mindful of broader processes in the political economy of the world system that promoted either a more general shift toward cultural conservatism or an instability in political loyalties conducive to the growth of conservative movements. In the United States and western Europe, heightened economic competition in the world system and a slow down of growth in gross national product resulted in fiscally conservative regimes coming into power.[8] By coupling calls for reductions in social programs with appeals to individual morality, these regimes were sometimes able to enlist the support of fundamentalist groups who, in turn, gained a modicum of political clout in the bargain.[9]

This support, moreover, came largely from white-collar and middle-class fundamentalists whose economic fortunes depended more on keeping tax rates low by reducing government spending than on the various welfare programs that poorer fundamentalists might have desired. Not only in the United States, but also in Great Britain and Canada, conservative religion and conservative morality joined forces with the conservative economics of various political candidates. Fundamentalist politics thus formed in opposition to various sociomoral orientations of the modern state, but in support of economic policies favorable to the middle class.

In the developing countries of Latin America and other parts of the world, it might be noted, the consequences for religion were quite different, producing fundamentalism of a different hue. Shrinkage in global economic fortunes often led to domestic political instability. Core nations were sometimes less able or willing to take military action to prevent such instability, and indigenous class factions that depended on an expanding export economy were sometimes weakened by budgetary crises, foreign debt, and fluctuations in trade. In the face of this instability, various class factions both in and out of power sometimes looked to fundamentalist groups with faithful constituencies for support.

Higher Education

Perhaps the most puzzling feature of the social environment in which contemporary Christian fundamentalism appeared is the relatively high levels of education that exist in modern societies. If fundamentalism were truly a function of simplemindedness and a lack of exposure to modern ideas, as it is often alleged to be, then it should have diminished markedly as a result of growth in higher education. Especially during the third of a century after 1960, college attendance rose dramatically in the United States and in most other advanced industrial societies. And yet fundamentalism seems not to have diminished. Why not?

One answer is that it did in fact diminish, but appears not to have, because the remaining minority grew more vocal, stirring as it were to make their wishes known with their last dying gasp. That fundamentalism is on the verge of death is certainly an overstatement. But there may be some truth to the assertion that it is diminishing. In the United States, for example, surveys asking about biblical literalism have shown a declining proportion of the population who hold this belief. Still, it does seem puzzling that fundamentalism fares so well in the face of an ever more educated population.

For a clue to this puzzle, we might do well to consider the comparable question of why happiness seems not to have risen as economic well-being has grown. Analysts predicted it would because cross-sectional surveys showed strong correlations between higher incomes and happiness, just as they have between higher education and a rejection of fundamentalism. And yet studies over time show little change in the proportions who register various levels of happiness or unhappiness. Here the solution is obvious. Happiness is a relative concept. At any given time, those who are better off are generally happiest, but as overall economic development occurs, expectations shift, causing the less well off still to compare themselves unfavorably with the better off.

Fundamentalism may function in a similar way. Its roots may be less in the absolute stock of knowledge available in a given society than in the relative position of various segments of the population to that knowledge. Thus, we know much more as a society about history, the arts, other cultures, and the outer reaches of the universe than at any time in the past. But some people still know a lot more about these topics than other people do. An engineer in Duluth, for example, may know a great deal about the mechanics of his trade, and yet feel there is an alien world out there, located in the big cities and in universities and literary circles, about which he knows little. His religious views may be shaped less by the fact that he actually knows quite a lot about things than by the fact that he feels he doesn't. Furthermore, he does realize that he knows his own subject matter pretty well, is intelligent, has an advanced degree, and works in a well-paying profession. Thus he isn't likely to parrot what he hears coming out of the big cities and the art councils and the think tanks. Instead, he figures he may well be right and they wrong. His fundamentalism reassures him in this belief. Or, to make the same argument in more general terms, educational expansion in the United States has upgraded the overall level of technical and cultural knowledge, but has nevertheless left a great deal of internal variation, even among the better educated, and some of this group will continue to find fundamentalism an appealing view of the world.

To conclude this section, we might point out how counterintuitive these arguments may appear against the background of prevailing conventional wisdom about religion and social change. Over the past quarter century the United States has undergone significant economic expansion, political expansion, and educational expansion. The conventional wisdom would suggest negative consequences from all these developments for the likelihood of a strong fundamentalist movement occurring: rising incomes should make people more content with the secular world, government expansion should make them better able to realize their purposes through normal political channels, and educational upgrading should reduce the ignorance from which fundamentalism presumably springs. None of these predictions has been borne out. The reply from conventional wisdom would be to say: Yes, but fundamentalism might still be expected as a backlash against such modernizing forces. But if so, why should it be evident among the well off, the politically involved, and the better educated? My arguments have suggested that social reality is more complex than the conventional wisdom acknowledges. Fundamentalism has not been a direct psychological response to changing environmental conditions. Instead, these conditions have created new opportunities—niches—which fundamentalists have been able to use to their advantage. By extension, we would expect fundamentalism to continue strong in the twenty-first century as well, even if the culture of modernity also continues to spread. If the present argument is correct, then even educational and economic expansion will produce a cultured elite whose members nevertheless may be attracted to fundamentalism because they are in fact marginal relative to the position of some other privileged elite.

The Dynamics of Christian Fundamentalism

The main problem with focusing only on the environmental conditions in which fundamentalism arises is that these conditions often imply a kind of static, stable-state of society, whereas the very notion of something *arising* suggests the need for a more dynamic understanding. This problem is sometimes circumvented by conceiving of the social environment in more transitional terms, such as talking about economic "growth" rather than economic "prosperity." Nevertheless, the fact remains that fundamentalism is not just a "something" that responds to these changing conditions; rather, fundamentalism is itself a dynamic process, a movement that unfolds over time. As it unfolds, it also changes its relations to its environment.

To capture this dynamic sense of the movement itself, some investigators, at least of other kinds of movements, have tried to identify typical phases through which all movements must go. There is, for example, an early phase of assembling in which people simply gather and try to articulate their grievances; later perhaps, a leader emerges and helps put these grievances into specific demands; eventually, the leader may die, causing the movement to face problems of succession. Such models can be useful for understanding a very well defined movement—for example, the Free Speech Movement that began in Berkeley, California in 1964, or the Moral Majority movement that Jerry Falwell brought into being in the late 1970s.

But fundamentalism is generally a broader social phenomenon, a result of a whole variety of specific movements, and rooted in longer-standing cultural traditions. Usually it does not go through such neatly identified stages. To understand its dynamics we must take an additional step back, seeing it somewhat more abstractly.

Population Ecology

For this reason it may be more helpful to draw theoretical inspiration from a different source: the work of population ecologists who have been concerned with ways in which more loosely scattered aggregates of species, individuals, social characteristics, and even organizations adapt to their environments.[10] In this literature three conceptual moments in the process of adaptation are generally identified: production, selection, and retention. Production refers to the phase in which new movements and countermovements come into being, thus enlarging the overall range of variation in available belief systems. Selection refers to the process by which these various movements seek out distinct niches in the social environment, adapting to its differential resources, and thereby resulting in some movements being able to flourish better than others. Retention is the phase in which movements begin to gain greater control over their own resources and thus become institutionalized as more stable features of the social environment itself.

  Although it may seem that these processes are the work of blind forces in the larger society, they actually depend on the day-to-day decisions of movement leaders and the willingness of their followers to commit time and energy to these movements. What these processes sensitize us to especially is the fact that religious movements are always in competition with other movements—other fundamentalist groups, nonfundamentalist religious movements, and secular organizations attempting to make claims on individuals' time and energy. Thus, the future of any particular set of beliefs is likely to depend on its ability to compete for scarce resources with contending belief systems.

Uncertainty

One of the ways in which we can gain a better grasp of the dynamics of fundamentalism in the United States, therefore, is to look at the general uncertainty that has plagued the moral order of our society since the 1960s. Starting in that decade, if not earlier, expectations about moral commitments and the moral communities sustaining those commitments became increasingly ambiguous. Young people went away to college, developed different occupational expectations from their parents, lost ties with their communities of origin, and confronted a variety of new challenges in ethics and life-styles. From the beginning the splashier movements that experimented with political radicalism and countercultural lifestyles were opposed by ultraconservative religious and political movements. New belief patterns were produced, in short, greatly expanding the range of options from which young people could choose.

Put differently, the changing economic and political conditions discussed in the preceding paragraphs did not only generate new resources and opportunities. They also generated uncertainty. Old rules sometimes lost the resources needed for them to be reinforced. New rules were largely up for grabs. How to live was the issue, as the emphasis on lifestyle experimentation in the 1960s indicated. This period was not particularly auspicious for fundamentalists. But it was out of this uncertain time that fundamentalists began to hone their new sense of concern for the moral order.

Social Selection

The selection process began almost at once and extended itself during the 1970s and 1980s. Many of the fringe movements that appeared on the religious scene in those years gradually failed. Some did so as a result of idealism that made it difficult for collective decisions to be made or for viable economic bases to be established. Among the more conservative Christian groups, many also failed but were often absorbed into established churches. Over a longer period, the human costs associated with experimentation in such activities as drug use and sexuality also took their toll, resulting in a relative shift in emphasis to those movements that cautioned against these activities. Even a liberalizing movement as successful as the feminist movement often produced conservative countermovements. Thus, the net result of this selective process was to leave a number of fundamentalist movements in relatively good shape.

The exact manner in which social movements are produced and selected, it should be noted, depends greatly on the degree of heterogeneity already present in a society. As a general rule, we might posit that the likelihood of fundamentalism being present at all is increased by higher levels of heterogeneity, whereas the likelihood of fundamentalism becoming a powerful and unified movement is greater where some, but limited, heterogeneity exists. The reason why heterogeneity heightens the likelihood of fundamentalism being present at all is that distinct social niches are more readily available for it to occupy. In the United States, regional, ethnic, and religious diversity all contribute to the likelihood that fundamentalism will be able to find at least limited niches to occupy here and there: orthodoxy in Jewish communities around New York City, militant Catholic fundamentalism in isolated ethnic enclaves around Philadelphia, or fundamentalist Baptist offshoots in the Midwest and South. But for fundamentalism to solidify as a major national movement, the boundaries defining some of these niches must either shrink in importance or be drawn along the same lines as other social divisions. Fundamentalism has been able to gain national prominence in places such as

Guatemala or the southern United States, for example, because whole regions could provide unified constituencies as localistic, familial, tribal, or political divisions diminished in importance.

It is worth speculating—although to my knowledge no empirical data exist—that the reemergence of fundamentalism in the United States in the 1970s and 1980s was nurtured in some degree by the persistence of one "ethnic" enclave and the demise of others. The one that persisted was the southern (largely Baptist) Bible belt. As the South gained a new industrial economic base in these years, many of its churches and meetinghouses gained new resources as well as a sense of entitlement in national political affairs. Their constituents played an identifiable role in politics, much in the same way that the so-called Celtic fringe did in British politics a century earlier.

The ethnic enclaves, that diminished were the smaller conservative sects that had emerged from various waves of immigration, such as Dutch Calvinists and Scottish Presbyterians. As migration and intermarriage broke up these enclaves, some of their members probably shifted religious loyalties to larger fundamentalist bodies, such as fundamentalist Baptist churches or Assemblies of God churches. We do know, in a broader sense, that denominational barriers eroded significantly during the period after World War II and that this erosion contributed to the emergence of a division in American religion between religious liberals and religious conservatives. It may have helped solidify the fundamentalist wing within the broader conservative spectrum as well.

Institutionalization

Retention has also been accomplished with considerable success by American fundamentalists. One of the most significant ways in which fundamentalism institutionalizes itself, giving it power over its own destiny, is by identifying a stock of specialized knowledge over which it is the sole or chief arbiter. Students of elite culture (meaning people with educational credentials and professional knowledge) have had a field day debating the concept of "cultural capital." As if by magic, this concept provides a name for the advantages that go with attending Exeter and Yale and being able to read items correctly from a French menu and discuss the latest Broadway play. Those things are all like money in the bank, a kind of capital investment from which we can draw to get ahead in life. But fundamentalists have their own forms of cultural capital. It may consist of resources that to the outsider seem like nothing—being able to recite Bible verses from memory, knowing all the stanzas of "Amazing Grace" by heart, saying "Amen" at the appropriate time, praying a long spontaneous prayer in public with considerable fervor and sincerity, or having been acquainted with a family who went to Africa as missionaries.

These are valuable forms of cultural capital in fundamentalism, and despised in the outside world, precisely because they are commodities the fundamentalist community can produce and certify without much in the way of resources that are in scarce supply in the wider world. Fundamentalism is, in this sense, a variety of what Clifford Geertz has called "local knowledge." [11] It exists in local settings and depends largely on the interaction of the group to be understood. It is not so much a medium of exchange that can be used in universalistic transactions (like money) but a vehicle of restricted exchange, a carrier of meanings that do not easily permeate external boundaries. They reaffirm the group, giving it resources over which others cannot easily gain control.

This aspect of fundamentalism is especially important in underdeveloped societies or in less-developed segments of advanced societies. Where resources are scarce, the capacity to control them becomes all the more important. Especially in competing with more established religious institutions, fundamentalism often has an advantage in such situations. One might wonder, for instance, how fundamentalist sects have been able to convert so many areas of Latin America in view of the much stronger and better established position of the Catholic church. Part of the reason is that fundamentalist churches use local lay preachers and generate enough commitment to the local body that a kind of mutual aid society emerges among their members. If a more established international church is already suffering from scarce finances and leadership, these newer competitors can make strong inroads.

The greatest challenge that fundamentalism has faced in recent years in advanced societies has come mainly from its attempts to "go public," as it were. People have long believed the world was created in seven days. But when those beliefs cease to be the result of local teachings and are presented in the terms of universalistic scientific publications, then they are more easily turned over to the credentialing agencies of the larger society.

This is perhaps one reason why pentecostal varieties of fundamentalism appear to be growing more rapidly than their more cognitively or doctrinally oriented cousins. Rather than attempting to formulate doctrines and moral statements along rational and even scientific principles, pentecostal churches are more likely to emphasize the inherent nonrationality of faith, its emotionality, and the experience of warmth and caring among the body of believers. Here, participation generates its own resources, as warmth and caring feed on themselves. External authorities, especially those representing the cold, uncaring worlds of bureaucracies, corporations, big governments, and rationalistic universities, can make few compelling claims against the resources of these churches.

The main point of these considerations, then, is that fundamentalism in the United States has been in competition with other religious and secular movements, all of which were in their own ways responding to the moral uncertainty in our society. In this competition, fundamentalists enjoyed certain advantages, partly because of the heterogeneity of the environment giving them protected niches to occupy, and partly because of their own strategic use of resources. They also have their own forms of cultural capital and are generally able to retain control over the interpretation of this capital. At the same time, there has been a basic tension between using these resources for the internal benefit of their own community and exposing them to the critical winds that prevail in the more universalistic arenas of American politics. The fate of fundamentalism in the next century will surely depend heavily on the ways in which leaders resolve this basic tension. In the short term, forays into the academic or political life of the wider society may heighten fundamentalists' visibility, but in the long term their strength is likely to be secured by maintaining control over their own cultural resources.

The Culture of Christian Fundamentalism

We obtain an understanding of the social sources of fundamentalism by viewing it in relation to the conditions and processes just described, and yet somehow fail to gain a very good sense of what all this has to do with fundamentalism specifically. Fundamentalism is, after all, a distinctive set of beliefs and practices, or as I suggested in the last chapter, it is a language, a discursive style, a way of talking, of communicating something important to oneself and to one's fellow believers about the sacred, about how to live, and even about how to act out one's values in broader social settings. Our accounts will be vacuous if they do not in some way take into consideration these characteristics of fundamentalism.

The Meaning of Life

Like any religious orientation, fundamentalism is not so much about prospering or growing or governing, although it may be those things too, but about living, and knowing how to live, so that life has transcendent meaning and value. Accordingly, fundamentalism is concerned with the symbols and concepts and languages that give meaning to life.[12] Indeed, its distinguishing feature is the assumption that life has meaning only in relation to certain of these frameworks, especially the historic role of Jesus in atoning for the sinfulness of humankind, the authority of the Bible as God's unique and inerrant revelation of divine truth, and the importance of following certain moral prescriptions for behavior and belief that are taken as pleasing to, or in keeping with, the divine will.

　　To say that fundamentalism holds itself to be the unique (or exclusive) framework in which life has meaning is to imply immediately that it also sets itself over against, or in contrast to, various other frameworks that are false, errant, deceptive, and capable of leading people astray. Perhaps to a degree more evident than in most other systems of belief fundamentalism is thus a framework in which polarities abound. The believer exists in a world of right and wrong, good and evil, light and darkness, mammon and God, flesh and spirit, demons and angels, worldly temptations and heavenly salvation.

Polarities

Fundamentalists are of course enjoined to seek the light and shun the darkness. But to understand fundamentalism in this way only is to miss its essence. Few people of any faith or of no faith at all would deny wanting to side with goodness as opposed to evil. Nor is it even accurate to say that the fundamentalist wishes more acutely than most to "love good and abhor evil." The difference lies not so much in the fact that fundamentalists conceive of polarities but in the way in which these polarities are understood. They are understood as sharply opposing contrasts and they are associated with a number of distinct cultural connotations.

If the sharpness of polarities in fundamentalist thought is sometimes taken as a cognitive style, the cultural connotations associated with these polarities are nevertheless matters of social construction. To take the most obvious example, during the second half of the twentieth century, communism served as a favorite symbol of evil for many fundamentalists, and even today it is possible to receive direct mail solicitations from fundamentalist preachers calling for mass campaigns of vilification against individual college professors who espouse Marxist perspectives.[13] But earlier in the century, urban life and often the Roman Catholic church or Jews served the same purpose. As we move into the twenty-first century, we are likely to find fundamentalist hatred shifting toward other targets, such as Muslims, environmentalists, the New Age movement, or politicians of certain parties.

My point is not that fundamentalists are always on the lookout for innocent victims to satisfy some deep hunger to vent their hatred. That may or may not be the case. The point needing to be understood is that fundamentalist discourse constructs the symbolic worlds in which its adherents live. It does so partly by responding to the real environment in which it finds itself: fundamentalists did not have to invent communism as an object of hatred; it was already there, and they were not the only ones to hate it. But fundamentalism does engage in a creative act when it constructs these objects. It selects some features of its environment, attaches negative valences to them, and ignores others.

We might call this selective, constructed world the "social horizon" of the fundamentalist. It, rather than the social environment in the more external way in which I have described it in previous paragraphs, is the world in which the fundamentalist lives. It is a world constructed and maintained in discourse. It depends on the conversations and Bible studies and sermons and church dinners in which the fundamentalist participates. But it also articulates with the external world (that is, with the social horizons in which nonfundamentalists live). It gives the fundamentalist an understanding of what is going on in the world and why it is happening.

What I am pointing to is the fact that fundamentalists are themselves social analysts. Like academic social scientists, as we try to understand the social conditions that led them into national prominence, they too attempt to diagnose the social characteristics of their world. Their diagnoses and ours do not always coincide, of course, but there is a degree of articulation between the events happening in the social environment and how they have chosen to talk about it. The moral uncertainty to which we referred earlier was not a product entirely of their invention; they merely helped put it on the national agenda. The same was true of the fiscal conservatism that began to influence American politics in the 1980s. Fundamentalists responded positively to these appeals, but also reinterpreted them, turning them into moral capital.

Were it only that fundamentalism constructs a social horizon in which to live, we would still not have much to say about its distinguishing characteristics. But fundamentalism, as we have already observed, imposes a basic polarity on its social horizon. It is, in this sense, a form of cultural criticism. It selects much from the secular world to vilify, terms it polluted and uninhabitable, and identifies a life that is more worthy of pursuing.

This is what some have referred to when they say fundamentalism is essentially antimodern, or that it poses a counterdiscourse to the discourse of modernity. Fundamentalism does define itself in polar opposition to modernity. But this view also needs to be qualified in two important respects. First, it does not reject modernity entirely; it rejects it selectively. A North American fundamentalist, like an Ecuadorian fundamentalist, may lash out against alcoholism, and yet feel comfortable taking sleeping pills, drinking coffee, or working for a multinational corporation that rapes the environment. To say that fundamentalists are simply antimodern misses the extensive degree to which they are also modern. Second, fundamentalist discourse does not define its basic polarity simply around a past versus future orientation, as some observers imply. Fundamentalists do not see the train of civilization moving along the tracks into the future and call for putting the engine in reverse. Instead, they envision switching points along the track and call for the train to move in one direction into the future instead of another.

We must also be careful when we say fundamentalism poses itself as a counterdiscourse, for that implies a dominant discourse out there somewhere that simply exists apart from fundamentalist constructions. Fundamentalism is not a monolithic counterdiscourse consisting of principles and ideals that differ from some external discourse. Rather, it is internally a dialogic construction. It consists of an internal conversation between its own view of Christian fundamentals and its own view of something opposed to these fundamentals. It does not simply respond to modernity; it caricatures modernity, redefining it in a way that heightens the contrast between its evils and the good life provided by a belief in Christ.

Motivation to Action

Seeing fundamentalism as a form of cultural criticism helps us to recognize its creativity and its vitality, rather than dismissing it as some form of mental retardation. But in defending the creativity of fundamentalism, we must not neglect its simplicity either, like the anthropologist who tries to turn primitives into sophisticated scientists. The reason that fundamentalism often appears to be simpleminded is that it, like all forms of cultural criticism, is designed to motivate people toward taking some action. It is not a purely intellectual (or anti-intellectual) exercise concerned with spinning out theories of society; it is a call for action, a plea for a changed life-style. To invoke this plea, it often adopts a rhetorical style that moves from the complex to the simple, from the chaotic to the commonsensical.[14] It accuses its opponents of making life more complicated than it needs to be. One merely needs to find the simple truth.

But the truth it seeks is anything but simple. This is where the critics of fundamentalism, who charge that it only provides ridiculous certainty in the face of true complexity, fail to understand it. Just as a Marxist vision of the perfect classless society can produce libraries filled with complex discussion and debate, so fundamentalism envisions a life-style that takes at least a lifetime to figure out.

The other feature of fundamentalist culture that is often misunderstood is that it does not set up a polarity between good and evil only to identify itself with the light and distance itself from the darkness. This tendency toward self-righteousness is what nonfundamentalists object to more than anything else. And fundamentalism is no more free of it than any other right-seeking and truth-seeking belief system. But the point that critics and naive adherents both ignore is that the emphasis in these phrases is not so much on right and truth as on seeking.

The fundamentalist riles his advocates by asserting not only that there is a better life but also that he knows what this life is. In doing so, he seems to side with the good. But closer inspection of fundamentalist discourse shows that the believer is always a seeker, a pilgrim, someone who is striving after the good, but never (at least in this life) having attained it with perfection. Evangelist Pat Robertson disturbs the secular consciousness when he declares that God told him personally to run for the presidency; but even Robertson poses as a seeker, someone who does not understand the will of God but is willing to follow it to see where it leads.

This brings us, then, to the final feature of fundamentalist culture that must be understood if we are to recognize its potential for the future. The seeker, the image of the pilgrim set upon a journey in faith, is also a cultural construction. It is, to be sure, a function largely of the polar theological or moral discourse in which it is framed. But it also draws on material from the surrounding social environment. If Jesus or the Good Samaritan or some other biblical figure serves as a "type" in the technical sense of the word in which fundamentalists use it, that type nevertheless takes on some of the admired characteristics of its culture and negatively illustrates others. For example, in a society such as ours that values knowledge, the model Christian—even for the fundamentalist—often becomes someone who knows his Bible, studies it dutifully, and faithfully takes notes during the Sunday service. Or, as has often been observed, the fundamentalist image of Jesus in our society may reflect the therapeutic motif by stressing the intimacy and warmth of the Christ. As social conditions change, presenting new challenges in the next century, the figure of the model fundamentalist is also likely to undergo significant modifications.

Coda

There is perhaps a normative lesson to be learned from considering the past and immediate future prospects of fundamentalism. If accounting for fundamentalism helps us understand it coldly, analytically, and intellectually, we can also recognize that fundamentalism is not as foreign to modern culture as it or its critics like to make out. For the critic, it may be most helpful to understand that fundamentalism is more sophisticated in its own right and less a gut reaction to the dominant culture than generally supposed. For the fundamentalist, it should be important to see that every cue, every guideline, every moral model is not simply being taken literally from holy writ; literalism notwithstanding, fundamentalism is very much a matter of cultural interpretation.

9

Fundamentalism and Its Discontents

The title of this chapter suggests that I am going to consider the ways in which fundamentalists express their discontent toward the malaise they envision in mainstream modern culture. Fundamentalists are the perpetual malcontents, the reactionaries, who dislike what they see in the movies, what they read in the newspapers, and what they know to be going on in liberal churches. Indeed fundamentalism first appeared, historians tell us, because some Americans could not keep up intellectually with the scientific developments of the nineteenth century, and because their rural WASP-ish way of life was being threatened by the cities and by new ethnic and religious groups. Contemporary fundamentalists are simply the latest wave in the psychological history of being left behind. Their women stay at home, schooling their children and protesting against abortion, Kristin Luker's book on the subject suggests, because they haven't the educational background or career opportunities to make something better of themselves.[1] Christopher Lasch, in his book on progress and its critics, which is by no means unsympathetic to the cultural conservatism of fundamentalists, also depicts them as reactionaries, desperately clinging to their marginal cultural existence in the petty bourgeoisie and the upper working class, hanging on by such a thin thread that they cannot embrace the ideals of civilization advanced by great thinkers and social reformers for more than a century.[2] And so it would not be difficult to consider the fundamentalists' discontents, asking whether they will last into the next century, or finally be relegated to the scrap heap of history.

It would not even be unfashionable to tackle this question, given recent efforts in the social sciences to rehabilitate fundamentalism from some of these stereotypic views. In her highly nuanced book *Bible Believers* Nancy Ammerman conceives of fundamentalism less as a relic of the past than as a creation of modernity. It could not exist, she asserts, without modernity.[3] Her point is that fundamentalism developed fairly recently and in a kind of dialectic tension with modernity. Anthropologist Susan Harding, drawing on extensive field research among fundamentalists in Lynchburg, Virginia, credits fundamentalists with an even more creative role in this dialectic. They have, she argues, developed a sophisticated "counter-discourse" in their apocalyptic writings that provides an alternative to the theory of cultural change presupposed by most cultural modernists.[4]

But these efforts still present only half the story. If there is indeed a dialectic of some kind between fundamentalism and modernity, then the other side of the coin is to see how modernity has been influenced by fundamentalism. Given its numeric preponderance, we might be content to say that fundamentalism was merely the tail being wagged by the dog of modernity. A true dialectic, however, suggests that modernity isn't just a dog because of itself; it is a dog partly because it has a tail.

I would, therefore, like to turn the issue around and suggest that liberal and moderate Christians have often let the fundamentalists define their agenda, so that it is they who are acting out their discontents with the fundamentalists. In other words, my concern in this chapter is really with religious liberalism—the nonfundamentalist constituency in mainstream or old-line churches that makes up a significant majority of the ways in which people define their faith. I want to ask if liberal Christians have not sold themselves short by letting themselves become the reactionaries of our time. This is a question, it seems to me, that merits serious attention if the mainline churches are to remain a significant cultural force in the twenty-first century.

I am going to try to answer this question by considering three of the issues it raises: first, whether and in what manner liberals have in fact let fundamentalists define their agendas for them; second, the cultural forces that may keep fundamentalists going in the future, allowing liberals to continue defining themselves in reaction to fundamentalism; and third, what the possibilities may be for liberals (and moderates) to seize the initiative. Before doing so, however, I must make clear that my approach is not that of the theologian. I am not, for example, concerned with showing that liberals are theologically less liberal than they think, or that they are on less or more solid ground than the fundamentalists in terms of biblical scholarship. My approach is that of the cultural sociologist, a maverick breed of academic deeply indebted to recent literary criticism, such as the work of Mikhail Bakhtin and Frederic Jameson.[5] The sociological point, especially in Bakhtin, is that the social world is itself figured in the text.[6] Indeed, looking at the dialogic structure of texts can be a way of seeing some of our assumptions about the social world. In a general way, that is what I want to do by looking at liberalism's implicit dialogue with fundamentalism.

How Liberals Let Fundamentalists Set the Agenda

Truth or Progress

Despite the fact that they are so often depicted as naive simpletons, fundamentalists have one enormous advantage over liberals when it comes to setting any theological or programmatic agenda: fundamentalists are the bearers of tradition. Who claims to preserve the historic gospel that has been taught over the centuries? Who claims to believe in the historic Jesus and the historic truths of the Bible? Who wants to return America to the faith of its fathers? Who speaks on behalf of traditional moral values? The fundamentalists. That is high ground on which to stand.

By comparison, liberals must occupy the slippery slope (as fundamentalists see it) of moral relativism and faulty human judgment. Or, as liberals prefer to see it, they are the true sojourners, leaving their encounter with God at Sinai to wander in search of the Promised Land. They are called to be the progressives, the innovators, the seekers after a deeper, more elusive knowledge of God than that known by the fundamentalists.

There is a certain irony evident here already, of course, for fundamentalism is, as Nancy Ammerman observes, scarcely a century old, whereas the institutions in which religious liberalism is embodied are generally much older than that. It should be the liberals, not the conservatives, who claim to occupy the high ground of tradition. But fundamentalists saw their opportunity. At the end of the last century, when modernists had become fully enamored with pursuing the gleaming city of progress, the fundamentalists stole in at night and took the high ground for themselves. It has been hard for the liberals to get it back.

The liberal identification with progress does have a certain appeal even today. We can look to the wonders of modern medicine and say that some things have surely gotten better. We like to think the billions we are investing in science and technology is getting us somewhere. It is nice to have religionists on board the ship of progress, helping to steer it through the uncharted waters of new moral challenges. The only problem is: these waters are indeed filled with uncertainty. We need safe havens when storms arise, not just heroic bravado in face of the torrent.

Beyond that, liberalism has difficulty even in claiming the future for itself, because that future, the one envisioned by the progressives, is still very much in the hands of the scientists and the rational technocrats. They are the true bearers of progress, guiding the ship with up-to-date navigational equipment; the religionists are only the chaplains, offering ceremonial prayers each morning and evening. They are in as precarious a position as the timing of their prayers would indicate. Embrace science too little, and the captain terms them fanatics and leaves them in port.

Embrace science too much, and passengers begin asking them questions they cannot answer, like "Wouldn't a few more doctors and engineers on board make more sense than these clowns?"

It is probably much easier, caught in this position, to fight the fundamentalists than the scientists. "Yes, we are religionists too, certainly we do not claim to be scientists, but we are definitely not like those fundamentalists, who aren't even smart enough to figure out what science is. They've made spirituality much too simple; we believe it to be more complex."

Simplicity and Complexity

This reply, however, raises a second way in which liberals let fundamentalists define the agenda and, in so doing, occupy the higher ground. Liberals are fond of charging fundamentalists with oversimplification and pointing out the need for complexity. That's how it goes. The starting point is what fundamentalists say. Their simple formula is reported as a point of departure. Then an appeal is made for greater complexity. Sometimes an attempt is even made to provide a complex answer. The answer is surely more complex than anybody can assimilate, at least hearing it from the pulpit. Maybe the fundamentalist view is damaged in the process, but the liberal view doesn't come across very well either.

Let me illustrate. It is always dangerous to take things out of context. What follows is part of a sermon preached by a very competent pastor. A rhetorician would say the sermon reveals deft craftsmanship at a number of points. It is thought provoking when read. It causes the eyes to glaze over when heard. Why? The text is Luke 4:1, the passage about Jesus spending forty days in the wilderness and being tempted by the devil. Having started with several hints that the story seems simple but is so complex as to defy interpretation, the pastor builds to a climax, expressed in the following sentence: "I think that each time I'm really serious about Christian believing I'm driven again into the wilderness where I experience my humanity in all its limitations, and where I experience the struggle with whether or not I will believe that God *really loves me,* or whether I will seek security in the tyranny of my authoritarian conscience, where my life is governed primarily by fear of punishment and hope of reward." There are several things to note about this sentence. All I want to note here is that its sheer length—seventy-one words—makes it almost incomprehensible.

Lest this illustration seem completely unfair, here is another example: a different text, a different pastor, a different denomination, a different location. Again, the entire movement of the rhetoric is from simple to complex. The sermon opens with a four-word assertion: "Everybody loves a parade." Its main point, which comes only two sentences from the end, is expressed this way: "To those to whom truth has been revealed, who continue in the tradition of the Holy One's followers, the call is not only to offer words of praise, confessing that Jesus is Christ the Lord, but to offer our lives as the instruments of this Lord of peace and justice." You get the point. Or did you? The sentence has five major clauses involving forty-nine words.

What makes these sentences so complex? Partly it is the fact that the speakers themselves regard the truth to be complex. The whole rhetoric of their sermons moves, as I said, from the simple to the complex. They tell us the truth will at first sound simple, but it is really very complicated. And they show this in their construction of sentences. This, however, is not the only reason for the complexity.

Were you to read these sentences again carefully you would notice that both are complex because they contain an internal contrast of the form: not this, but this. The "not this," moreover, is the ground occupied by fundamentalism. You would see this more clearly if you had the whole sermon before you, but note what the "not this" is even in the two sentences themselves. In the first, the speaker contrasts believing that "God really loves me" with seeking "security in the tyranny of my authoritarian conscience, where my life is governed primarily by fear of punishment and hope of reward." Who thinks this way if not the fundamentalist? In the second text the speaker contrasts the desire "to offer our lives as the instruments of this Lord of peace and justice"—what could sound more liberal than "peace and justice"?—with those who only "offer words of praise." Is not the latter the happy, naive fundamentalist who sits all day in the comfortable pew?

The Role of the Devil

Let's push the point a notch higher to reveal something else going on here. Elaine Pagels writes provocatively (although provocation is not her intention) that the early Christian understanding of Jesus would have been impossible without the simultaneous resurgence of beliefs about Satan.[7] Her thesis, supported by other examples ranging from Martin Luther to Saddam Hussein, suggests that Satan occupies a pivotal role in Christian and secularized Christian thought right up to the present. But what, we must ask, plays this role in liberal religious circles where Satan and sin are seldom mentioned at all? The best clue comes from her insight that Satan, unlike earlier Hebrew concepts of an external source of evil, is an "intimate enemy," somebody we know well because it is one of us, a member of our own tribe, but the personification of all that opposes us. Do not fundamentalists play this role? And if Pagels is right, are not liberals dependent on them occupying this position?

It is instructive to note that the first sermon I quoted was about Jesus being tempted by the devil. In the sentence itself the speaker puts himself in the wilderness, and the sense that God loves him is there in a positive way: surely the authoritarian conscience, the voice of the fundamentalist, is that of the devil. In other sermons the equation is often not this direct. And yet the temptation, the evil, to be avoided is clearly defined in reference to fundamentalism. Here is another example: "many conservative First World Christians preach a Gospel which declares that the spiritual message of Jesus is incompatible with seeking economic and political justice." The sentence comes near the beginning of the sermon. A few sentences later, in case we did not understand who these conservatives might be, the speaker explains that this line of argument is heard from "conservative American Christians like Michael Novak and Richard Neuhaus, who are sophisticated intellectuals, on one end of the spectrum and Jerry Falwell of the fundamentalist fringe on the other."

Fundamentalism and the Future

So what do fundamentalists have going for them? What makes them so strong that liberals keep attacking them? Will they continue setting the agenda in the future? Part of the answer to these questions is implied in what I have already said. If early Christians needed Satan, liberal Christians of today need fundamentalists. Every time they construct their logic in a way that starts with fundamentalism, they help perpetuate it. The more they protest, the healthier their intimate enemy remains. Only the death of liberal Christianity would do in the fundamentalists for good.

Pragmatism and Success

In good liberal style, though, it is worth arguing that the reasons are also more complex than that. Let us acknowledge the simplest—and probably most important—of these first. Fundamentalist churches have witnessed spectacular growth, while liberal churches have been skidding into oblivion. Or so it seems. Should these trends continue, there will indeed be plenty of ways that fundamentalists can continue setting the agenda. In the meantime, they have forced liberals into the unenviable position of having to argue against two of the strongest themes in modern western culture: pragmatism and the success ethic.

Here is an example. The speaker is a pastor in a liberal denomination; I will not say which one, only that it, like many, has not been noted for its growth in recent decades. He says: "Just as there is a 'market-driven economy,' it appears that the more successful churches are in a similar way driven by the market—they are market-driven churches. Their success comes from providing the services that the religious consumer is seeking. The outrageously successful contemporary churches succeed by providing services. . . . This works fine in regards to the task of a church to figuratively 'comfort the afflicted.' But it doesn't work so well when it comes to the shadow task of 'afflicting the comfortable'—to confront, to challenge, to stretch spiritually and morally." We know intuitively who the "outrageously successful" churches represent. Is there a twinge of envy here as well?

Don't misinterpret what I'm saying. Somebody needs to lift a critical voice against pragmatism, the success ethic, and other such prevalent assumptions. That it is difficult to do so doesn't mean liberals should quit trying. I am merely pointing out that it is difficult because these are indeed prevailing assumptions. Liberals miss the point if they think fundamentalists are the ones fighting an uphill battle against the entrenched forces of modernity. It is the liberals who are fighting both modernity and fundamentalism.

Rational Attacks

Even apart from their numeric growth, another reason why fundamentalism has a lot going for it is that liberals' criticisms of it are generally so off target as to have little effect. Many liberals seem to think the main thing fundamentalists have going for them is simplicity and security. Implicitly, many liberals also seem to think fundamentalism will crumble as soon as anybody launches a logical, rational attack on their beliefs. For example, if fundamentalists are clinging desperately to the security of an authoritative Bible, then they will fall away the minute someone brings in historical criticism or raises questions about the canonization process.[8] Perhaps a hard core of the most insecure will remain, but others will troop thankfully after their liberal rescuers. An obvious reference for this kind of argument, of course, is Bishop John Shelby Spong, who writes in his book *Rescuing the Bible from Fundamentalism* that the "major function of fundamentalist religion is to bolster deeply insecure and fearful people," and that the way to rescue people from this nonsense is to make more readily available "the biblical scholarship of the past two hundred years."[9]

But this is to misunderstand fundamentalism in several ways. First, it assumes that the need for security is somehow located more among fundamentalists than among others, whereas in reality it is probably —if we believe Abraham Maslow—a universal need. Indeed, given their uncertain journey through the wilderness in search of innovation and progress, we might have supposed liberals would be the ones most subject to needs for security, and we might even venture that liberals take as much comfort in saying there are no answers as conservatives do in saying they know the answers. Second, it overestimates the extent to which people are guided by rationality and logical consistency, especially in matters of faith, and it assumes that liberals really understand such things, whereas in fact they probably do not (in fairness to Bishop Spong, he admits as much) and (to speak the unutterable) liberals may not even be any smarter than fundamentalists. Certainly, liberals spend less time and devote less cognitive energy to doctrine and intratextual examination of the Bible than fundamentalists do. Third, this view also misunderstands what fundamentalists devote their cognitive energy to: they do not try to come up with rational arguments for how things go together, and why historical criticism makes no sense; instead, they focus on intratextuality within scripture itself, and they avoid or have sophisticated ways of explaining away its internal problems. Even more to the point, they tell stories and give personalized applications, rooted in the authority of the speaker in the text, or the preacher, rather than drawing abstract rational principles.

Teaching the Children

Still another reason why fundamentalism is likely to continue defining the agenda is that fundamentalists do a highly effective job in transmitting their beliefs to their children. As we know, much of the reason for the decline in liberal churches, apart from demographic and social class factors, is their failure to retain the few offspring they produce. Fundamentalists do better perhaps because they beat their children into submission, whipping them with authoritarian arguments every time they try to speak up. If we have learned anything from Lawrence Kohlberg's studies of moral development or from James Fowler's research on stages of faith, though, it is that the simple, black-and-white cognitive styles generally associated with fundamentalism are the ways in which most children tend to think. In other words, fundamentalists have a natural advantage in this area.

Children of liberal parents, in contrast, either learn nothing simple enough for them to understand, leaving the fold to pursue something (might we say "simple") like monetary success, or else they turn at some point to twelve-step groups or cults that resocialize them religiously by starting out with simple concepts. Part of the reason why liberals so often wind up reacting to fundamentalism, then, is that they were themselves raised as fundamentalists (Bishop Spong being but one prominent example).

Liberals also react, often with special vehemence, because fundamentalism does produce its own discontents. Its strong communal traditions restrict young people when they want to move away, or when they need to rebel as adolescents, or when they decide to experiment with sex, or when they think new thoughts and break away to explore other traditions, or just when they find that life is more complicated at forty than they thought it was going to be at twenty. Perhaps it becomes complicated when their daughter gets pregnant, or their son has AIDS, or their best friend is being beaten by an alcoholic husband. As people mature, they may well feel constrained by fundamentalism, and liberalism provides an alternative. It says to them, we are not fundamentalists, we are more mature, sophisticated, and we understand things better, and we can help you more in the future.

We could certainly mention other reasons why fundamentalism is such a ready target for liberals to identify themselves in opposition to—the fact that fundamentalists generate strong commitment that provides community for their members and brings money into their coffers, the fact that they have adapted rather well to science and technical rationalism in devising recruitment and evangelization strategies, and the fact that their public visibility in community and national politics has often generated a great deal of anger and emotional arousal. For all these reasons, liberals may become even more inclined to let fundamentalists define their agendas for them in the future.

Can Liberals Seize the Initiative?

To answer this question, it may be helpful to consider the two alternatives to fundamentalism I mentioned in passing just a moment ago: cults and twelve-step groups. Both appear to have grown dramatically at various points during the past quarter century and may do so again in the future. There are some lessons to be learned from both.

Cults and Twelve-Step Groups

The so-called new religions of the 1970s, studies have revealed, often turned ex-fundamentalists into neofundamentalists, just providing a different sort of cult belief. But some of them did work, and they did so, it appears, for three reasons: first, they drew on and created a distinct past of their own, an alternative rooted in a different religious tradition entirely, but still a distinct past, rather than just a vague vision of secular progress; second, they involved people in fairly tight and well-defined communities, so that they again were not just part of the broader secular culture, and they could develop a deeper personal identity, undergo resocialization, learn new values they had not known as children, and develop a specialized language rooted in new experiences and stories; and third, they focused a great deal on the nonrational—that is, on ritual and feeling—getting people out of their heads, thus avoiding having to say: No, this is what fundamentalists said but we have a different view.

As for therapy and twelve-step groups, many of them also function like cults, substituting something similar to fundamentalism for chemical addictions. There is a strand too that is simply reacting to fundamentalism, such as Fundamentalists Anonymous, or in the case of codependency literature, telling people to be less compulsively responsible in the way that a fundamentalist might be. But for all these limitations, these groups do provide some clues: an emphasis again on strong community; deep resocialization involving learning how to tell stories, a deemphasis on cognition and an emphasis on feelings and emotional support; and a lot of countermainstream discourse, such as talk about not getting too stressed out or becoming too materialistic and the need to think for yourself instead of succumbing to social expectations.

Lessons

One lesson from these two examples, then, is that liberalism needs to become a counterculture to secularism, instead of a reaction to fundamentalism. It needs to present itself as a third way; and in this, it has clearly been strongest when it has engaged in activities like the peace movement, because this was more an antisecular movement than a reaction to fundamentalism. Another clear implication is that strong commitment to small groups and communities is important; and these are probably going to succeed better if they do not try to teach people how to think in nonfundamentalist ways, but rather provide support and feelings and personal stories, and if they provide a positive image of faith journeys.

How then can liberalism be true to the doctrinal insights that come from historical criticism, systematic theology, and the like? Complexity and pluralism, even universalism, can all be achieved in drama and literature, better than in the hegemonic discourse of science and rational argumentation. The story can make important theological points about deep human values. But the insight of historical criticism is that people need to think about the meanings and invent symbols and trust God for guidance in these matters. Stories are pluralistic, letting people come up with their own moral implications; literature is countersecular in that it upholds ideals, and finds ways to challenge the assumptions of modernity, often through postmodernity. So theologians have rightly explored postmodern criticism.[10] And pastors probably do well when they return to the narrative style of preaching.[11]

Dialogue

Having presented some negative examples from sermons earlier, let me conclude by giving a positive example. I wish it were possible to reproduce the entire sermon, because it touches on so many of the points I have raised. All I can give are a few excerpts. The sermon was preached in a Baptist church deeply committed to the liberal wing of American Protestantism. It was presented in the form of a dialogue between the minister and a young woman graduating from high school and being commissioned, in a sense, to leave the church of her youth and go off to college. The dialogic structure of the sermon, with the listener literally giving voice to her own views, substitutes, it appears, for the kind of imaginary dialogue that often places fundamentalists in this role. Like a loving father, wanting to impart some knowledge of the family heritage, the pastor speaks of his desire to answer all her questions and, at the same time, of his reluctance to give a lecture about "Baptist distinctives." Instead, he decides to make some connections, as he says to the young woman, between "your story and our story." His language is simple, nonthematic, storylike, but it also does a masterful job of reappropriating tradition in the name of liberal religion, of emphasizing the importance of community, and of evoking an identification between the listener and this community that is stronger than any rational argument could provide.

Reminding her of how much she values her own personal freedom, he observes that she has much in common with her Baptist ancestors. "They used a term for it," he says: "Soul Liberty." Elaborating: "Soul liberty means your own freedom to shape your faith in light of your participation in a faith community, in light of your experience of God in Christ, and in light of scripture." He also emphasizes the way in which the church has functioned as a community—a countercommunity. "You cited our becoming a sanctuary church, our inclusive language, and political involvement. This is yet another connection between your life story and our Baptist story. For our Baptist forebears were considered radicals, and for that they were imprisoned, banished, and tortured." Among other things, he also speaks eloquently of how the congregation itself becomes a community of memory, and how she will carry on that tradition. He says: "Let us be aware of how the community is in individuals." "As a high school senior grows up in our church," he says, "and then comes the time to leave in pursuit of individual goals, the community goes with that person." "Community," he concludes, "is anchored within your memory as you become increasingly aware of the connections between your story and the Commonstory."

IV

Political Challenges: Christianity and Conflict in the Public Realm

10

Faith and Public Affairs

In this chapter I want to consider the public role of religious faith, or what some have called "public religion."[1] To identify something as public religion implies, of course, that there must be something else that we might term "private religion." But as soon as we draw this distinction we realize how much we have been conditioned by living in the modern, post-Enlightenment age. Martin Luther would not have known what to make of such a distinction. For him, the public and the private were a seamless web, not only because his leadership placed his private convictions under public scrutiny, but because the culture drew no line between the two.[2] What Luther believed in his heart was something he did not hesitate to confess openly, not as self-disclosure in the manner of Rousseau's *Confessions*, but as conviction about divine knowledge that should be declared and, if necessary, disputed.[3]

Our culture provides for a much cleaner distinction between the public and the private. Faith is, we commonly observe, a subjective orientation, derived from our unique personal experiences, and lodged in the interiority of our consciousness.[4] We do not expect anyone else to believe exactly as we do, and we may well feel it an imposition to have someone probe too deeply into what we believe—like a successful businessman in Chicago who affirmed to one of my graduate students who was interviewing him that he was a devout Christian evangelical, but when asked to give a few sentences describing his beliefs, refused. We shield our deepest convictions from the public eye. And yet we know that religious faith is present in the public arena as well. It has been throughout our nation's history, and it undoubtedly will be in the next century. Most observers, in fact, argue that our society would be diminished if religion were not a part of our public values, but there is also disagreement about what its role should be.[5] We need to consider what its role has been in recent decades, and what that may tell us about the future.

The Polarization of Liberals and Conservatives

Historians at some point in the future will probably look back on the last third of the twentieth century and note the enormously pluralistic ways in which American religion has contributed to the public arena. They will emphasize the role of pastors in the civil rights movement, the religious dimensions of unrest surrounding the Vietnam War, the way women struggled for greater inclusion in clergy and leadership roles, the controversies that arose over homosexuality, the efforts of born-again Christians to rid the public square of moral refuse, the courts' rulings on school prayer and the teaching of creationism, and the ways in which religious convictions animated the public debate on abortion—and, being historians, they will point out that all of this had happened before. But if they look more closely, they will also see some important changes.

I have argued, along with a number of others, that one of the most important of these changes has been the deepening polarization between religious liberals and religious conservatives.[6] Some prefer to say progressive and orthodox, or old-line and evangelical, but whatever the specific terms, the arguments are much the same. There is a discernible gap between those who define themselves as religious liberals and those who think of themselves as religious conservatives. In opinion surveys, people in fact appear comfortable defining themselves in these ways; the two sides represent about equal proportions of the American public; and there are now fewer people in the middle and more at the two extremes than there were even a few years ago.[7]

Private and Public

Those who have tried to probe the meanings of these self-definitions have found that they often pertain to the private, interior religiosity of the self. A conservative Protestant, for example, will refer to believing in the historical reality and bodily resurrection of Jesus, and will talk about the necessity of believing in Jesus to receive salvation. A liberal Protestant will mention Jesus less often, talk about God, but perceive of God through a rich symbolic layer of interpretation that emphasizes grace, hope, and goodness. Both may feel a deep personal sense of spirituality in their lives, but conservatives may express this as a relationship between themselves and an object-entity outside themselves, whereas liberals may speak more subjectively of the divine being within their own consciousness or worldview. Often the differences are subtle, the beliefs vaguely expressed, with the cues coming from different usages of language that give off slight indications of differences in degrees of certainty, or in distinctions drawn between the natural and the supernatural, or in ways of understanding the Bible. There may be deep, insuperable epistemological differences, but it seems just as likely that the differences are marked by linguistic subcultures more than by sustained theological reflection.[8]

It is at the public level that the distinction between religious liberals and conservatives is most clear. Indeed, we might suspect that public pronouncements are often the source of labels that individuals then opt for as ways of describing their private religiosity because they intuitively feel closer to and more comfortable with a whole variety of issues and statements publicly associated with one label or the other. Studies have mostly confirmed what we already know from the media and from personal experience: religious liberals and conservatives differ in their views on abortion, welfare spending, national defense, communism, whether prayer should be permitted in public schools, and a host of other issues. They often have negative impressions of each other as well, and these images are reinforced by public statements found in the secular press, in religious magazines that cater to one group or the other, and sometimes in the pronouncements of clergy and other religious leaders.[9]

Roots

To appreciate fully the character of this division, we must recognize that it is not an inevitable fracture, somehow built into the nature of religious thought itself, but is a product of specific social and cultural forces. Such conflicts have of course been present in many periods of American history, but they are also episodic, coming in distinct waves, revolving around specific issues that differ from one episode to the next, and having definable beginnings and endings. Typically they have been most extreme when forces in the wider society were also at work, such as the geographical and political forces shaping the Jacksonian period, and the rural-urban or agricultural-industrial conflicts in which the fundamentalist-modernist controversies were embedded a century ago. It is important to see that specific historical forces are at work because human effort may then be effective in reshaping these tensions.

Mention of the fundamentalist-modernist controversies may suggest that the present tensions are at least a century old.[10] But, as I have argued elsewhere, there appears to be a significant discontinuity between that period and ours.[11] During the 1930s, 1940s, and 1950s, many factors in American society helped to mitigate the tensions between religious liberals and conservatives. After the Scopes trial in 1925 the fundamentalists were very much in disarray as an organized movement, and the economic pressures of the Great Depression and World War II made it difficult for them to do much more than function as small separatist denominations deeply divided from one another. The vast majority of people who held fundamentalist beliefs in their private lives probably stayed in the mainstream denominations, and these denominations especially after World War II were caught up in evangelistic and church building campaigns, in continuing battles with Roman Catholics, and in Cold War fears of communism that provided a great deal of centrist activity.

It was not until the 1960s, and even then only gradually, that the issues currently separating liberals and conservatives began to take on their divisive significance. Prospects of a thaw in the Cold War after 1965 began to separate liberals and conservatives in their views on communism; clergy activism on behalf of the civil rights movement often aroused opposition from conservatives who claimed to dislike the tactics of the movement and who may have been prompted by other concerns as well, but found considerable support from religious liberals, especially the young and the better educated, who found in social justice a kind of mission for the churches. The Vietnam War prompted similar divisions involving the issues of both communism and protest tactics.

Other factors played a role as well: the enormous rapid expansion of higher education during the 1960s created a widening cultural gap between the college-educated young and those both old and young who had not been to college, and this gap reinforced the division between the more liberal religious views of the better educated and the more conservative outlooks of the less well educated. Evangelicals, though, were already gaining strength as a national movement, partly because they had repudiated fundamentalist separatism, forged national organizations, developed an educated leadership, and seen their numbers swell largely as a result of demographic increase and greater success in retaining the religious loyalties of their young. By the middle 1970s, when the end of the Vietnam War permitted American politics to focus again on domestic issues, the stage was set for a major confrontation between religious conservatives and religious liberals.

Crystallizing Forces

With the advantage of hindsight, we can now see that several decisive events helped to crystallize and deepen this division over the next decade and a half. The failed presidency of Jimmy Carter, an evangelical Christian with liberal social and political inclinations, was certainly one important development. Had the OPEC oil embargo, the ensuing recession, the hostage crisis, and a number of other episodes not led to his downfall, it is at least possible to imagine a much stronger centrist position in American religion today, or at least a more complicated crossing of the lines between religious and political perspectives. The *Roe v. Wade* decision on abortion in 1973 undoubtedly constituted another significant turning point. Coupled with the long struggle for ratification of the equal rights amendment, it helped to mobilize sentiment, especially among women, on both sides of the abortion and women's rights issues. Homosexuality, at first raising questions about membership and ordination in religious organizations, and then with the AIDS epidemic increasingly being associated in the public mind with disease, drug problems, and social decay, was probably a more divisive issue even than many people were willing to admit. Even something as minor as Internal Revenue Service noisings about possible investigations of Christian schools on discrimination charges did a great deal to mobilize formerly passive evangelicals and cause them to become a more significant voice in public affairs.

Some of these events obviously could have had different outcomes, and even together, it is not clear that they provide an adequate account of the polarization between liberals and conservatives. There were deeper geological forces at work in American society pulling religious communities apart and realigning them in new ways. The educational changes to which I have alluded provide one of the clearest examples of these deeper forces. They were hardly driven by religious considerations, or even strictly by the institutions of higher education themselves, having instead much broader roots in the competitive drive for technical superiority in world markets and the growing dependence of military advantages on technology. The expansion of the federal government during and after World War II—again a phenomenon not limited to the United States—was another important factor. We cannot understand fully the significance of cases such as *Roe v. Wade* or the numerous court cases dealing with church-state issues except in the context of this wider supervisory role being played by the federal government. Even something like the declining tensions between Protestants and Catholics, and between Christians and Jews, which permitted alliances among conservatives or liberals across these earlier divisions to be made with greater ease, were linked to a much broader range of social developments, including greater regional migration, the suburbanization of the population, and more interfaith marriages among the college-educated young.

One reason for being interested in the division between religious liberals and conservatives, therefore, is that an analysis of the sources of this division helps to bring into perspective a host of other relationships between American religion and American society since World War II. It serves as an interpretive key around which a number of other, seemingly disparate developments can be organized. In other periods, denominationalism or interfaith tensions have provided the same kind of organizing framework. For social scientists, the notion of secularization has provided perhaps the most popular way of thinking about such developments, but with increasing evidence that most concepts of secularization are too restrictive, or not well matched to the sorts of questions that arise when looking at changes only over a couple of decades, alternative frameworks become all the more important. At some future time, when our imaginary historians do their retrospective work from a new vantage point, some other framework may prove even more helpful.

I say this largely to dispel the criticism that an emphasis on liberal-conservative polarization fails to take sufficient account of other characteristics of public religion in the United States, such as the continuing presence of Jimmy Carter–like evangelicals occupying a middle ground by espousing liberal political views, or the so-called new pluralism being brought into being by Latino and Asian immigration.[12] These, too, are an important part of American public religion, and in a sense, their very importance is heightened by the wider tensions between liberals and conservatives. When the extreme positions become strident and familiar, it is often more valuable to seek out alternative voices so that their words can be amplified. Yet, this larger division does help put into perspective many of the salient features of American religion and raises questions about how they are related to one another.

The Character of Public Religion

We come, then, to the question of what specifically the current split between conservatives and liberals may tell us about the character of public religion, now and in the future. Of particular importance is the question of how these two factions conceive of the public. How do they define America, its history, its purpose, its goals, and the place of faith within these conceptions?

Underlying Agreement

Let us first acknowledge that the two factions share many assumptions about the character of American society, and that included in these assumptions is an implicit agreement that disagreement is acceptable. I am referring in part to what Robert Bellah, following Rousseau, has termed our "civil religion."[13] It is this implicit cultural framework that tells us it is important in the first place to have a conception of our nation's past, its present identity, and its future purposes. The civil religion defines a myth of origin that populates the founding times with sacred or larger-than-life characters and separates it from real time; it legitimates our sense that some people—white males, property owners, or in more recent times women and African-Americans, but not convicted felons or illegal aliens—are members in good standing of the national collectivity; and it tells us we are a people with some stature or mission in the world.[14]

Substantively, the American civil religion may include other assumptions on which both conservatives and liberals can agree in principle. For example, the two share basic agreement on the principle that no religious test should be required for formal citizenship or the holding of public office, even though they might in fact favor rather different religious views when it came to treating someone like a citizen with full rights or voting for a specific political candidate. The two might also agree that a society in which some respect toward a higher conception of the divine is acknowledged is probably a better society than one in which no sense of the divine is present—even though the two might differ in their definitions of what this divine entity should entail.

But I also have in mind something other than the civil religion as an underlying cultural premise for the liberal and conservative conceptions of public religion. It is probably best captured in the slogan about agreeing to disagree. We may cherish consensus and, failing to achieve it, throw up our hands and resign ourselves to being in disagreement. That might be the outcome of a discussion between spouses who love each other deeply. But in American public life we generally take a much more positive attitude toward disagreement. In politics we expect Republicans and Democrats to disagree about virtually everything. Sometimes we tire of their rhetoric, but we worry more when we think the two have become like Tweedle-dee and Tweedle-dum, failing to express genuine differences, and we would worry even more at the prospect of a single-party political system. In the economic arena we expect even more disagreement, believing that intense competition between firms accrues to our benefit as consumers by keeping prices down. Increasingly, our public culture is also dominated by the struggles of athletic teams against one another.

So it is perhaps not unexpected that things should be no different in the religious sphere. To be sure, we have norms of tolerance that augur against Catholics and Protestants gunning it out as they do in Northern Ireland, just as we do to prevent Democrats and Republicans from slinging real mud across the aisle in Congress. This is sometimes what we emphasize when we speak of pluralism in American religion: diversity reigned in by a live-and-let-live attitude. But pluralism hardly captures the more positive emphasis on competition that pervades most of our society. At some level, we expect there to be genuine struggles and conflict, not just a passive acceptance of disagreement. Were we to be completely honest about it, we would be disappointed if religious groups of some kind weren't slugging it out with each other in some way. And this is part of what legitimates and even encourages the conflict between religious liberals and conservatives.

They struggle with each other, as we know, over the hotly contested issues of the day, such as abortion laws or the ordination of homosexuals. They also struggle to define America in a deeper sense. Each has a vision of what America has been and of what it should be. Insofar as they articulate different myths of national origin and different definitions of national purpose, it seems fair to say that they differ over the character of American civil religion itself. But if civil religion is taken, as it is by some, to be the underlying ground bass of the culture that is by definition consensual, then we can still identify two very different public theol-

ogies or strands of public religion. They are part of our story of ourselves, providing the narrative framework in which we are likely to cast
interpretations of ourselves well into the future.

On the Liberal Side

Liberal public religion must be understood, because of its disproportionate location in the hierarchies of old-line denominations, as having developed from the long traditions of church-state relations in Scotland,
England, and northern Europe in which religious leaders made statements on public issues. In these traditions it was accepted both that religious bodies would attempt to define the collective interest and that it
was possible for them to do so because of formal recognition and publicly supported institutions. Much the same was true in the Catholic regions of Europe as well, although their influence on the American story
came much later.

Were we to trace the evolution of these church-state relations in Europe, we would see that conflict between Protestants and Catholics and
among various factions of each played a decisive role in shaping religious
understandings of the polity. Indeed, what we generally consider to be
Enlightenment conceptions of the polity, including Lockean contractual-
ism and the more communal liberalism expressed in Rousseau's discussion of civil religion, were very much reactions to the intense religious
struggles of the preceding two centuries. Add the rising influence of deism
and rationalism, and we have the main ingredients on which the public
theology of the United States was originally founded.[15]

The liberal version of American civil religion has varied in the degree
to which it identified something unique about the American experiment,
but it has always embedded that experiment in a much wider notion of
human rights and responsibilities. What made the United States special
was simply that it had the opportunity to embody the universal moral
sensibilities on which people of goodwill everywhere could agree. Ideas
about moral sentiments, traceable especially to the Scottish moralists,
identified a lawful and beneficent order that was not only an external
reality in the universe but an internally or subjectively knowable reality
as well. It is to this conception that much of the so-called optimism
about human nature that is often identified with American liberalism owes
its origin. Because of this subjective sense of moral order, reasoned deliberation among people of goodwill can be expected to result in agreement
about the common good.

Three important practical implications follow from this conception.
First, the moral order is not something that sits heavily on human society, needing to be imposed externally through the coercive powers of the
state on an unwilling, recalcitrant population; it rather is something to
which an informed citizenry will give voluntary assent, much as civic
humanists would argue, because they know it is in their interest to do

so. Second, the deliberative process gains a kind of ultimate sanction, in the sense that public knowledge of otherwise private moral sensibilities is gained through this process. As reasonable people come together to discuss matters of common concern, the will of God, we might say, becomes manifest. And third, though less readily put into practice, there is a kind of inclusiveness built into this conception of the moral order, because it is not limited to people of a given national or religious heritage. By bringing people of other ethnic, racial, religious, and political persuasions into the deliberative process, they too can become partners in defining the moral order.

We can of course see how some of the more substantive planks of the liberal religious platform fit together with these assumptions as background. Certainly the deliberative process of the various synods and assemblies of most of the old-line denominations fits this model, but so does their feeling that religious values can be brought into the secular public sphere without having to be voiced in specific religious terms or needing to be mandated with a strong legislative code. People can especially be trusted in their private lives to find what is morally right. Tolerance for including new racial and ethnic groups in the political process follows from these assumptions as well, and even the idea of using diplomacy rather than military force in dealing with foreign powers makes sense in these terms.

On the Conservative Side

The conservative strand of American civil religion should not, by conceiving of the origins of liberalism in this way, be thought of as a minority or totally reactive orientation. In adopting a somewhat more pessimistic view of human nature, it too draws heavily on Reformation theology, and its view is not as negative as sometimes portrayed. The heavy emphasis on individual conversion in conservative Protestant circles, for example, also assumes that some subjective sense of a beneficent moral order can be found. But conservative civil religion places greater emphasis on the externality of that order and limits its discovery to a more restricted sphere. It is still the chosen few, the regenerate, who can claim divine insight, and they do so less through reason and impulse than by learning principles that have already been laid down and by paying heed to the institutions in which these principles are understood.

Conservative public religion has also been shaped by the history of its associations with the old-line denominations and secular institutions. Many of its current leaders are products of sectarian splinter groups that reacted historically to the universalism and rationalism perceived to be taking over in established denominations. They also defined themselves in opposition to the secular optimism evident in academic settings, to what they perceived as moral relativism, and against these same influences taking precedence in legal and political debates. Fearing that individuals generally did not have a reliable moral sense built into them, they believed it necessary to have strong churches, strong moral instruction in the schools, and even legal sanctions to ensure public decency. But recognizing the importance of having a myth of origin, they also argued that America had originally espoused these very ideals. Pointing to the theocratic orientations of the Puritan colonies, they argued that America was in fact founded on strong biblical principles, that there was a special covenant between this new nation and God, and that many of the founders were dedicated believers.

These assumptions give a great deal of coherence to conservative civil religion as well. The story of America is not one of gradual elevation in moral insight, but of degeneration away from an initial high-water mark and brought about by the leadership of established religious and secular institutions turning away from the biblical order. But America still has a special mission to fulfill as far as God is concerned, whether this be fighting communism, opening other countries to the work of missionaries, or keeping the land itself free of moral decay. Seen in this light, it is no inconsistency to be fearful of government intrusion in religious matters but at the same time to espouse a strong system of legislated morality.

What of the Future?

Having summarized the two versions of American civil religion in this way, I may seem to be suggesting that the two will simply continue to exist in an uneasy tension with each other in the indefinite future. I have tried to suggest, however, that both versions were also conditioned by the social circumstances under which they arose, and thereby implied that they may well be influenced by these conditions again. To understand how these conditions may already be producing revisions in the historic patterns, we need to look again at some of the developments I mentioned earlier as factors leading up to the current tensions between liberals and conservatives. If these factors have heightened the tensions in recent decades, they have done so in part because of their effect on the assumptions undergirding each conception of public religion.

Decline of the Old Line

The liberal strand in American civil religion has been influenced negatively by two developments and positively by two developments. Negatively, it has been influenced by the declining strength of the old-line denominations and by a concurrent erosion of the moral optimism it inherited from the eighteenth century. Each of these developments is relatively familiar. The institutional decline of old-line denominations consists chiefly of numeric losses amounting to as much as a fourth or a third of total membership, but also of the growing pluralism in American society more broadly, the end of the so-called Protestant century, with Catholics, Jews, Muslims, adherents of new religions, and secularists all

demanding greater public recognition. The decline of moral optimism is
sometimes associated with the dispirited mood created by declining
memberships but is certainly traceable to the failure of modernism and
the devastation of the two world wars. It is also evident in a different
sense, though, that does not so much involve a loss of optimism but a
displacement of this optimism from reason to the even more subjective
and intuitive level found in modern expressivism. In this view, goodness
may still be part of human nature, but it is found in more idiosyncratic
ways, involving less public deliberation and more private exploration of
the inner self. On the positive side, liberal civil religion has been reinforced mainly by the inclusionist movements within the United States to
which I have already referred, especially those of African-Americans and
women, and by the greater internationalization of world culture since
World War II. The inclusionist movements have often tapped the moral
universalism of liberal civil religion and, in the process, given it new
vitality and urgency. The world scene has done much the same, drawing
on liberal civil religion for legitimacy in addressing such issues as nuclear
disarmament, world peace, and environmentalism.

The net effect of these developments on liberal public religion has
been to generate a kind of stridency, coupled with an embattled mentality, and perhaps an imbalance between the private and the public as well.
The stridency can often be seen in the urgency attached to particular
issues and the vehemence with which liberal religious leaders attack their
conservative counterparts. It can perhaps be understood by the fact that
the issues seem to have expanded, taking on global importance, just as
the resources of old-line institutions have been declining. These factors
may also underlie the embattled remnant mentality that has arisen on the
liberal side. Whereas it was once able to buttress its optimism with a
feeling that it was in the majority, it is not uncommon now for liberal
issues to be raised as if by a prophetic remnant. Using the rhetoric of the
prophetic tradition, it also adopts at times what might be termed a language of excess, that is, a critical style that questions whether the rational
deliberative procedures of established institutions can any longer be effective, needing perhaps to be replaced by dramatic confrontation, radically populist procedures, or the symbolic identification of visionary alternatives. And the possibility of an imbalance between the public and
the private is suggested by the fact that so much of the new urgency has
come from the outside, as it were, by social movements raising issues
about social justice and human rights, whereas the interior sense of moral
principles has, as I indicated, become more hidden, more highly personalized, and more difficult to bring to bear on formal discussions of public
morality.

Going Public

On the conservative side, a similar set of challenges seems to be at work,
redirecting and reanimating its public theology. Its assumption that sec-

ular society cannot by itself, through reason alone, discover the basis for a beneficent moral order seems to have gained adherents in conjunction with a widespread perception that chaos is on the increase. Evidence to this effect comes from warnings about global warming, the AIDS epidemic, statistics on abortion and divorce, among many other signs of moral decay. In the face of such decay, rationally understandable principles of moral and social conduct, derived from biblical sources, provide an attractive alternative. And yet the numeric increases in some conservative denominations have generated almost the opposite orientation from the disillusionment evident in some old-line denominations: a kind of instrumental triumphalism that assumes eventual victory, at least in legislating moral standards, and that links definitions of moral right with measures of popular appeal or effectiveness.

But if liberals are finding themselves uncertain in their private religiosity, conservatives are more likely to face the same difficulties as they attempt to turn private certainties into public doctrines. Having less confidence in the ability of rational people to arrive at desirable definitions of collective values, they are perhaps of necessity drawn more toward the politics of power plays and interest group pressures, despite the fact that this orientation underscores divisions within their own ranks. In a sense, then, the more strident posture and the language of excess adopted by some liberals play into the hands of conservative leaders who argue that power politics are indeed the only way to proceed.

One implication, if this analysis is correct, is that the future of public religion in the United States is likely to see a continuation of the conflict between liberals and conservatives, even if particular issues come and go, because both traditions are in a state of internal ferment and uncertainty. Until each side is able to come to terms with its past and gain greater clarity about its own vision of America, negativism toward the other and a reluctance to engage in reasoned public debate seem likely to prevail.

A correlative development also seems likely. With the separation between private and public religiosity that is evident in both the conservative and liberal frameworks, public religion may well become the domain of activists, clergy, and other leaders who have some professional or political stake in advancing particular issues, while the majority of believers become increasingly content to let these few play that role. Focusing on their own internal quests for fulfillment and spirituality, the rank and file may be happy that something is being done about public issues. But, as I discovered in interviewing volunteers, they may disclaim the knowledge or skills needed to participate in public life themselves.[16] And, without their backing, or even the sense that private motivation and public morality must be closely connected, we must wonder whether public religion can have much of an effect in steering our society into the future.

11

The Future of the Religious Right

Having considered the broader cultural orientations of the liberal and conservative wings of American public religion, I want to turn in this chapter to a more specific examination of the so-called New Christian Right, asking what role it may play in American society in the early decades of the twenty-first century.[1] In doing so, I am mindful of the fact that most observers of American religion (and politics) were caught by surprise when the religious Right emerged into national prominence in the late 1970s.[2] To make predictions now may be to shoot arrows off into the night with no better likelihood of them hitting the mark than before. And yet, we do know considerably more about the character and social location of the religious Right now than we did when it first appeared. Perhaps this knowledge can be helpful in suggesting the directions it may take in the years ahead.

My approach will be to look back over the conditions that helped bring the New Christian Right into being, asking whether these same conditions are likely to perpetuate it into the future, or whether conditions may be changing in ways that will alter its course. I do not assume that the religious Right (or any social movement) is simply a product of the social conditions under which it emerges.[3] Indeed, many of these conditions, as we shall see, are the accretions of the movement's own activities—its history, reputation, and repertoire of resources. I do maintain, however, that the religious Right is not free to do entirely as it pleases. It cannot accomplish its goals by sheer dint of imagination. Rather, it has to adapt to its environment, garner resources, respond to and challenge the issues with which it is confronted. These are the features of its interaction with the social environment that we must try to understand.

We must pay heed to these conditions whether we are active leaders and supporters of the religious Right, fellow travelers who feel that its aims somehow make a difference to our well-being, or opponents seeking ways to block its ambitions and aspirations. For my own part, I have been deeply concerned about the divisiveness in American religion to which the religious Right has contributed. At the same time, some (perhaps much) of this divisiveness can be attributed to spokespersons in the wider society who understand little of the outlook and origins of the religious Right. Examining the conditions that will guide the trajectory of the religious Right in the years to come, therefore, is not so much a way of promoting its cause or aiding its enemies but of increasing our understanding of the society in which we live and the vital place of religious faith within this society.

In earlier works I have suggested a number of social conditions and processes that gave rise to the religious Right or that produced some of the other characteristics of American religion and culture to which it responded.[4] As one attempts to account for something new that is still on the ascendancy, one is often tempted to pay attention only to those factors that contribute positively to its rise. Other factors that may inhibit its further development, or even lead to its downfall, tend to be neglected. We are now at a critical juncture when a more balanced assessment of all these various factors needs to be made. In what follows I shall pay special attention to the social, cultural, and religious conditions that have proved particularly important in accounting for the rise of the religious Right, but also consider the nuances in these and other factors that may channel the religious Right in various directions and augment or diminish its strength.

Before turning to this analysis, I should also assert my disagreement with many casual observers of American culture who believe that the religious Right is simply defunct. To be sure, the dissolution of the Moral Majority in 1989 and the eclipse of religious television, together with other developments in domestic and foreign politics in the 1990s, signal a moment of uncertainty in the fortunes of this movement. But we should also recognize that most of the issues to which the movement has devoted attention are still unresolved and there is still a strong core of leadership on which the movement can draw, as well as a loyal constituency.

Predisposing Circumstances

Analysts of social movements know the importance of looking at conditions that may, by themselves, have little to do with the shaping of a specific movement but in combination with other factors become enormously consequential. I believe there are at least three such characteristics of American religion generally that must be a part of any discussion of the religious Right: the "this-worldly" orientation of American religion, its conviction that values matter, and its massive institutional resources.

An Orientation toward This World

The so-called this-worldly orientation of American religion (indeed, of Christianity in the modern West, to follow Max Weber's characterization of it) refers to its belief in the sanctity and significance of the present life, as opposed to the view in some religious traditions that only the life to come is important.[5] In American Christianity this orientation takes a variety of forms: from extreme beliefs holding that the life to come is simply a metaphor compared with the final reality of the present one, to various arguments about works in the present life leading to rewards in the afterlife, to concepts of God's kingdom and will for the earth. These variants are sometimes critical in channeling religious energies in specific directions. But the fact that American religion on the whole takes an active orientation toward the present world is of the foremost significance. Historically it has called believers to be concerned with the relation between faith and society. It encourages the faithful, individually and through their churches, to be interested in public affairs.

The religious Right is an expression of this orientation in American Christianity. The movement itself is an effort to address social concerns from the standpoint of biblical teachings. It orients its constituents not toward some passive existence spent preparing for the life to come but toward active engagement in social service and moral reform. Thus engaged, the movement also becomes subject to the wider influences of the society in which it exists. That is, the religious Right does not try to isolate itself from the wider society; it confronts, engages, and resists, but in these very activities exposes its flanks to broader political and cultural forces. Its this-worldly orientation, therefore, makes it more susceptible to many of the other social conditions that we shall consider presently.

It is of course peculiar in one sense to say that the religious Right includes a this-worldly orientation, for many of its constituents are fundamentalists. And of all religious groups in the United States, fundamentalists are generally thought to be the most other-worldly. Indeed, one of the hallmarks of American fundamentalism in the twentieth century has been its premillennial eschatology, a belief that envisions Christ's kingdom replacing the present age rather than coming into being through some evolution of the social order as we know it.[6] Why, if the present world is going to vanish in the twinkling of an eye, would fundamentalists care about political and moral reform?

The answer is varied, reflecting the diversity within American fundamentalism itself. Many of the leaders of the religious Right are fundamentalists in other ways, such as their belief in biblical inerrancy, but have shifted toward a postmillennialist rather than a premillennialist eschatology. This view is probably especially pronounced in denominations with roots in Calvinism or the English Reformation (including Presbyterians and Baptists). It is also more characteristic of leaders identified with the more mainstream evangelicalism that began in the 1940s and 1950s as opposed to sectarian fundamentalism. In other instances, premillennialism is still the eschatology of choice, but its other-worldliness has been tempered by doctrinal and practical considerations. Doctrinally, the premillennialism taught especially in Baptist contexts holds that believers should prepare for the Second Coming of Christ but avoid making specific predictions as to its date. In some teachings, believers are also encouraged to wage battle with the moral evils that may precipitate Armageddon and the end of the age, if only to allow more time for the heathen to be converted before the return of Christ. In other interpretations, dispensationalist theology has emphasized the age of the church during which God's work is to be conducted through the activities of believers in the church. And the practical considerations (which often take on cynical overtones) have to do with pastoral ambitions, building programs, and fund-raising drives: in the crudest form, large structures can only be justified by deferring the expected return of Jesus.[7]

These variations have, it should be noted, produced divisions within the ranks of the religious Right and its potential constituents. Fundamentalists with a strong orientation toward inner piety and spirituality as a way of preparing for the day of the Lord are probably least active in New Right causes. Those with a strong sense of corporate warfare between the church and forces of evil—with apocalyptic implications—have probably been more active in the religious Right. And those with pentecostal orientations have probably been a mixed group. For some, an emphasis on the purification of the church, as signified by the biblical account of Pentecost, has encouraged active efforts to resist evil and purify the wider society as well. For others, pentecostal beliefs have led more toward a conception of inward renewal and personal holiness.

In the future, the religious Right will be enhanced by the overall this-worldliness of American religion, but also be conditioned by doctrinal variations within this general orientation. Beliefs of such subtlety as to be little understood in the wider population will shape the likelihood of coalitions emerging across a broad spectrum of the religious Right.

An Emphasis on Values

The seriousness with which values are taken in American religion is also an important predisposing factor, but one that can be dispensed with more easily. We have always believed that what a person is, believes, thinks, and values has an enormous impact on not only that person's behavior as an individual but also on the well-being of our society collectively. This is part of the individualism built into our culture. It is also very much a feature of American religion. What the churches do, their teaching and preaching, makes a difference to the body politic because values count. Thus, it makes sense to worry not only about such things as poverty programs and national defense but also about the political implications of ethics, personal morality, what people read or see on television, and the values they learn in schools.[8]

When the religious Right came into being, the eyes of many public officials had turned away from this concern with values. Everything seemed to be "structural" and required "policy" solutions. Even today, there are many in the universities who think government programs are the only way to accomplish anything of importance. But the religious Right was also part of a broader reorientation in public life toward bringing values back in. After Watergate, and then again with the numerous public scandals in the late 1980s, it became evident that values do make a difference. Leaders on the left as well as on the right began calling for closer consideration of values and morality in public life.

This reorientation is, however, a mixed blessing as far as the religious Right itself is concerned. On the one hand, it will ensure that a large segment of the population believes that values and morality and teachings do matter, as opposed to purely structural solutions. On the other hand, when everyone—right and left—is talking about values, the distinctive claims of the religious Right tend to be muted. Its potential strength, therefore, may be diminished by having a less distinct identity.

Institutional Resources

The other predisposing condition I mentioned earlier—the massive institutional resources of American religion—refers simply to the fact that churches constitute a tremendous potential force in American society.[9] Were the religious Right to attempt the same activities in, say, Sweden, it would be up against insuperable odds.[10] Habits of religious giving and participation in religious activities are too weak there to give any religious movement much support. In the United States, things are vastly different.

For the immediate future, these resources are likely to remain in abundance. People join churches and attend Sunday worship services in about the same proportions they did a generation ago.[11] But over the long haul, some diminution in these commitments seems likely. Though still only a minority, the numbers who claim no religious beliefs has grown steadily over the past two decades. Large proportions in our society also believe it is possible to be spiritual without any participation in organized religion.

It would, however, be imprecise to conclude that these trends will simply reduce the overall strength of the religious Right. In the past, rising numbers of people without faith have generated controversies about religious beliefs being taught in schools or observed in public places. These controversies will likely continue and will generate reactions from the religious Right. Whether 85 percent of the public believe in God rather than 90 percent, in short, will make less difference than whether that 10 or 15 percent are perceived to be a legal and educational threat to the rest.

Organizational Factors

What I have just been discussing focuses largely on the cultural climate of American religion but also suggests the importance for the religious Right of the way in which American religion is organized. In this section I want to highlight three such factors: the declining significance of denominationalism, the role of special purpose groups, and networks among religious leaders.

The Declining Significance of Denominationalism

Over the past half century, denominationalism has declined seriously as the primary mode of identification in American religion. Indications of this decline include increased interfaith and interdenominational switching, heightened tolerance across faiths and denominational boundaries, ecumenical cooperation, and a deemphasis in many denominations on distinctive teachings and specific membership requirements. This decline, I have argued elsewhere, helped clear the decks for the division that has emerged more recently in American religion between conservatives and liberals.[12] Relatively speaking, the latter have been a more important source of identity and of public controversy because of the diminishing importance of other, cross-cutting cleavages.

For the religious Right, declining denominationalism has made it easier for mobilization to occur across group boundaries. Conservative Presbyterians and conservative Baptists were better able to join forces than if their denominational distinctives had kept them apart. A weakening of boundaries between the major faiths also made it possible for conservative Protestants to garner support from conservative Catholics and Jews.[13] The same was true on the liberal side of the fence.

Denominationalism seems likely to continue its decline in the foreseeable future. But the other side of the coin also needs to be emphasized. Churchgoers may care little which denomination they attend, but for clergy and church administrators, denominationalism makes a great deal of difference. Career opportunities, pension payments, and the policies of judicatories and legislative bodies depend on it. In the past few years, denominationalism actually seems to have been staging a minor revival, perhaps for these reasons. Conservative bodies, most notably the Southern Baptist Convention, have been struggling mightily over the theological destiny of their denominations, and liberal bodies such as the

Episcopal, Presbyterian, and Methodist churches have launched evangelism campaigns in an effort to regain membership losses.[14]

Should this revival of denominationalism continue, it will, I believe, have two significant implications for the religious Right. One will be a reduction in the energy available for religious Right activities: in conservative denominations, because more energy is being spent fighting internal battles, and in liberal denominations, because more attention is being devoted to causes such as evangelism and church growth that conservatives can espouse. The other implication is that denominational organizations will continue to provide a staging ground, perhaps a more decentralized one, but a staging ground nevertheless for the political and moral campaigns of the religious Right. This possibility can be explained better in the context of the other two organizational factors I have identified.

Special Purpose Groups

Special purpose groups are the religious counterpart of interest groups in American politics. Their number has grown considerably over the past quarter century and is likely to continue growing. Organized around the particular aims of a like-minded group of people, these groups do not try to unite a heterogeneous body of believers in the way churches do. Consequently, special purpose groups contribute potentially to the separation of believers into those championing either conservative causes or liberal causes. In the past, they have played an important role in the work of the religious Right.[15]

Newspaper stories about special purpose groups (a Christian Bikers' Association for motorcycle enthusiasts, for example) suggest that special purpose groups are continuing to flourish. But one of the distinctive characteristics of these groups is that they come and go as interests change. Compared with denominations and even local congregations, they are inherently unstable. The religious Right, therefore, cannot count on these groups for indefinite support. Rather, energy will have to be expended to start new groups that reflect changing issues and interests, and old groups will have to pass out of existence.

Some question has also arisen, given the polarization of American religion into conservative and liberal factions, whether special purpose groups might just as well try to bridge this gap, rather than contribute to it. They can, of course, try. But my own interviews and informal conversations with leaders of special purpose groups suggest a doubtful prognosis for these attempts. In part, the problem is ideological. To pursue an objective zealously, one has to believe zealously in its truth. As the leader of one group told me, when you know you're right, why should you compromise? Or as another person stated in a letter to me, mixing gasoline and water isn't going to get you where you need to go. In part, the problem is also strategic. Special purpose groups depend on having a clear objective and a distinct constituency. As the leader of one liberal group whom I challenged to use less divisive language told me, "I see your point, but we know what language our contributors respond to." For these reasons, I doubt that the efforts of special purpose groups, either on the right or the left, will be much diminished by new groups trying to take more moderate positions.

Leadership Networks

Networks among religious leaders are the other organizational factor we must understand. The origin of the New Christian Right owed much to preexisting networks of independent Baptist clergy who could be pressed into service as state and local chairmen of the Moral Majority. Denominationalism, in this case, contributed positively, rather than negatively, to the movement's initial success.[16]

These networks, I suspect, will be increasingly important in the future. National campaigns have proved enormously expensive in the past and these costs will be harder to cover in the future if religious television ceases to be as effective a revenue-generating mechanism. National campaigns have also proved problematic in the sense of producing adverse publicity in the national press and resulting in relatively few legislative or judicial victories in Washington. Indeed, the thrust of many legislative bills and court cases has been to press action back on the state and local levels. And this is precisely where clergy networks can be a valuable instrument. Presbyteries and regional associations bring members of the clergy into contact with one another. Through these contacts, they can coordinate efforts even without a massive centralized organization in the nation's capital.

Sources of Societal Strain

Thus far, I have concentrated largely on factors and conditions that may be thought of as potential resources for the religious Right. But resources make very little difference unless there is some crisis or grievance against which to deploy them. We need to say more about how broad characteristics of American religion translate into actual movement resources. But first, we must consider some of the changes in our society that have resulted in crises—or at least strains—capable of generating responses from the religious community. For brevity's sake, I will concentrate on the effects of educational expansion, the welfare state, and upheavals in domestic politics.

The Growth in Higher Education

Educational expansion was, as we know, extraordinarily rapid in the 1960s and 1970s. Increasing numbers of students went off to college and, perhaps as much from the "going off" as from the colleges themselves, adopted a more liberal, secular, and privatized religious orientation. As recently as the mid-1980s, having been to college was the most significant social predictor of whether one was a religious liberal rather than a religious conservative.[17] Some of the fervor of the religious Right, for this reason, also registered a kind of social class dimension: the educationally disadvantaged struck out at the pretensions of the educationally advantaged, to put it in the crudest terms.

But educational expansion has slowed remarkably since the 1970s. Going away to college now puts young people in a less turbulent environment than it did in the 1960s and 1970s. Campus cultures have become more conservative, or at least more business oriented, resulting in less rethinking of basic familial values. Furthermore, the move into higher education among religious conservatives that was already evident in the 1970s has had important consequences of its own. At present, religious conservatives and religious liberals are scarcely distinguishable as far as levels of educational attainment are concerned.[18]

What does all this imply for the religious Right? As with some of the other developments I have mentioned, the probable consequences are mixed. Over the long haul, higher education does seem to have a liberalizing and relativizing effect, which may shift many of the Right's potential constituents toward a moderate, middle-of-the-road, live-and-let-live orientation. In the short term, though, the rising educational levels of religious conservatives constitute a net plus for the religious Right. Better-educated people are more likely to vote, have more money to give to causes of their choice, tend to be more active in community and political organizations, read and keep abreast of societal issues, and provide leadership skills. In the short term, their educational parity with religious liberals is also not likely to render them entirely content with their social position. Religious conservatives are still more likely to have come from educationally disadvantaged backgrounds, to live in regions of the country where educational opportunities are less available, to have attended less prestigious institutions and majored in more technical and practical subjects. For all these reasons, they are likely to feel at least some resentment toward those who have been more privileged.[19] Resentment of course is not the only factor in the mobilization of the religious Right. But it surely has been one, and will likely continue to be.

The Growth of the Welfare State

The welfare state grew rapidly during the 1960s and 1970s just as higher education did. In taxation, regulation, court cases, defense, welfare provision, health, education, and the formulation of public policy more generally, government simply became a more intrusive element in everyday life.[20] Consequently, groups wanting to achieve some goal increasingly organized themselves to press government with their demands. Groups opposing prevailing tendencies did too. The religious Right was generally suspicious of big government and its various social programs. But to oppose this political entity, the religious Right had to organize as a political entity itself.

On the surface, the successes of the Right (religious and secular) during the 1980s can be seen as a curtailment of the bureaucratic welfare state. Ronald Reagan came to office on an antigovernment ticket. Regulatory agencies were dismantled, taxes were reformed, and free enterprise was extolled. But for all this, the period witnessed very little in actual government reduction. New programs replaced older ones; the same was true of taxes. Big government, it seems, has become a way of life. And it will continue to be in the future.

The religious Right will probably continue to play a game of insider-outsider with government (a topic that merits consideration on its own).[21] And the religious Right will probably be more effective in mobilizing support if it poses as an outsider than as an insider. There is, after all, a broad tradition of skepticism in American religion toward big government. But something akin to the religious Right—that is, as a religio*political* organization—will probably also continue into the indefinite future. A politicized, government-dominated society will, in short, produce a politicized religion.

Political Upheaval

Upheaval in domestic politics is not a phenomenon showing linear growth, like higher education and the bureaucratic state. It refers instead to the instability or cyclical dynamic in American politics. Leaders of the religious Right have been able to gain headway in the past because some of their issues and some of their champions rose in prominence. At the same time, this sort of dynamism in American politics introduces a great deal of uncertainty into the fortunes of a movement like the religious Right. One has only to mention the different religiopolitical styles of Ronald Reagan and George Bush or Newt Gingrich and Dan Quayle, to see the significance of this uncertainty. Unexpected military crises, Supreme Court decisions, and deaths add to the unpredictability of American politics.

My point here is only to suggest that the religious Right came into being partly in response to upheavals produced by events such as the civil rights movement the Vietnam war, and the 1973 Supreme Court decision on abortion. Similar upheavals in the future could greatly augment or greatly diminish the strength of the religious Right.

Resources that Can Be Mobilized

Having considered some aspects of the broad social environment, we can now turn more specifically to the religious Right as a movement. As such, it has been effective only insofar as it has been able to muster the resources necessary to respond to its environment, and to respond actively in a way that sometimes transforms this environment. Rather than viewing the religious Right as a monolithic entity, therefore, we need to focus on each of its specific resources, asking how this component of its overall apparatus may fare in the years ahead. At the risk of neglecting some important components, let us focus attention on several that may be especially subject to the vagaries of social change: people with sympathetic orientations, grass-roots leaders, a nationally visible elite, communications media, time and money, and the wielders of power.

Sympathizers

A broad base of people with sympathetic orientations is important to any movement, even though only a small minority ever become active in the movement. The religious Right has depended heavily on this base for financial contributions, letters and petitions, votes, and symbolic support such as that registered in opinion polls. Although relatively small numbers ever expressed outright support of the Moral Majority, for example, a much larger proportion of the public gave lip service to the issues it supported, such as prolife policies, the campaign against pornography and sexual permissiveness, and strong national defense.[22] At present, this base of support seems fairly secure. Polls suggest at least as many people identifying themselves as religious conservatives as in the past, if not more.[23] Studies also suggest a strong interest in profamily issues, concern about sexual infidelity, and a commitment to traditional standards of honesty and integrity.

Grass-roots Leaders

Grass-roots leaders are, as I have already suggested in discussing clergy networks, plentiful as well. Despite a general decline in voter participation and involvement in partisan activities, the American public continues to be actively engaged in a wide variety of volunteer efforts. Clergy can play an especially prominent role as grass-roots leaders. So can laity with special skills, such as lawyers and business elites. Where some people often misjudged the religious Right in the past was to think of it as a gathering of misguided hillbillies without the savvy to accomplish anything.[24] With rising levels of education and an additional decade of political experience, it ability to organize itself effectively at the grass-roots level with be even greater.

Elites

A nationally visible elite was created for the religious Right around such figures as Jerry Falwell and Pat Robertson. With Falwell's retreat from

politics and Robertson's anemic showing in the 1988 presidential campaign, serious questions need to be asked about the future of this elite.
Certainly individual names can be put forward as possible successors to
the national leadership. These individuals may experience relatively short-
lived careers in the public eye as well. What needs to be asked, therefore,
is not who they will be but from what category of persons they will be
selected.

Let me venture two guesses. First, both the history of the religious
Right itself and what we know from public opinion more broadly suggests that the future figurehead of the religious Right probably should
not come from the parish clergy. Falwell was always limited by the demands of his own church and by the view that he was sectarian because
of his Baptist identity. In this comparison, television ministers such as
Billy Graham and Pat Robertson have been able to reach wider audiences
by virtue of not manifesting such a visible sectarian identity. But even in
Robertson's case it proved difficult to bridge the gap between pulpit and
politics. One can, for instance, think of writers, counselors, lobbyists,
and business people who might have greater success.[25] Second, it proved
in both these cases a handicap for the national leadership to speak so
clearly through the accents of the American South. The strongest constituency of the religious Right may well be located in the southern Bible
belt. And yet its audience is sufficiently diverse that a leader from Washington, D.C., or California, or the Midwest will probably be a better
choice.

Religious Television

Communications media have been vastly important for the religious Right.
Direct-mail solicitations using computerized mailing lists helped it come
into being in the first place. Magazines, newsletters, and radio played a
role too. But it was clearly religious television that gave the movement
its widest exposure.[26] People with doctrinal sympathies watched and found
support for their social, moral, and political concerns as well. But people
without these sympathies also watched, and they came away with a deeply
negative impression. The very style was wrong for them. For people used
to attending religious services, the hand-waving, shouting, angry rhetoric, and emotional display seemed quite ordinary. But for people conditioned to watching *The Tonight Show* and *Family Ties,* such broadcasts of
religious fervor seemed, well, embarrassingly strange. This, together with
the fact that secular television, commentators and news people became
the natural interpreters of religious television, made it a remarkably divisive force in American religion.[27]

Had the religious Right not enjoyed the technologies of religious
television, it might never have become the powerful movement it did.
But eventually the time came to pay the piper. Like a bubble on Wall
Street that turned people into instant millionaires but just as easily bank-

rupted them, religious television made and nearly unmade the religious Right in a few short years. Not only did it strike an ax through the center of American religion, it also made the religious Right itself far too vulnerable to the whims of a Jimmy Swaggart or Jim and Tammy Faye Bakker. It also put the religious Right too much in the hands of Jerry Falwell and Pat Robertson for its (or their) own good.

In the future, therefore, we might ask whether the religious Right will be better served by opting for quieter media. Traditionally, the churches have made a serious impact on American culture by preaching and teaching, by training children in basic religious values, by sustaining people in the religious community itself, and by augmenting these media with books and magazines and tracts and personal visitation. Doing things this way seems slow and old-fashioned in an age of television. And yet, we also know that television evokes quick responses but transmits little in the way of enduring commitments. Perhaps Jerry Falwell, in turning his attention to teaching and preaching, came again to that realization.

Labor and Power

Time and money are the most tangible resources a movement like the religious Right must mobilize to be effective. As I already suggested, these may be more plentiful in the future than in the past because of religious conservatives moving up the social ladder educationally and professionally. They may even increase as a result of the baby-boomer generation moving into retirement, although this will obviously be dampened if a smaller proportion of this generation holds conservative religious views. The women's movement will perhaps be the major limiting factor for the religious Right. In the past it has relied heavily on women in the churches for voluntary labor both in the churches and in political activities organized by the churches. In the future fewer women will be free of economic responsibilities in the labor force and thus fewer will be available for these voluntary activities. It is little wonder, then, that the religious Right has often adopted issues that ran contrary to women's inclusion in the labor force.

The wielders of power, finally, are (as I have already indicated) a very decisive factor in the fate of a movement such as the religious Right. We cannot emphasize too much the personal role played by Ronald Reagan in embracing religious broadcasters, giving moral support to the conservative clergy, and drawing religious Right leaders into his administration. Reagan was sincere in these efforts, even if a great deal of substance was not accomplished as a result. We hear a lot from political analysts about the variations in presidential styles. Perhaps a religious movement headed by television preachers was the perfect match for a president known as the "great communicator." But for other presidents, we may well imagine that different styles will require a different sort of movement.

Factors that Dampen Movements

I have touched at several points previously on factors, such as a shrinking constituency, that may dampen the fortunes of the religious Right in the future. Declining institutional resources in American religion, a preoccupation with denominational squabbles, and relativism as a result of more people attending college may sodden the hopes of movement leaders in some general way. But there are also some things that movements do themselves—which in retrospect can be seen as driving nails into their own coffins.

Winning

One that we might not think of immediately is the problem of winning. Suppose the religious Right achieved all its goals. It would then have no reason to exist. This prospect seems remote. But suppose abortions were completely outlawed and prayer and Bible reading were returned to the schools as mandated policy. What then?

I raise this prospect partly to suggest that the religious Right may well diminish in the future because it has already achieved some of its purposes. Jerry Falwell could perhaps disband the Moral Majority in good faith by asserting that it had succeeded in placing moral issues on the public agenda in a serious way. But I also want to insert a more cynical point by raising this prospect. Most movements, I believe, never really hope to accomplish their stated objectives. Nobody was more surprised than Lenin when the Bolsheviks were swept into power in 1917. And nobody would be more surprised than Jerry Falwell if the Supreme Court suddenly reversed itself on all the issues Moral Majority had opposed. The religious Right, like other movements, has pursued some objectives, hoping to achieve others. Maybe the Family Protection Act would never pass, but championing it would at least bring family issues to the public's attention. For the future, the religious Right will have to pursue the same strategies if it hopes to perpetuate its existence—always champion specific policies, but keep them just beyond reach. Returning prayer to the school room might well be a good issue to pursue.

Losing

The only thing that may be worse for a social movement than winning is losing. In reality, losing may not even be as bad as winning: for example, Prohibition was probably worse for the temperance movement than its repeal. But suppose a movement does lose. What if case after case goes through the courts only to tell the religious Right that it was on the wrong side after all? We love winning enough that such a defeat would undoubtedly ferret out a lot of the movement's fair-weather friends. It would not, however, signal the end of the movement.

Were the religious Right somehow to lose, either through actual defeat or through other issues taking priority on the public stage, I suspect it would not so much die as retreat into quieter pastures. A different scenario is certainly possible. When the student counterculture began to die in the early 1970s, its dissolution was accompanied by a variety of offbeat, more radical, even violent offshoots, such as Synanon and the Symbionese Liberation Army. We might see the religious Right dissolving into radical clusters of skin heads, neo-Nazis, and self-appointed destroyers of adult bookstores and NC-17–rated movies. But I doubt it. That specter has been put forth by the press. But it betrays only misunderstanding of the religious roots of the movement. Its constituents are largely law-abiding, white middle-class suburbanites whose jobs, let alone their religious upbringing, deter them from going more than ten miles over the speed limit, never mind committing a felony.

The more likely outcome, the quieter pastures to which old religious Righters might retreat, is the church itself. Long after the repeal of Prohibition, temperance advocates quietly sent in petitions from their churches. The rallies and saloon smashing ended; the petitions did not. In this sense, the religious Right may have a long future indeed.

New Issues

Short of such unlikely events as total success or defeat, the religious Right may also find itself weakened in the future by crosscutting issues. As I have shown elsewhere, the religious Right became a powerful force in American religion during the 1980s partly because the issues it embraced—prolife, antipornography, antihomosexuality, opposition to the equal rights amendment, and a few others—all overlapped neatly with one another. People who supported one plank of the Right's platform generally supported others as well. The same had not been true in the 1960s. Then, religious people were active on both sides of the civil rights movement and on both sides of the antiwar movement. But the two issues cut in somewhat different ways religiously. People who agreed on one issue disagreed on the other.[28]

The intrusion of some new issue on the public agenda could weaken the religious Right in the same way. The prospects of this happening are not as great as they were in the 1960s because the civil rights issue at that time still brought to the surface strong regional differences between North and South. Most issues at present would fall along the lines already in place. The religious Right must be careful, however, for these lines are always somewhat fluid, as the secular Right has found to its dismay.

Finally, the religious Right always runs the danger of being weakened by internal disputes. Some observers of the Pat Robertson candidacy in 1988 believed his chances were limited by the fact that Falwell supporters tended not to turn themselves energetically in Robertson's direction.[29] Other divisions will continue to haunt the religious Right in the future. Creedal fundamentalists who place heavy emphasis on the rational aspects of the Bible are often skeptical of pentacostalists who pride themselves on emotion. White fundamentalists have failed largely to enlist black fundamentalists in their cause. Protestants and Catholics, for all their affinities on issues of abortion and pornography, are still divided on other grounds. This is not to say that the constituency of the religious Right may not, indeed, be a "moral majority." But neither is it the monolithic specter that liberal critics have often made it out to be.

A Cautious Forecast

In conclusion, then, let me draw together the various arguments I have made, first, by stating again the uncertainty with which any such forecasts are made, and second, by offering what seems to me to be a plausible scenario for the religious Right in the years ahead. This scenario will, in my view, include a strong sector of the American population that remains firmly committed to the churches and wants a society in which moral values are respected. It will be a constituency composed primarily of white middle-class suburbanites, many of whom are in the lower echelons of the middle-class, but an increasing number of whom will be college-educated professionals. Most will have families and be devoted to the virtues of the nuclear family. Some will be mobilized by fear—fear that religion is being pushed from the political arena, fear that the pious are in danger of disenfranchisement, fear that the truly moral are being marginalized by the forces of anarchy and social decay. But the majority will participate in politics from a sense of entitlement, knowing that religion has a rightful place in American politics as long as it is willing to play by the rules of democracy—"a right to a stall," as Hodding Carter has written, "to many stalls, in the civic marketplace."[30]

Their leadership will be centered in the local churches, but connected locally and regionally through clergy networks and alliances among special purpose groups. At the local level, they will work to keep their schools strong, their communities clean, and their politicians from swaying too far to the left.

If this scenario sounds much like the religious Right of the present, it differs in the character of its organization at the national level. It will perhaps be headed by a Christian author or administrator without denominational or regional limitations. It will, above all, be more decentralized and less visible to the public at large.[31] Some of its branches will work at lobbying in the nation's capital. Others will seek to influence state legislatures and municipal councils. Still others will fight legal battles, but few of these cases will reach the Supreme Court; if they do, they will be decided on grounds that will not set far-reaching national precedents. In other words, the courts themselves will encourage a more decentralized style of political action in the future than in the past. In addition—although this is perhaps only wishful thinking—the religious Right of the future will be less concerned with achieving its ends through politics alone and more devoted to the ideals of service, caring for the poor and disadvantaged, promoting community, reconciliation, and the transmission of values through teaching and training the young.

12

Religion and Symbolic Politics

Individuals with deep religious convictions—conservatives and liberals alike—will undoubtedly continue to make their voices heard in the public arena. In the century to come, just as in the century now ending, faith will prompt Americans to be concerned about the direction of our society. But what shape will these concerns take? How effective will people of faith be in expressing their concerns?

We can address these questions better in the years ahead if we take stock of ourselves now. Recent decades have produced a myriad of attempts by religious groups to influence public affairs. From the efforts of clergy in the 1960s to advance the cause of civil rights to the protests organized by religious groups in the 1980s against abortion, the last part of the twentieth century has given us ample opportunity to consider the ways in which religious convictions can make a difference in public life. I would like here to consider what can be learned from the experience of one prominent example of these efforts.[1]

When the Reverend Jerry Falwell announced in 1989 that he planned to devote the next decade of his life to the furthering of Thomas Road Baptist Church and Liberty University, the movement known as Moral Majority that he had initiated a decade earlier came to a formal conclusion. Its work was by no means over. Many of its leaders hoped to continue their efforts on its behalf in other ways. But the formal dismantling of Moral Majority did mark a significant turning point. It brought an important chapter in the efforts of conservative Christians to influence American politics to a close.

We can now view that chapter from the vantage point of history, asking the reflective questions that can only be raised by considering it an episode of the past. From this perspective it becomes possible to ask, as I have done in the preceding chapter, whether the conditions that brought the so-called New Christian Right into being are likely to perpetuate it in the foreseeable future. But here I want to reflect on the religious Right from a broader perspective, viewing it not so much from the vantage point of a navigator trying to chart a course through the unknown waters of a river flowing into the future, but through the eyes of a surveyor trying to map the wider contours of the valley through which the river flows. I am interested in what we can learn from the religious Right about the ways in which religious convictions can—and cannot—be brought to bear on the political process.

Put a different way, the questions I am raising in this chapter are: What worked for the religious Right? What did not work for it? Some of the things it tried to accomplish succeeded marvelously well. Others failed miserably. Why? I am not, however, proposing to survey its record of accomplishments in terms of specific bills passed, votes turned out, candidates elected, or court cases won. Such matters have produced a small library of scholarly investigations already.[2] And these investigations, while enormously intriguing, demonstrate one conclusion with clarity: we often cannot say whether the religious Right was effective or not. For even when there was apparent success, the outcome was often more a result of larger societal processes than of the movement's efforts itself.

My interest in asking what worked and what did not, therefore, is to use this question as a device for considering the broader norms that govern religion's involvement in the public sphere. For example, what tactics do religious groups feel compelled to use in order to be perceived as playing by the rules? In any specific case, these tactics may succeed or fail in producing the desired outcome. But the fact that they are used in the first place tells us something important about how we think the game should be played.

I believe this is an important matter to address because some of these rules are well established in our cultural heritage and others are very much in flux. As an example of the former, we have time-honored constitutional provisions regulating the relations of church and state. We also have a more informal, but deeply rooted, tradition of distrust toward the powers of central government. But how these traditions are interpreted is continuously in change. In recent years, the growth of governmental functions has altered some of our understandings. So have changes in the marketplace. And of course new technologies, especially in mass communication, have contributed to uncertainties about the rules of political engagement as well.

The religious Right provides an exceptionally good case for examining these changing rules of the game. Naturally it illuminates somewhat different realities than would be the case from looking at, say, the civil rights movement or the ways in which new religions have confronted public policy. But the religious Right is a particularly instructive case for considering how believers with firm convictions in the divine truth of their cause confront the pluralism inherent in American public life. The religious Right underwent changes that are themselves valuable lessons in the pragmatic norms of public policy. It also provides a helpful case for considering how morality functions in the public arena. Above all, it represents a movement that was remarkably adept in the use of symbolism for political purposes.

Politics and the Public Sphere

Thus far I have used terms such as politics, political process, public policy, public arena, and public life interchangeably. Before proceeding further, we must distinguish more clearly among the meanings of these various words. We must do so because how we view religion influencing our society depends greatly on which of these we have in mind.

Terminology

Politics refers to all the formally organized or institutionalized ways in which a society governs itself. In the United States it subsumes an enormously complex variety of entities, including not only the three branches of the federal government but also the comparable ways in which government is organized at the state, county, and municipal levels. Political parties must of course be included as well. In attempting to influence politics or the political process, therefore, religious groups generally focus on such activities as running or supporting candidates in electoral campaigns and lobbying or in other ways communicating with their elected and appointed officials.

Public policy can be defined as the outcome of the political process with respect to specific substantive issues. National defense, the provision of public safety, various infrastructure items such as transportation and communications, protection of the environment, and numerous entitlement programs compose much of what we consider public policy. Politics is generally regarded as the means of implementing policy, rather than an end in itself, even though these means, once instituted, often influence the kinds of policies that are likely to be initiated. What political scientists call "administrative capacity" is regarded increasingly as an important factor in shaping public policy. For instance, the implementation of social insurance and welfare programs early in this century varied greatly from one advanced industrial society to another largely because of the various states' preexisting capacity to administer such programs.

Terms such as "public arena," "public life," or "public sphere" refer to something broader than either politics or public policy, namely, the ongoing discourse that takes place in any society about its collective values.[3] How a society views war, life, learning, ethics, and progress are all likely to be part of its public sphere, but only some of these values may be expressed in specific public policies. The important distinction here is between "public" and "private," not in the sense of government-operated versus a for-profit operation, but as the values concerning people collectively and corporately versus those values deemed to be located within the individual's personal life and therefore subject only to individual choice, taste, or discretion.

New Right Objectives

In drawing these distinctions it should already be evident that they help considerably in sorting out the various ways in which the religious Right has tried to influence the society in recent decades, as well as the concerns that have been expressed about these efforts. Although some concern has been voiced about the religious Right trying to obtain political power for its own sake, for example, it is abundantly clear that the religious Right has been much more interested in using politics to implement public policy than vice versa. Some political clout as such has perhaps been gained by virtue of the religious Right's efforts to enlist and mobilize evangelical voters, and some administrative capacity has perhaps been achieved that will transcend specific issues, if federal court nominees, executive branch offices for religious and moral affairs, and grassroots political party machinery can be taken as examples.[4] But most of the religious Right's energies were directed toward specific issues, thereby leaving it with little in the way of formal political structure that may endure beyond these issues. The suddenness with which Moral Majority was disbanded and the speed with which Pat Robertson's state and local machinery evaporated after his failed quest for the presidency in 1988 attest to this possibility. At this point, the public affairs office of the National Association of Evangelicals, which preceded the religious Right and encompassed a wider range of issues, seems to be among the few enduring agencies representing the interests of religious conservatives in the nation's capital. By comparison, religious liberals have been able to maintain at least a more enduring presence through the lobbying efforts of their various denominations.

The distinction between public policy and the wider public sphere is also helpful for understanding the religious Right because much of its energy was directed toward specific policy initiatives and yet its successes in these areas were more limited than in affecting the public agenda more broadly. Indeed, it can be seen in retrospect that a significant source of conflict within the religious Right was precisely the question of which was the more important approach to take. Leaders with experience in secular politics generally took the position of focusing on specific policies, while the religious leadership was often more inclined to take the broader approach. As a result, accusations between the two have often been bitter, especially as both sides attempted to determine why the movement did not accomplish more. As political operative Paul Weyrich observed at a conference on the subject, "I was not interested in just putting things on the agenda, I wanted to win."[5] In his view, the movement failed miserably because he and others from the secular arena were never able to teach the preachers involved how to get from point A to point B.

Reinforcing a Public Agenda

Criticisms

Whether Weyrich's diagnosis is correct, or whether the movement failed for other reasons, it does seem fair to say that the key outcome of the religious Right was not so much passing specific bills or winning specific court cases as influencing the public agenda. Certainly it did not succeed during the decade of its most concerted efforts in obtaining a legislative or judicial ban on abortions, nor was it successful in winning passage of the Family Protection Act, and by the end of the 1980s the American Civil Liberties Union was engaged more actively in litigation against positions favored by the religious Right than it had been at the start of the decade and was still winning a disproportionate share of these cases. Political scientist Kenneth Wald, who has followed the religious Right closely, said of it a few years ago, "For the most part, the record has been one of failure."[6] Robert Booth Fowler, also a political scientist who has written extensively on the movement, came to the same conclusion in a more recent statement:

> Has there been any significant advancement on the national or, indeed, on many state levels of the central [New Christian Right] agenda? No. Has the family been strengthened the way the NCR envisioned? Has prayer entered the public schools, the movement toward gay rights been turned back, pornography been seriously attacked, or the Constitution amended regarding abortions? We know the answer is also no. Even on abortion, where the record is best, the NCR is reduced to the old and once contemptible (in their eyes) strategy of depending on the Supreme Court to do their work for them as public opinion slowly turns more and more pro-choice.[7]

The various explanations that have been given for the religious Right's failure focus some of the blame on factors internal to the movement itself, but in general suggest a dismal outlook for any conservative religious groups trying to shape public policy in the United States. Having remained aloof from the grubby world of politics for most of the twentieth century, conservative religionists have relatively little experience to draw on when it comes to public policy. The very fervor from which their convictions derive renders them subject to accusations of fanaticism and sectarianism. They are often internally divided by these same sectarian traditions and face strong opposition from the agencies of liberal policy, including spokespersons from the mass media, universities, and the political establishment itself.

Accomplishments

And yet the religious Right did succeed in placing a number of its issues squarely on the public agenda, a feat worthy of note in itself, Weyrich notwithstanding.[8] If it failed to pass specific legislation, it at least made the public more conscious of a wide range of religious, moral, and social issues. Abortion may not have been outlawed, but even liberal religious leaders have come to deplore the immorality of abortion at the same time that they oppose government intervention as the means to deal with this immorality. Prayer has not been reintroduced to the public schools, but it is prevalent in other areas of public life, and textbook companies make efforts to include statements about creationism in science books and about religion in history texts. Even the mass media have become sensitive to concerns of the religious Right. At a special briefing held at NBC headquarters in New York in 1981, I was told that the networks were unimpressed with the fundamentalists' efforts to clean up television. A decade later, much of the blatant sexual innuendo to which the religious Right had objected was gone from network programming, and prime-time television seemed to be a platform for warnings against drugs, alcoholism, pornography, AIDS, and sexual permissiveness.

The religious Right cannot take complete credit for these changes, anymore than it should bear the entire blame for its failures. The 1980s was one of those periods, which historians tell us come about every twenty years, when the public mood shifted decidedly to the right, after the liberalism of the 1960s and 1970s. The baby-boomer generation that had found sexual experimentation to its liking in the 1970s grew up, got married, had children, and decided that sexual fidelity was now in its interest. AIDS ushered in—almost overnight—a new Victorianism that blended well with the moral views of conservative Christians. Ronald Reagan, assisted only marginally by the religious Right, brought a new spirit of governmental conservatism to the White House and at least gave lip service to the claims of the evangelical Right. It is more accurate, therefore, to say that the religious Right reinforced a certain public agenda, rather than creating it, but it is also appropriate to recognize that it did play an active role in this process.

If there is a lesson to be learned from the 1980s for the future of religious politics, then, it is that symbolic politics should not be ignored. This is the kind of activity in which religious groups may be able to engage most successfully; indeed, it may be most compatible with the needs and interests of those groups themselves.[9] For religion is fundamentally about values, not about settling matters of public policy. We do not want our policy makers to be devoid of value considerations, but neither do we want our seminaries and churches to become halls of public administration. When professional expertise is the norm for getting things done, it makes no sense to expect the local pastor to figure out where to route a new highway or come up with solutions to the debt crisis in Latin America. But in a democracy, religious leaders can make an enormous impact by keeping the specialists and the public alike aware of the moral and spiritual dimensions of these issues. To this end, we can also learn from the religious Right by considering some of the specific ways in which it tried to shape the public agenda.

Insiders and Outsiders

One of the more interesting dimensions of the symbolic politics in which the religious Right engaged was the way in which images of insiders and outsiders were drawn. Religion has often played a critical role in democratic societies by bringing outsiders into the political arena. One thinks, for example, of E. P. Thompson's argument about Methodism doing this for the British working class in the nineteenth century, or in our own society of the way in which the Catholic church gave immigrant groups a voice in public affairs in many of the industrial cities of the Northeast.[10] The process always begins with some segment of the population who have been excluded from the public arena by virtue of their religious identity *and* some combination of ethnicity, region, and social class. Their common religious bond helps create unity across the full spectrum of this societal segment, and through its organizations and leaders, gives them a way to become legitimate members of the wider society. As Will Herberg observed in his book *Protestant–Catholic–Jew,* ethnic immigrants in the United States found that through their identification with one of these three religious communities, they could more fully think of themselves as Americans as well.[11] But in doing this, people of faith have to be skillful in manipulating the boundary between insiders and outsiders. They want to be insiders, and yet they may actually be more effective by posing as outsiders.

Antielitism

The reason this sort of posturing—the symbolism of insider and outsider—may be as important as the actual social location of any particular group is that Americans have a long tradition of respect for the common person who is a victim of oppression, or disadvantaged in some way, and a strong heritage of disdain for the privileged elite, especially when this elite is synonymous with government. Americans pride themselves on helping the down-and-out, or at least argue that democratic principles should favor the rights of minorities; they worry about totalitarianism, centralized power, and the monolithic authority symbolized by large bureaucracies. Indeed, there is surprising convergence on these views between political liberals and political conservatives. For liberals, the rights of minorities are more sacred than the fear of bureaucracy; for conservatives, anxieties about centralized control are stronger than the concern for minorities. But both outlooks favor the same result: it is advantageous to pose as an embattled minority and to deplore the overweening power of government—even when one happens to be part of that established power. Thus, it was not only the antiestablishment liberals of the 1970s counterculture who called for a return of power to the people; it was conservative Republican president Ronald Reagan in the 1980s as well.

The Politics of Exclusion

The religious Right was most effective posing as outsiders trying to become insiders. Being conservatives, its leaders did not adopt the rhetoric of an excluded minority (quite the contrary: they chose the term "Moral Majority"), but they identified their constituents in populist language as the people, the good citizens, the heartbeat of America who had been pushed aside by a minority of intellectuals and bureaucrats. They used the symbols of political power—the flag, the Liberty Bell, the Capitol— to show that they wanted to be heard in the public arena. But they also cultivated the image of the outsider: holding rallies on the *steps* of state houses, pushing to the forefront leaders who were ministers rather than politicians, speaking in the accents of the rural South, launching their own organizations and newspapers, and advocating legislation that had no hope of passing. Even their ties with Ronald Reagan did not diminish this image, since he too posed as the Washington outsider.

The religious Right began to falter when it became uncertain about its outsider image. With its political operatives wanting to win, rather than be voices crying in the wilderness, some of its leaders became part of the Washington establishment and others began assimilating into the machinery of the Republican party at the state and local levels. Increasingly, one faction of the movement was pulled toward the *realpolitick* of the moderate Republican center, while another faction remained further to the right, steadfastly arguing for the purity of its moral principles. The gap separating these two factions was clearly in evidence by the time the Moral Majority disbanded in 1989. And when leaders of the religious Right succeeded in securing a meeting with President George Bush in November 1990, the outsider faction (which perhaps paradoxically included Robert Duggan of the National Association of Evangelicals and Richard Land of the Christian Life Commission of the Southern Baptist Convention) wanted to convince the President that his administration was morally bankrupt, while the White House wanted to include representatives of the insider faction (notably, Jerry Falwell) to show that it already had the support of conservative religionists.

Preachers and Politics

The lesson in all this for the future of religious politics is probably that religious groups will have more success in speaking to the public sphere as outsiders than as insiders or as groups with a mixed or divided image. The reason is the populist antigovernment sentiment to which I referred earlier. There is also a healthy suspicion in our society of preachers becoming too closely involved with politics. Nobody disagrees, for example, when preachers deplore the horrors of war, but they do not want preachers deciding whether one weapon system or military skirmish is better than another. Operationally, this is the true meaning we have come to associate with separation of church and state. We do not mind the church's values being voiced in the political arena. We do mind religious specialists trying to be politicians—much in the same way we would mind them being surgeons or engineers.

If I am correct, this argument also bodes well for the continuing influence of religion in our society. Even though the vast majority of Americans claim to believe in God and belong to some religious organization, nearly all religious bodies have been able to present themselves as outsiders.[12] Catholics and Jews have long done this in relation to the so-called Protestant establishment. Blacks have done the same thing relative to whites. Evangelicals and fundamentalists continue to portray themselves, in reality, as a moral minority.[13] And increasingly, the membership declines suffered by the mainline denominations have encouraged their leaders to pose as an embattled remnant as well.[14] All these groups have the organizational means to make their voices heard in the public arena and can legitimately pose as outsiders to the dominant secularism of governmental and business institutions. But they must remember that being an outsider is as much image as it is reality. People admire Mother Teresa because she is an outsider to the materialism of Western culture. They admired Martin Luther King, Jr., because he represented an embattled minority. They may admire a ghetto priest who lives in poverty to help the poor or, in a curious way, even a radio preacher who warns in broken English that the Day of Judgment is at hand. But people will not admire, nor fundamentally respect, the prophets who hold pulpits in luxurious suburban churches, enlist Madison Avenue to raise donations, and sit in the meeting rooms of government agencies and large corporations.

The Politics of Morality

If being outsiders is the way to be heard, there is still the question of what can be said. Here again the religious Right provides a lesson with broader implications for the future. Morality proved to be the most powerful rhetorical weapon of the religious Right. The movement not only brought morality back into the national discourse, but experienced considerable success in getting the media to censor themselves, in bringing values and religion back into the classroom, and encouraging discussion of the importance of the family. Its detractors were correct in pointing out that these were only some of the moral issues that might have been targeted. For example, precious little was said by the religious Right about the immorality of poverty and racial injustice or the immorality of nuclear weapons. But the very fact that other groups began talking about these issues using the language of morality was testimony to the power of this rhetoric.

Morality versus Politics

Of course "morality" can be a flabby, overused word that means nothing. It does little, for example, to say that a war is moral if there is no framework in the wider public for understanding what this means, and the same is true when a peace activist says war is immoral. Religious groups need to play a continuing role in informing the public about these meanings. But there is at least strong reason to believe that framing questions as moral issues is a good place to start.

One reason is that morality bespeaks a different kind of commitment than politics, or related terms such as justice or equality. In *Habits of the Heart,* Bellah and his associates found deep skepticism in the American public toward the language of politics because it so often conjured up an image of self-interest.[15] The people they interviewed felt that individuals and groups participated in politics chiefly to feather their own nests. To call something a political issue was thus to suggest that people were fighting over it to gain power for themselves or for economic reasons. In my study of compassion and individualism in the United States, I found much the same objection to the concept of social justice.[16] Even people who were deeply involved in caring activities felt uncomfortable with this concept: it was a legal or economic term in their minds, something that only experts could understand, and it was not a motivating concept because they were all too aware that things in real life are seldom just or equitable.

Morality versus Religion

In much the same way, morality also connotes something different from religion. Critics of the religious Right were quick to suggest that it was not really concerned with morality but with religious dogma. Fearing that it was compromising separation of church and state, they charged it was attempting to bring *sectarian* views into the public arena. By implication, these views were matters of personal choice—indeed, chosen by the relative few—and therefore should not be imposed on anyone else. But the religious Right was largely successful in diverting these accusations by keeping the focus on morality. Moral issues were those on which people of many different faiths could agree. They might have been part of religious traditions in the past, but could be understood and appreciated even by people who had abandoned those traditions.

To be sure, there are many different views in American culture about what morality is and to what it applies. But it is an appealing concept because it indicates that things are right or wrong, and in a society that has largely retreated into the safe havens of empiricism and ethical know-nothingism, there is a deep thirst for such moral tutelage. We admire people who are willing to take a moral stand, even if we disagree with them. Moreover, morality has come to be personalized in such a way that it provides such guidance largely without raising questions about absolute right and wrong. In other words, morality tells individuals how to lead their lives, or how to think about questions of right and wrong, unlike social and political theories that try to tell us what the whole society should be doing. We thus demonstrate a desire to lead moral lives, but we are unwilling to say that everyone's notion of morality should be same.

The religious Right came into being in the aftermath of the Watergate scandal when morality was beginning to be a matter of public concern. It rode the crest of this concern through the 1980s as one ethical scandal after another hit the business community, and the nation came increasingly to worry about the immorality of sex, pornography, drugs, and a younger generation seemingly being raised to think about nothing else but rock music and television. The public did object to a religious Right leader such as Jerry Falwell telling them that his morality should be theirs as well, and they reveled in the spectacle of his peers, Jimmy Swaggart and Jim and Tammy Bakker, admitting to immorality in their own lives. The public did not object to the religious Right emphasizing moral issues, though, and it was not uncommon to hear liberal critics of Jerry Falwell admitting quietly that they respected him for speaking out, especially as his stridency became modified by a greater respect for cultural pluralism and civil liberties.

Religious groups attempting to influence the public arena in future generations will increasingly face the question of why their moral claims are any better than anyone else's, especially when absolutes are no longer taken seriously. They will have to struggle with questions of relativism, of making morality so personal that it carries no authority for the wider society, and with finding alternative bases, such as pragmatism or arbitrary historical precedent, to legitimate their moral claims. But we can be sure that morality will continue to be an issue of vital importance to the public mind.

The Power of the Holy

The religious Right's ability to wage even symbolic warfare was, as I have suggested, contingent on larger developments in the society. It did not simply advance its various causes as moral issues because it suddenly decided to do so. The time was ripe, for a variety of reasons: the wider swing toward social and political conservatism in the late 1970s and 1980s, the leadership vacuum in moderate and liberal evangelical circles that provided an opportunity for ultraconservative activists to emerge, and even the advent of religious television programming and broadcast capabilities. In trying to learn from the religious Right, therefore, we must also pay some attention to these institutional and cultural factors, asking whether conditions will again in the future make the time ripe for religious groups to mount a concerted effort to influence public policy.

Taking a somewhat longer view of American history would suggest that religious groups have been able to penetrate the public arena under the most diverse social circumstances. The abolitionist movement, the Social Gospel movement, Prohibition, the civil rights movement, and the religious Right could hardly have developed under more diverse conditions politically, economically, and culturally. The role of these wider factors was more to channel religious energies than to impede or promote them. The issues, whether slavery or alcoholism, were created by broader societal forces; the religious response was to help sharpen and define these issues. The energy came from within the religious community itself, drawing both on its organizational resources and its cultural heritage.[17]

The organizational resources that contributed to the rise of the religious Right included a national network of clergy, a means of communicating with a wide segment of the laity, and ample facilities. The clergy network provided leadership and a means of coordinating activities both within and across denominations. The civil rights movement depended on such a network just as much as the religious Right did. Communication with the laity flowed largely from central locations through television broadcasts, direct mail, and various denominational periodicals and newsletters. Facilities included the thousands of church basements and fellowship halls that—as events in Eastern Europe demonstrated even more vividly—provided vital meeting space at the local level. Facilities also included the finances to pay clergy salaries, print leaflets, send donations to national organizations, and transport delegates to political meetings.

In the future all these organizational resources will continue to be important as religious groups try to influence the public agenda. Litigation and legislation do not come about simply because some good-minded person decides an issue needs to be addressed; they come about because organizations are there to help these people raise money, hire lawyers, and mount political efforts. In addition to local congregations, the role of church colleges, seminaries, and publishing houses should not be overlooked either, especially as means of influencing the public mind without necessarily engaging in politics. On the whole, the religious community may be weakened in the future by declining financial contributions and growing indifference to its regular services, and yet there will continue to be pockets of growth and vitality—pentecostal Catholics, Asian and Latino immigrant churches, and residential communities for the elderly, to name only a few.[18] The issues raised by these groups are likely to be different from those of the religious Right, but they are sure to influence the public agenda.

The cultural resources that contributed to the rise of the religious Right included not only the aforementioned political and moral interests but also the distinctive theological traditions of its churches. Students of social movements have long noted the importance of cultural repertoires to the success of these movements.[19] Revolutions succeed or fail at least partly because of the effectiveness of their slogans. And churches are an important repository not only of slogans but of visual symbols, hymns, and moral arguments that can congeal a movement into united action. Even though a relatively small percentage of the American public claimed to support the religious Right, a much larger number could understand and appreciate its rhetoric. Just as people could recognize the biblical imagery used by Dr. King during the civil rights movement, they could sense something familiar in Jerry Falwell's language of evil and moral outrage.

In the end, then, any effort to project from the experience of the religious Right into the future must take into account the sheer power of the holy. Being able to declare that the Lord has spoken carries enormous weight, especially in a culture where the next highest authority is individual taste. Despite all the secularity evident in American culture, the future will still be a time when people yearn to hear the voice of God.

V

Cultural Challenges:
The Possibilities of Faith
for Constructing
Personal Lives

13

The Quest for
Identity

Religion in the twenty-first century will, as I have argued, continue to play an important role in American public life, animating social movements and reform efforts of all kinds. It will do so because it is well institutionalized and because our culture legitimates its involvement in the shaping of collective values. There is always the danger that public religion and private religion will become separate, the one voicing opinions that are not felt deeply by the vast majority of American Christians. Public religion cannot persist without its private counterpart. We have already considered (in chapter 3) some of the challenges religious institutions face in trying to continue their role as sources of Christian identity. But let us turn the question around and ask, from the standpoint of the individual, how important the quest for identity will be. Where will people look for identity? How will their identity be shaped by their work and their intellectual concerns?

A Story

My first day of teaching at Princeton I passed around a sheet of paper to the undergraduates in my class asking them to write down their names. Eventually the sheet came back with the names as requested. But after each name was a curious two-digit number preceded by an apostrophe.[1]

These numbers, I soon realized, corresponded to the students' expected year of graduation: class of '76, class of '77, and so on. So much were these numbers a part of the students' sense of who they were that they attached them voluntarily to their names.

As I learned more about their subculture, I came to understand more clearly what these numbers symbolized for Princeton undergraduates. When a student is admitted to Princeton, he or she immediately is accepted as a member of one of these classes, and whether that student ever graduates or not, the label becomes part of his or her identity. For almost 250 years, students at Princeton have been following this custom. Thus a sense of one's place in history is an important aspect of these numbers. Especially at the annual P-rade, when thousands of alumni return and march under the banner of their respective class years, the students' link in the long chain of graduating classes is memorialized.[2] And the same is true as the student looks toward the future. In the twenty-first century there will presumably be classes of '01, '02, and so on, to carry on the tradition.

What can we learn from this example about the nature of personal identity in our society? The Princeton case has nothing to do with religion. And yet, seeing Princeton students ascribing these numbers to themselves and watching their annual alumni parade, one senses that there is a religious, or sacred, or mystical quality present. Certainly it is a powerful enough force to help bring in the millions of dollars Princeton receives annually from its loyal alumni.

The Character of Identity

Importance of the Quest

The first lesson this example suggests is simply that having a personal identity remains terribly important in our society. Some years ago I tried to gauge how salient the question of personal identity is by asking a representative sample of residents in several California communities how much they thought about the question "How did you come to be the way you are?" In response, 32 percent said they thought about this question a lot, another 32 percent thought about it some, an additional 24 percent considered it important, and only 12 did not think about it or consider it important.[3] In another study, this time in a representative survey of the nation at large, I found that 94 percent of the American public consider their efforts to "fulfill their potential as a person" important, and 60 percent consider it very important.[4] More recently, I found in another national survey that 88 percent of the American public consider "taking care of yourself" to be very important—which to me also suggests how much we value our personal identity.[5]

But we do not have to trust surveys to recognize how prominent the quest for identity is in our culture. Princeton students are scarcely alone in affixing symbols to their name to give them added identity. Think of the many titles, abbreviations, and acronyms that do the same thing: Dr.,

Rev., MSW, CPA, Ed.D., Esq., and so on. These fixtures are the counterpart of what names themselves often used to include. As we know, many of our commonest names came into being because they identified a person's trade: Smith, Cooper, Black, Wood, Tanner, to name a few. And many less common names gave people identity by referring to their place of origin; in my own case, for example, to a people who migrated eastward to the flatlands along the Warthe River from a village north of Berlin called Wuthenow.

The quest for identity is also clearly evidenced by the time, energy, and money we devote to this pursuit. Parents of Princeton students may spend as much as one hundred thousand dollars to give their offspring this part of their identity. For the rest of us, such costs may be calculated in anything from the time we spend reading self-help books, to the money we spend on therapists, to the energy we devote to succeeding in our jobs or cultivating excellence in a hobby. It does not seem likely that our interest in the question of identity will fade anytime soon.

Varied Sources

A second lesson we can learn about identity is that it comes not from one, but from a variety of sources. Being at Princeton may be the most significant source of identity for my students, but most of them have other identities as well. Their ethnic heritage, the town they hale from, sports they excel in, careers they aspire to—all help define who they are.

We know this from systematic studies as well. When asked where their identity, self-worth, or sense of fulfillment comes from, people in our society mention a wide range of sources: their families, close friends, work, efforts to be successful, finances, volunteer activities, and hobbies. People play multiple roles in life and thus have multiple identities.

Recognizing that our identity comes from multiple sources is critical whenever we consider the importance of any one of those sources, such as religious faith. We need to ask how much the various sources contribute. We also need to be aware that it is the mix itself that gives us our unique individuality. Part of what we take pride in is the fact that we have put our lives together in a way that nobody else has.[6]

Achievement

The third lesson my Princeton example suggests is that identity in our society is increasingly something we achieve rather than something simply ascribed to us. Princeton students take special pride in those numbers behind their names because they feel they have *earned* the right to be at Princeton. They attribute this aspect of their identity to years of hard work and self-discipline. They chafe at any suggestion that inherited wealth might have had something to do with their present status.

Social scientists tell us that the shift from ascribed to achieved identities is one of the hallmarks of modern society.[7] In premodern communities, people did take the names of the town in which they were born and identified strongly with their kin group. In modern societies, the individual tends to be more clearly differentiated from these communities of origin, drawing identity from the choices one makes and the skills one learns.[8] The fact that our highly advanced economy depends on the learning and application of such skills tends to reinforce this achievement-based mode of deriving identity.

History

My Princeton students also illustrate a lesson about identity's roots in history. Even though they take pride in being at Princeton as a personal achievement, and even though some of them are the first members of their families ever to have attended college, their identity still depends on the historical lineage in which they participate as Princeton students. The prestige that has come to surround the institution over time is conferred on them as members of that institution, thus heightening their sense of personal pride in their achievements.

This historic dimension of identity has often been neglected in discussions that focus on the shift from ascribed to achieved identities. It is true that people in modern societies often pay more attention to the present and the future than to the past, deriving more of their identity from the goals they hope to achieve than from the roots from which they sprang. And yet most of the goals to which we aspire are valued, and therefore able to confer a valued identity upon us, because they have some continuity with the past. Even aspiring to be an explorer of outer space gains some of its credibility from the stories we learn as children of pioneers and explorers in the past.

Community

There is also a lesson to be learned about the importance of community for identity. Each of my students is justifiably proud of his or her personal accomplishments; indeed, the individualism and the competitiveness that pervades our culture more generally is often evident in the extreme among these students. They are nevertheless part of a community and the very symbols they choose to express their identity reflect this community: they wrote down numbers given to them by the institution and locating them within its ranks as students of a certain class, not some symbol such as a scrawl or a unique design that was completely of their own making.

This too is often an ignored feature of identity in our society. It is easy to emphasize the fragmentation of our society that manifests itself in extreme individualism, geographic mobility, and detachment from stable and enduring communities. In comparison with the families and neighborhoods that gave people identity in the past, we look at broken homes and a mobile population and assume that personal identity must come entirely from within ourselves. But that assumption depends on too limited a view of community. To confer an identity, communities do not have to be stable, enduring, or consensual. A broken home still confers an identity. We need to pay more attention to the kind of identities our communities confer, but certainly their importance should not be neglected.

For all these reasons, I believe the quest for identity will continue to be a prominent feature of our lives in the twenty-first century. We shall still find the quest important, and despite changes that may be as sweeping as the ones witnessed over the past century, our identities will come from multiple sources, depend heavily on our individual achievements, but also link us with history and communities.[9] The question is: Will religion continue to play a significant role in this pursuit?

Religion and the Pursuit of Identity

Writing from the perspective of that most atypical of decades—the 1950s—Will Herberg argued that religion had been, was, and would continue to be a vital part of Americans' personal identities.[10] In his view, religion provided a vital link between individuals and the larger society. Americans wanted to feel that they were in fact Americans, but in a large national society it was often difficult to feel this attachment very directly, so religion served an important mediating role. Part of what it meant to be an American was that an individual had faith in God and expressed this faith by being a member of one of the established religious communities. It gave people a better sense of who they were—a sense of the way in which they were legitimately American—by identifying themselves as Protestants, Catholics, or Jews. Americans might have a rather shallow commitment to their particular faith tradition, Herberg noted, but they would nevertheless remain loyal to this tradition because it was part of what a good American did.

Problems with Herberg

In retrospect, it is possible to see that Herberg's argument made sense of certain features of his time but in other respects was woefully misleading. Empirical research demonstrated that most people did in fact identify themselves as Protestants, Catholics, or Jews, and most claimed to believe in God, even though they often knew little about the Bible and participated sporadically in organized religious activities. Some research also supported Herberg's argument that the grandchildren of immigrants would return to the faith of their forebears in order to reclaim their ethnic roots in the midst of an increasingly vast and faceless society. The limitations of Herberg's study lay partly in the fact that it reflected the heightened Americanism of the cold war period in which it was written, and partly in the fact that even then it ignored so much of everything else on which personal identity depends.[11]

My earlier point about multiple identities raises particularly troublesome problems for Herberg's thesis. Perhaps being an American in the 1950s meant being religious, but what else did it mean, and how important was being religious in comparison with these other identities? For most people, being an American probably meant being against communism, believing in democracy, working hard, living in a safe neighborhood, and providing for one's family. Being a Protestant, Catholic, or Jew was only one among many sources of identity. A generation or two later, identity still comes from multiple sources, but the share that comes from religion may be even less because the lines defining Protestants, Catholics, and Jews have become less clear.

Fluid Identities

Not long ago I attended the sixtieth birthday party of an acquaintance who had been a devout Roman Catholic all his life. Held in the church hall following a Sunday afternoon mass, the party included many of his fellow choir members, and one speaker after another rose to say something about him, about who he was and what made him special. Here I thought would be strong testimony of the role of faith in shaping one's identity.

From the speakers' remarks it soon became evident that religion was indeed a key ingredient of this man's identity. One speaker was a priest for whom the guest of honor had served as an altar boy, another told a joke that contrasted Catholic guilt with that of Protestants and Jews, another sang an Irish melody with lyrics adapted to the occasion. But what impressed me more was that even this man, for whom faith was so much a part of his identity, was just as deeply many other things as well: married to a non-Catholic of German origin, he was genuinely ecumenical; schooled in philosophy, he regarded himself not as a Catholic intellectual but simply as a scholar; and of course he was a proud father, proud of having been of special value to some of his students, proud of his job, and proud of his friends.

Such people are increasingly typical because religious distinctions have become fluid, and with this fluidity, other sources of identity have become relatively more important. At an earlier time this man might have been encapsulated in a Catholic subculture: reared in a Catholic neighborhood, educated in Catholic schools and at a Catholic university, married to a Catholic woman, and employed by a Catholic institution. But for a growing proportion of the American public, such subcultures are breaking down. Mother belongs to one religion, Father to a different one, they switch denominations several times while growing up, mingle with children of different faiths, hear religion described at school in a way that makes all faiths interchangeable, eventually marry someone of a different faith, and live in neighborhoods and work in organizations that include people of all faiths and of no faith at all.

The fact that identity is so often achieved, rather than ascribed, also has serious implications for how we understand its relation to religion. I suppose Herberg's Protestants, Catholics, and Jews of the 1950s might have regarded their religious identity in some ways as having been achieved. They were at least the descendants of immigrants who had made the difficult transition from one culture to another, achieving in the process the identity for themselves of Jewish *Americans,* or Irish Catholic *Americans,* or German Baptist *Americans.* But Herberg was more interested, rightly I believe, in the ascriptive qualities of religious identity in the 1950s. Being a member of a religious community was like living in a particular town or state; it was an ascribed identity that linked the person to the larger society.[12]

Choosing an Identity

This view told only part of the story in the 1950s and tells perhaps even less of it today. For Protestants, religious identity has always been understood to be a matter of choice, and therefore as much achieved as ascribed. A child may have an ascribed identity by virtue of growing up an Episcopalian, but at some point the child is supposed to decide whether he or she really believes in the church's teachings. For Catholics and Jews, religious identity has always depended more on the ascribed status acquired by birth into a particular kind of family. But in both traditions children are also encouraged to achieve the requisite depth on which a mature faith depends by learning appropriate religious teachings and rituals. The "new voluntarism" that encourages people to pick and choose until they find the religious identity best suited to their tastes is evidence of the growing emphasis on achieved rather than ascribed religious identities.[13] So is the growth witnessed in recent decades in evangelical and fundamentalist churches, where achieved learning is emphasized; another, more broadly based example is the popularity of self-help devotional guides and religious books.

The shift toward achievement in American religion can be regarded as a way of adapting to the wider achievement ethic in American culture, and in this sense may secure religion a place in the panoply of sources from which people derive their personal identities. It nevertheless puts religion in direct competition with all the other sources of achievement from which identity can be acquired, and religion may fare badly in this competition because so little effort goes into it, compared with the effort on which our other achievements are based. Princeton students put their university at the center of their identities because they view it as the culmination of years and years of hard work. They often relish the fact that they are Protestants, Catholics, or Jews, but only in the same way that they mention being from New York or Iowa. Religion is a part of who they are, but not a part of their deep being, not a part of the identity that consumes their time and energy.

A Link to the Wider Society

In fairness to Herberg, though, we must focus squarely on the question that interested him most. He was not concerned with religion as part of our entire personal makeup, but with its capacity to link us to the wider society. And this question continues to be as important now as it was in the 1950s. When so much of our identity is private and unique because it depends on our own achievements and the peculiar mix of our individual experiences, perhaps religion can still play a special role by attaching us to something outside ourselves.

Time and Space

This is where the role of history and community, as we have seen in previous chapters, becomes especially important. Whatever else one may know about religion, it is clear that religion places one in time and space. It is not purely a matter of choice or of personal construction. This is why the authors of *Habits of the Heart* were so distressed by the woman they interviewed who created her own religion, naming it "Sheilaism" in reference to herself.[14] Religion may give comfort, as it did for Sheila, and help that person reach out to others in need. But religion has always claimed to be an external reality as well, operating in history and through communities of people. Insofar as America has been peopled by religious communities of all kinds, these communities help individuals feel they are a part of our nation's larger being, past and present.

Will the same feeling be there in the future? It is difficult to give an optimistic answer to this question. In recent decades there has been a widespread, if unintended, effort to exclude religion from our understandings of the nation's history. Schoolbooks present the Pilgrims as entrepreneurs searching for material wealth and a comfortable life, not as members of a religious community. The religious motives that inspired Martin Luther King, Jr., to lead the civil rights movement are often neglected. So are the more negative aspects of American religious history, such as its role in legitimating slavery or the oppression of Native Americans. Without these stories being told, the coming generation of Americans is increasingly likely to regard spirituality, if they regard it at all, as a subjective element of their personal identity, rather than a link with the history of our nation.

Alternative Sources of Identity

This does not mean that individuals will cease to feel attached to their society, however. The flag to which children pledge allegiance each morning in school will continue to induce these collective sentiments, especially when it is reinforced by televised images of our nation's capital, its leaders, its war heroes, and its various historical sites. Being an American will continue to mean citizenship in these symbolic ways, even if the lack of effort among all but those who fight in the nation's wars means that citizenship is not taken as seriously as the roles one works hard to achieve.

Being an American will also be defined by those institutions that religion has always tried to keep in an appropriately limited perspective— the institutions of the marketplace. We shall consider these forces in the next chapter. Here, it is worth noting that role models supplied by religious communities, such as pastors, priests, rabbis, nuns, Sunday School teachers, and saints, are increasingly being replaced by images supplied by advertising and the mass media—images of cartoon heroes and rock stars. These will continue to provide children with a sense of what it means to be an American. When they ask themselves, Who am I? they will be able to answer in terms of the visit they took to Disney World, their identification with a lead singer in a popular recording group, or the slogan some company has printed on their T-shirts. There will always be ways to identify with being an American. But the quality of these identities may become increasingly shallow in the years ahead.

14

Maladies of the Middle Class

Although a substantial minority of Americans live below the poverty line, and a few enjoy enormous wealth, the vast majority constitute the middle class. It has been the middle class that has shaped American Christianity in the past, and it will continue to do so in the future. Most Americans attend middle-class congregations and most clergy minister to the middle class. If we are to understand the culture of American religion in the twenty-first century, therefore, we must not neglect the special role of the middle class.

The distinguishing feature of the middle class is its obsession with work and money. This is not to say that the poor and the wealthy are uninterested in either; many of the poor are gainfully employed and desperately concerned with making ends meet, and many of the wealthy have earned their riches and work hard at protecting their investments. But the middle class is fundamentally defined by its pursuit of careers, the preparation of its children to participate in the labor market, and the close connection between its material well-being and its values.

To say this is not to suggest that Karl Marx was after all correct in his diagnosis of capitalist society. The middle class was in fact Marx's great oversight. It is positioned between the bourgeoisie and the proletariat, sharing but minimally in owning the means of production, and yet experiencing more control over the productive process than Marx ever imagined. The middle class is actually an enormously diverse social category, being as much influenced by ethnicity, neighborhoods, religion, and type of industry or occupation, as by its economic standing relative to the rich and the poor. Its values must, as Marx realized, be understood in relation to its obsession with the material life, but these values are shaped by other forces as well.

One of these forces in the past has been the church. Always concerned with the material life as well as the spiritual, the church has powerfully influenced Americans' conceptions of work and money. We all know the story well. Puritan teachings extolled work as a supreme virtue. The same teachings encouraged frugality, rather than the pursuit of wealth, but frugality coupled with hard work often became the means of accumulating wealth. During the nineteenth century, the Puritan heritage lost much of its distinctiveness, gradually resulting in a more generalized ethic of work, saving, and sobriety. The middle class tried to live morally, encouraging those poorer than themselves to do the same. The moral life focused heavily on such virtues as ascetic discipline, hard work, the avoidance of laziness and idleness, devotion to a calling, and stewardship of one's material possessions.

Many of these teachings have continued to be part of the churches' ministry to the middle class. Respectability is the hallmark of the middle-class church, and the tokens of respectability include fine dress, attractive transportation, capacious homes, well-educated children, and successful careers. Clergy emulate these values in their own lives, serving at least implicitly as models of a certain kind of respectable morality. The churches, too, maintain the same morality in their emphasis on carefully orchestrated stewardship appeals, the application of computerized financial accounting techniques, and polished buildings-and-grounds programs, all in the name of honoring God.

But this is only part of the picture. While middle-class respectability continues to dominate much of American religion, it is also becoming clear that many people are suffering the costs associated with their material obsessions, and a growing number are looking to the churches for help in dealing with this suffering. People are beginning to question whether affluence alone is enough and whether the quest for middle-class respectability is itself sufficient as a basis for life. They may still be devoted to the desirability of middle-class values but yearn increasingly for something more. What they thought would be a better life, gained through hard work and material accumulation, is proving not only to be more difficult to attain than they had imagined, but also less satisfying when it is attained. It is not an overstatement to say that many are making the frightful discovery, to borrow words from novelist Milan Kundera, that "the only reason [they were] better was for want of anything better."[1]

The Challenge of Materialism

One of the greatest challenges facing Christians in the twenty-first century will be to face up to the realization that materialism alone is not enough. Economic conditions themselves may facilitate this process. Few of the world's dominant empires in the past have been able to maintain their economic prowess for more than a century: Spain in the sixteenth century, the Dutch Republic in the seventeenth, France in the eighteenth, and Great Britain in the nineteenth, all diminished in relative prominence after less than a century at the top. The United States may be no exception, especially as it bears the costs of policing the world and loses an increasing share of its markets to countries with lower labor costs. But even if affluence continues, Christians need to pay closer attention to the maladies associated with maintaining their middle-class lifestyles.

These maladies might be calculated in such familiar litanies as the number of broken homes, abused children, alcoholics, and drug addicts that make up the middle class. Or they might be discussed with reference to the outcasts, such as the homeless and the jobless, who suffer the effects of a callous economic system or government policies more concerned with tax cuts and military spending than with economic justice. The churches have, to their credit, focused much attention on these various problems. But too often these problems attract only polite interest because they are depicted chiefly as the problems of others. Christians are encouraged to minister to the needy when they should be encouraged to take a closer look at the travail of their own lives.

Work

The place to begin in trying to grasp more fully the travail of the middle class is work itself. At the start of the twentieth century, the typical working American put in fifty-one hours a week on the job; today, that figure has shrunk to about forty hours a week.[2] In the process, most jobs have also become less demanding physically, automation has eased the routine chores of daily life, leisure time has become more important, and social observers point to alarmingly high numbers of American families who spend hours and hours each week watching television. Surely work itself is not the problem; if anything, the issue even as Americans see themselves is one of a deteriorating work ethic. Says pollster Everett Ladd, "Again and again when asked, [Americans] profess to see a decline in willingness to work hard and in the inclination to take pride in one's labor."[3] And yet this perception attests more to Americans' continuing commitment to the work ethic than anything else.

The fact is most Americans are taking their jobs as seriously, if not more seriously, than ever before, and many middle-class Americans are putting in such long hours that they have little time for anything else. "Every minute of my day is schedule oriented," says dentist Fred Moreland, "I'm under the gun from morning till night." Typist Julie Baines says the same thing. Although she decided to take in typing rather than pursue a career, so she could be at home with her three children, she finds she has to work most evenings to make ends meet. "It's a constant juggling act," she admits, "I seldom get any time to myself."[4]

Statistics bear out the impression that such cases are increasingly the rule rather than the exception. Between 1973 and 1985, according to Harris surveys, median working hours in the U.S. labor force actually increased by about 20 percent, from 40.6 hours a week to 48.8 hours a week, while median hours spent on leisure activity decreased by about a third, from 26.2 hours a week to 17.7 hours a week.[5] These increases in work hours were not being picked up by official estimates because those counted only the time hourly workers were being paid for, whereas an increasing share of the population, like Fred Moreland and Julie Baines, was working in professions and other salaried or independent occupations. Thus, among all professionals the typical work week averaged 52 hours, among young people in their twenties and thirties with college educations it averaged 53 hours a week, and among proprietors of businesses and professional offices it was 57 hours a week.[6]

Working this hard has not diminished Americans' enthusiasm for their jobs and their careers. Indeed, most studies show overwhelmingly high levels of job satisfaction, especially in the professions and other white-collar occupations. And yet, when asked to choose between their work and other parts of their lives, most people say it is the nonworking hours that are most enjoyable. Consequently, surveys also document a large number of people who complain that they have too little time to do the things they really want to do. In one, for example, 41 percent complained of having too little time to spend with their families.[7]

What compounds the problem is that for an increasing number of families, both parents are now working this hard. At midcentury, only about one woman in three between the ages of twenty-five and fifty-four was gainfully employed; currently, 81 percent in this age group hold jobs outside the home.[8] And with household chores and parenting still falling more heavily on women than men, this means that mothers especially are feeling the pressures of having much too much to do.[9]

Often, as we know, it is the children who suffer most, and when they speak, they sometimes do so with eloquence. "Mommy," Julie Baines remembers her nine-year-old son calling to her one evening as she sat bent over her word processor in the corner of the family room, "if you had a dog, and you really loved this dog, and you worked real hard to earn the money to buy him the fanciest dog house and the best dog food, don't you think it would be better if once in a while you played with that dog?"

Materialism

The second malady that afflicts the American middle class is our love affair with materialism. It perhaps goes without saying that we are deeply devoted to the material comforts of American life. It is nevertheless worth taking stock of this devotion to assess the power of its grip. When we do, we realize not only that money and material goods have us firmly in their grasp, but that we are painfully reluctant to admit this fact to ourselves.

The lure of material possessions can be gauged in our spending habits; perhaps even more so, in our attitudes. According to one national survey, "making a lot of money" is very important to more than a third of the population, while three-quarters say it is at least fairly important to them. "A comfortable life" is an even more widely shared value, regarded as very important by three people out of four, and at least fairly important by 98 percent.[10] "Sure, I'd like to have a lot of money," says Walt Clinton, a computer salesman, "I'd like to have about $200,000 a year, just enough to be comfortable."

Like many middle-class Americans, Walt Clinton feels no awkwardness about his desire to be "comfortable." His parents were poor, and he worked hard from the time he was a teenager, so he feels he deserves everything he has. He does not really expect to win the lottery, but he figures he would be happier if he did. Still, he also worries that our society is becoming too materialistic. Like 86 percent of the people in the survey just mentioned, he thinks the emphasis we place on money is a serious problem in our society. And he is also typical, judging from the same study, in that his perception of money as a social problem does not seem to prevent him from wanting more of it for himself.[11]

This paradoxical—some might say, hypocritical—view of materialism, I should note, is also one of the perspectives we have succeeded in transmitting very effectively to our children. According to a national survey conducted for *Seventeen* magazine, a majority of teenagers think the world perceives their generation as being too materialistic, and nearly as many agree with this characterization. Even more—almost two-thirds— think kids today are too greedy.[12] And yet, other studies of the same age group show that being financially well off is one of their highest values, and the percentage aspiring to this value has risen dramatically during the past two decades.[13]

However we might wish to interpret these patterns, it does not seem likely that materialism is going to disappear anytime soon. The human psyche has an enormous capacity to withstand inconsistency. Thus, our worries about being too materialistic seem not to prevent us from wanting wealth. We cherish materialism and hate it at the same time. We may not go crying all the way to the bank, as the saying goes, but at least we go feeling guilty.

Stress

Combine this penchant for materialism with our drive to work harder and harder, and the result is an escalation of job stress, burnout, and related physical and emotional symptoms. A majority of the U.S. labor force, concludes a recent study conducted by the National Center for Health Statistics, suffers from stress on a regular basis, and this proportion is highest among people in upper-income occupations where as many as seven out of ten complain of frequent job-related stress.[14] Symptomatic of the problem, the number of stress-based workman's compensation suits has risen dramatically in recent years, as has the number of companies engaging professional counselors to screen potential employees for susceptibility to emotional problems before ever hiring them. In addition, alcoholism and substance abuse of other kinds appear to be rampant in the American work force, especially in its white-collar and professional echelons.

Jack Zellers is a highly successful attorney who specializes in leveraged buyouts. He likes his work and devotes most of his time to it, but he also thinks it is insane the way law schools crank out increasing numbers of graduates, and then law firms make them compete with each other for fewer and fewer positions. "It's like a pressure cooker," he says. "At one time you could have a life outside the firm, but now my life is just dominated by work. It's antithetical to my view of a balanced life."

If a growing number of Americans are buckling under on a day-to-day basis, the number of people who experience severe burnout is also rising. According to the best estimates, each year about one person in every ten changes occupations. Many of these changes occur for reasons other than burnout, of course, but the reasons given often suggest considerations other than sheer financial reward or career advancement. Among these are wanting to find more meaning and fulfillment, feeling trapped or bored, and hoping to make a greater contribution to society. But whatever the reasons, career change itself is often a source of added stress, anxiety, and even questioning of basic beliefs and values.

Diversions from Our Discontent

Before turning to the question of what the churches might have to say about all this, let us consider the two perspectives on these issues that have become decidedly more prominent in middle-class culture over the past century. Both of these perspectives supply meaning or legitimation to the economic habits of the middle class, but they also frame the issues in a way that diverts attention away from the deeper sources of our discontent. One is rooted in economic logic, the other in a medical framework.

Marginal Utility

The economic perspective emphasizes marginal utility. Give people a choice between working and not working, this perspective suggests, and people will choose rationally by estimating the marginal utility of the income earned from working over against the value they associate with leisure time. For most people, willingness to work will increase as long as added income rises accordingly, but eventually a point will be reached when they would rather have free time than extra money. Nuances of this perspective include the possibility that marginal income can be based on a lower wage scale than basic income (as clergy and college professors demonstrate when they take on added assignments to earn a few hundred dollars here and there), and that meaningful work can shift the equation (as it often does for professionals) by reducing the value they attach to leisure activities not connected with work itself.

Other nuances could be introduced as well, but the main point needing to be recognized is that this perspective essentially reduces life to a series of monetary calculations. The trade-off suggested between income and leisure time in effect places a monetary value on all time not spent working as well as the time a person does spend working. Implicitly this perspective suggests the following response to someone like Julie Baines when a child cries out to be played with: "Okay, I'll play with you for an hour—and this will cost the family budget $30.75."

The other point to be recognized about the economic perspective is that it is explicitly neutral with respect to the way in which leisure time is used. An hour spent shopping is no different in its view from an hour spent playing with your children. The values that might lead a person to choose one activity rather than the other are assumed to be outside the framework, matters of individual taste that money gives one the freedom to exercise. And yet implicitly the perspective does present its own values insofar as it turns things into commodities by placing a monetary value on them. The ways in which it does this are, of course, myriad—from encouraging leisure time to be packaged and sold as vacations or tennis club memberships, to imposing goal-oriented quality standards on the time one spends with one's children just as a manufacturer may set up quality controls for the consumer goods produced.

Health

The medical perspective has become the principal alternative to the marginal utility model, perhaps because it posits health as a much more basic consideration in balancing work and other activities, rather than focusing entirely on money. In my research, the one thing busy people said they took time for, or tried to make time for, was physical exercise. They did so both to keep physically and mentally alert and to alleviate stress and anxiety. It was also clear that physical exercise provided a symbolic boundary in people's lives. Working all day with their minds, white-collar workers said physical exercise was a needed contrast that helped them shut off their brains so they could relax.

Stress reduction techniques of all kinds also bespeak the prominence of the medical model. Recognizing that valuable workers may burn out, quit, or die young, more and more corporations have instituted programs to identify the early warning signs of overwork and job-related stress. Workers may be encouraged to take routine breaks, meditate, repeat formulaic prayers to themselves, go for a walk over the noon hour, sign up for biofeedback sessions, or enroll in scream therapy classes. The hope is that feelings, emotions, and other bodily signals can provide an adequate measure of when one has pursued the dollar long enough.[15]

But the medical model often plays into the hands of those who believe work and money are the highest aims of human life. Keeping fit can be a positive factor in closing the big deal and getting that next promotion. Stress management (note the administrative language) can be a way of getting through a rough afternoon, but it may be less useful in getting through life. In the right hands, medical considerations may actually be presented as an argument for working hard and making more money, rather than a reason for putting on the brakes.

"Does prosperity kill?" asks *Forbes* magazine. So say Marxist sympathizers ever on the look out for evidence that capitalism is bad for people's health, it reports. But better evidence conclusively supports "the commonsense notion that people are healthier when they are more prosperous." And how do we know this? By charting mortality rates against the business cycle. When this is done, it may appear to the naive observer that mortality is actually higher in times of boom than in times of bust. But of course we need to realize there is probably a three- to five-year lag between stress and death, so it is actually bust rather than boom that produces health problems.[16]

As I say, these two perspectives help the middle class legitimate its obsession with work and money, rather than raising fundamental questions about this obsession. The economic perspective suggests the need to limit one's work life and one's quest for money, but does so only by pointing out that if time is money, one may indeed opt for time instead of money. It does not say why one might prefer time instead of money. The medical perspective suggests a natural biological limit to the quest for money, but it too offers little guidance other than staying healthy. Taking time out to go jogging may be essential to keep up one's stamina, but otherwise one presumably can live by the motto "Shop till you drop."

Churches

In times past, churches and religious leaders would have had more to say on these matters. Limiting the material life would have been placed in the wider context of responsibilities to God, family, community, and self. But in our society the churches have often bought into the two perspectives I have just described. Time and money given to God are viewed in much the same way as any other leisure activity or family expenditure. Tax laws encourage these donations to be treated in economic terms, but so do pastors. The best reason they may offer for not working on Wednesday evenings is being available to serve on the finance committee at the church. Or the side benefit that might encourage people to pray more often is prayer's medical usefulness in reducing stress.

More likely, the churches say nothing at all about the material life, except to voice an occasional jab at the worship of mammon, adding hastily that there is nothing wrong with money as long as we do not love it too much. Even those most concerned about such social issues as peace, poverty, inequality, and economic injustice have been surprisingly blind to the economic realm. An overwhelming share of their attention has been focused on government, wanting it to do more, wanting it to do less, lobbying, sending it petitions, and treating it as the way to get anything done. And yet, by comparison, the economy is by far a more powerful institution in our society than government.

As a result, much of the American middle class seems to have forgotten even the most basic claims that religion used to make on the material world. Asked if their religious beliefs had influenced their choice of a career, most of the people I have interviewed in recent years—Christians and non-Christians alike—said no. Asked if they thought of their work as a calling, most said no. Asked if they understood the concept of stewardship, most said no. Asked how religion did influence their work lives or thoughts about money, most said the two were completely separate.

Ministries to and of the Middle Class

What were the moral claims that religious leaders once voiced to their prosperous, hard-working congregations? They were of course admonitions to work hard and prosper. There is much truth to the view that the Puritan work ethic spread widely through the American colonies, was soon shared in Quaker, Anglican, and Presbyterian communities, and eventually took on the cultural characteristics of Poor Richard, and later of Horatio Alger. But there was another part of the story.

Higher Values

Religious leaders also cautioned against the material life. Drawing on biblical distinctions between the spiritual and the material, they championed higher values that put work and money in a lower position. Work was understood as a means, not an end in itself. It was a means, not simply to the accumulation of wealth, but for self-improvement, happiness, and service. Work was thus not only gainful employment, but a disciplined orientation to all of life. Money was also a means, rather than an end. It was not understood as the inevitable outcome of hard work, but as a by-product that might or might not eventuate in material gain according to the will of an inscrutable God. It was thus important to keep work and money in their place, remembering always that duties to God, family, community, and even self came first. The material life was a necessary element of the human condition, but not the highest to which it should aspire. "We cannot live on work. We must have courage, inspiration, greatness, play," wrote Horace Bushnell in 1864. In his view it was the spontaneity and freedom evident in play that came closer, even than the sober devotion of work, to representing the true worship of God. "Religion," he counseled, "must, in its very nature and life, be a form of play—a worship offered, a devotion paid, not for some ulterior end, but as being its own end and joy."[17]

These arguments have perhaps never been proclaimed as loudly as the counsels of economic responsibility and productivity, but they provide a place to start in ministering to the middle class. They do so because people themselves are increasingly becoming aware of the need for moral restraint in their economic lives. Following the decades of greed and selfish ambition—which are by no means over—there is a groundswell of interest in rediscovering deeper commitments and more fulfilling pursuits. Julie Baines, responding to her son's eloquent plea for attention by putting her word processing aside and vowing never to let anything stand in the way of just enjoying her children, is but one example.

Moral Guidance

The middle class needs the moral guidance of the churches in charting its material commitments. Certainly it needs this guidance in matters of ethics, as the recent scandals that have brought major corporations and political figures to their knees indicate. But the middle class also needs the bold voice of moral authority in limiting its commitments to the workplace and the countinghouse. It needs to have better arguments than those provided by marginal utility calculations and medical considerations. It needs to know that it is right, good, worthy, legitimate, proper—whatever words are used—to hear the laughter of children, to alleviate the anguish of the poor, to explore the inner depths of our souls, and to seek God.

The churches can minister to the middle class by articulating these messages of faith and moral commitment, but they must also do their part in mitigating the pressures imposed by the economic realm itself. Day-care, nursery school, and latchkey programs are obvious needs as the number of dual-career and single-parent families increases. Many churches have responded actively to these needs. But there is room for much more to be done. Rather than limiting their financial ministries to the annual stewardship sermon, they need to explore ministries to professionals experiencing the trauma of burnout and career changes, provide support groups to counteract the stress of job pressures, and promote active discussion of the contradictions inherent in our views of materialism.

These are needs requiring ministries by the churches to the middle class, and within the middle class itself, as individuals and families provide services and support to each other. They fall within the realm of treating one's own maladies before railing at those of one's brother. But the middle class also has vast resources that can be used to address the needs of others besides its own members. One of the ways to promote healing is through service, and one of the paths to a heightened commitment to something other than material success winds through the by-passed alleyways of the desperately needy.

The danger of making moral arguments about the limitations of work and money, without keeping the needy clearly in mind, is the same danger that emerged in discussions of the so-called peace dividend. For many years, peace activists have argued that the money saved by curbing military expenditures would make possible social programs of major importance. But the trade-off between guns and butter, as it was so often described, was never as compelling to the middle class as the trade-off between guns and VCRs, between paying higher taxes for anything and a new boat, a new car, or a trip to Disney World. The same materialist calculations are likely in the realm of personal commitments as well. Too often, the people who opt for a shorter work week and a less costly life-style do so with the chief result being more time spent watching television, more time spent relaxing, and cutting back only marginally on consumer expenditures—as one man I talked to did in settling for a *used* BMW.

The desperately needy must not become merely a symbol of our own quest for meaning in life. But the middle class must share its resources if it is to have anything more than the hermetically sealed meaning of a self-serving social enclave. And doing so is likely to require genuine sacrifice—a word that has never been popular in economic circles, let alone in American politics. The time will perhaps come when sacrifice will be a necessity for all. In the meantime, a theology of sacrifice may be a high priority for the Christian to rediscover. If the twentieth century has not yet taught us to limit our material wants in order to gain the greater good, then the next century surely will force us to that realization. For what shall it profit us if we gain the whole world and lose our own souls?

15

Living the Question

During the twentieth century the United States undertook one of the most expansive programs of higher education ever witnessed. In the next century, whether such expansion continues or not, the college-educated person will make a major difference in shaping the future. So will the professoriate and those who administer the nation's colleges and universities. Their effect on American religion will be considerable. But what will this effect be? Is it possible to combine a deep personal commitment to the Christian faith with the life of the mind? Or is critical thought simply incompatible with Christian orthodoxy?[1]

Beware the Christian

Not long ago the *Chronicle of Higher Education* — the weekly newspaper that serves almost as a house organ for tens of thousands of college faculty and administrators—carried as its lead, center front-page story an article about the growing danger posed by evangelical Christians on the nation's campuses. One poor unsuspecting student, the article recounted, had begun attending services of an evangelical group on campus only to find "that her grades dropped, she lost touch with her friends, and her relations with her family deteriorated." Colleges need to be aware, the article cautioned, that many evangelical groups, while claiming not to be cults, use cultlike methods to attract and retain members, including deception, unethical recruiting, mind raping, authoritarianism, and dictatorial practices that tell students how to live, whom to marry, and what they can and cannot read.[2]

Reactionary Christians

The die was cast many years ago. In the 1890s the United States government made a fateful decision: if the nation's economy was going to compete effectively in world markets—this was long before we fell behind the Japanese—we were going to have to enter the modern era, which meant applying scientific methods in business, developing new technologies in industry, and promoting higher education among our nation's most talented youth. Land grant colleges, polytechnic institutes, and graduate research universities were launched with profusion. No longer would higher education be the preserve of church colleges and seminaries. Indeed, private benefactors added to what separation of church and state prevented the government from doing, offering church colleges generous grants if they would only shuck off their sectarian trappings and focus on secular liberal arts training. Caught up in the widespread belief that secular education and social progress went hand in hand, many churchmen embraced the new developments, calling for modernism in pulpit and pew. Only the fundamentalists held out, taking their very identity from the opposition they voiced to these dominant cultural developments.

As the twentieth century began, conservative Christianity was already at war, it seemed to many, with the prevailing values of an enlightened society. By midcentury, historian Richard Hofstadter could look back on the period and write in scathing terms of the anti-intellectualism espoused by this wing of American religion. Fundamentalists and evangelicals were, in his view, narrow-minded, dogmatic, and authoritarian. Not only were they content to believe in the superstitions and simplistic falsehoods of a time gone by; they were so threatened by the intellectual currents in the wider society that they were willing to wage war against it. They were prejudiced bumpkins from the farms and small towns, a subculture left over from the past like some Neanderthal creature, lumbering through the wheat fields and cow pastures without the intelligence to understand what educated people of the twentieth century were thinking.[3]

The Twentieth Century

The only problem with Hofstadter's analysis was that the twentieth century turned out to be more complex than he realized. At the same time Hofstadter was diagnosing the anti-intellectualism of conservative Christians, they were in the process of rediscovering a deeper tradition in their own past—a tradition of critical reflection that remained critical of secular thought but nevertheless recognized the importance of the intellectual life. While some leaders denounced secular knowledge as evil and called for a radical separation between believers and the world, the majority opted for active participation in the cultural climate of the twentieth century.

They identified themselves with many of the positive intellectual contributions of Western Christianity in the past—with the juristic approach to biblical literature of the Reformation, the dissenting political traditions of the English civil war, the emphasis on natural science and natural law of the Puritan divines, the studiousness of the Scottish Presbyterian moralists, and the social teachings of the American abolitionists. Believing that the same God who had created the soul had also created the mind, they founded and expanded Christian colleges and seminaries in which biblical studies and the human sciences could be brought together. They formed organizations to make their presence known in high schools and on secular campuses. And they encouraged young people to gain the academic credentials necessary to serve the needs of society and the world—in business, teaching, medicine, engineering, and the professions. They wanted to eradicate the village-idiot image of the fundamentalist, bringing the intellectual life to Christianity and making Christians intellectually respectable.

Their work was cut out for them. When the first opinion polls on religion began to be conducted in the late 1950s, the results documented that Christians who held orthodox beliefs were indeed far less educated than other segments of the American population.[4] Many did in fact live on farms and in small towns. Many of their parents were dirt poor—they were the remnants of the dustbowl, recent immigrants from Germany and Scandinavia, Appalachian coal miners, blacks, displaced migrants from the South, day laborers in the smoke-belching factory cities of the Northeast, sharecroppers in the Midwest. The tiny church colleges many of their leaders tried to nurture were indeed tiny, often little more than overgrown high schools with faculty members who were themselves poorly trained and poorly paid. Many of the better church-related colleges were rapidly undergoing a process of secularization that loosened their ties with sponsoring denominations and shifted their focus away from orthodox biblical instruction.[5] And in the secular colleges and universities, surveys of faculty showed few with sympathies toward these new recruits fresh from the pages of *Elmer Gantry.*

But social trends were not entirely against these new defenders of an orthodox Christianity. The 1960s and 1970s were a time of enormous expansion in higher education throughout the nation. Faced with stiffening competition in foreign markets and a continuing Cold War, American leaders poured billions onto the nation's campuses. Bright teenagers with good grades could obtain college scholarships more easily than ever before, no matter what their religious convictions were, and for many in the agriculturally depressed regions of the South and Midwest such scholarships were an attractive way out. Government loans made it possible for church colleges to expand dormitory space and for secular campuses to grow into the mega-universities that still dominate the Big Ten, Big Eight, California system, and a number of other states.

With large numbers promoting diversity, Christian students on these campuses could sometimes find kindred spirits, and with what was left of the proverbial Protestant work ethic, many were able to succeed.[6] By the end of the 1970s, surveys showed that much of the gap in education levels between self-professed Christians and others had been closed.[7] And during the 1980s this trend continued: whereas level of education had still been a key factor differentiating conservative Christians from liberal Christians in the middle of the decade, by the end of the decade the two were virtually indistinguishable in terms of education.[8]

At the end of the twentieth century, therefore, the connection between Christianity and the life of the mind is far different from that envisioned at the century's start. If the breach opened between faith and higher learning by the fundamentalist movement has not been entirely healed, the situation is at least one of Bible-believing Christians being found within the ranks of American higher education rather than peering distrustfully at the distant spires of academe from their benighted villages in the hinterland. The question can once again be asked with urgency: What is the relation between Christian conviction and critical thought? And: What may we expect of this relationship in the decades to come?

Tour of the Underground

I have always found it easy to tour the landscape of Christianity within the ivied walls more or less as a fellow traveler and, in this capacity, have always been put off by the arms-length reportage one finds in the *Chronicle of Higher Education* and other secular media in which naive journalists can scarcely distinguish a Christian from a Jew, let alone an evangelical from a fundamentalist. One of the mental tours I enjoy taking from time to time is a journey to the various spots in academe where I have encountered intellectuals who in one way or another profess to be Christians. Follow me for a moment as I retrace some of these steps.

My first stop is an exclusive restaurant in New York City. As I dine with a fellow social scientist from another university, he tells me he has come a long way in his thinking since undergraduate days when he attended an evangelical Christian college. He says he still believes in the "basics"—he does not elaborate—but is increasingly annoyed with the clergy. Then, pausing for effect and looking around to see if anyone is listening, he asks me never to tell anyone what he is about to say. He says he often feels depressed about his work as an academic, so much so that he has been considering dropping out, selling his house, and moving to Africa where he could teach children or maybe retrain as a paramedic.

A few weeks later I am at an international conference in Boston hosted by the American Academy of Arts and Sciences. The gathering includes scholars from all over the world, each of whom is an expert in one or another of the world's four largest religions. In turn they speak with surprising knowledge and yet with considerable detachment about their religion of interest. One young scholar speaks with slightly more passion than the others about the role of the church in Germany, points to the historic importance of Christianity in his country, and argues to the surprise of many that a religious revival is taking place in some segments of German society. That evening at a gathering in which he is not present, a colleague of his notes that he is an elder in an evangelical church in Germany.

As my journey continues I find myself at an academic conference in New Orleans. Over lunch a friend mentions that some sociologists are having an informal meeting later on and asks me if I want to tag along. I agree and several hours later we enter a hotel room where about ten people—all professors—are gathered. One suggests opening the meeting with a prayer and no sooner are heads bowed than he begins speaking unintelligibly; others follow suit, and I realize I am witnessing glossolalia firsthand. Soon the speaking in tongues stops as abruptly as it began, the host announces, "Gee, I guess we don't have any bread and wine, but here's some Coke and crackers to pass around," and everyone turns to informal chatter about their latest research project.

My final stop is at the home of a social scientist who teaches at a Christian college. We have retired there for some late-night conversation after a formal dinner with several of his colleagues—formal in every sense of the word; everyone abides by the college's rule against consuming alcoholic beverages in public, everyone bows their head and prays at the appropriate moment, everyone speaks positively about how nice it is to teach in a Christian environment. But now I am about to see the other side. My friend speaks openly of his reservations about the college's stand on everything from alcoholic beverages to biblical interpretation. He talks about quitting the local church his family has been attending in protest against its teachings on social issues. He speaks candidly of the difficulties he experiences when he tries to associate with faculty from the major secular research universities. And one by one he recounts similar stories for each of his colleagues.

I do not know how typical these encounters may be. My point is not to generalize about the typical anyway, but to point out the diversity that exists among Christians in higher education, just as it does in our whole society. Were I to say more about these various social scientists, it would become evident that they differ vastly from one another in interests, backgrounds, beliefs, and life-styles, and yet each is in some way identified as a Christian. What then can we say about the relation between Christianity and the intellectual life?

Faith and Critical Thought

The Puritan Contribution to Science

In 1938 Robert Merton, one of the leading sociologists of his generation, published an influential book in which he examined the connection between Puritanism and the rise of science in seventeenth-century England.[9] Merton argued that the Puritans had a special disposition toward scientific achievement because of their emphasis on this life as well as the life to come, their conviction that nature was the handiwork of God, and their commitment to the rational mastery of God's creation, including knowledge. It was a clever thesis reminiscent of—indeed, modeled after—Max Weber's argument about the special connection between ascetic Protestantism and acquisitive capitalism. But subsequent inquiries cast doubt on Merton's thesis. Royalists were shown to be as favorably disposed toward science as Puritans, French Catholics were every bit as devoted to science as the English, and other factors, such as antinomianism and rationalism, appeared to be as much at work as Puritanism.[10]

I take the Merton controversy to be an instructive metaphor in seeking close connections between Christianity and a particular style of intellectual orientation. Some have argued that Christian scholars may be inclined to accept rigorous empirical generalizations because of their belief that truth can be codified in simple propositions. Translated: Christians make better engineers than artists or, in the case of social scientists, better number crunchers than theorists. Some have argued that Christians may be less able than other scholars to appreciate paradox, subtle interpretation, and nuance for the same reasons. Some have suggested that Christian thought favors voluntaristic social theories more than deterministic ones; others have suggested just the opposite. My journey among my various Christian acquaintances—some of whom have themselves proposed such arguments—confirms none of these views.

The Question of Assumptions

The truth of the matter is that Christian thought, even evangelical Christian thought, is sufficiently diverse that no straightforward influence on the nature of intellectual work is readily found. Christians do not operate from some set of higher-order truths, such as the Trinity, redemption, or original sin, from which they derive notions about the sort of work to do and the best way of approaching it. They may make certain assumptions—we all do. But it has not been my experience that Christian scholars are any more likely than any other kind of scholar to take, say, an authoritarian stance toward certain deeply held beliefs, or argue from first principles in the face of empirical evidence or, for that matter, let new evidence readily upset favorite theories. The various people I introduced in my imaginary journey each expressed doubts, raised questions, and exhibited some critical distance toward the scholarly role itself. They did not abandon their intellect to be Christians. In fact, I would say they subjected their Christian assumptions, like everything else, to the dictates of their intellect. That, to me, suggests the more fruitful way of approaching the question of how Christianity and critical thought may intersect.

Living the Question

I have borrowed the much-used phrase "living the question" because it seems to me that Christianity does not so much supply the learned person with answers as it does raise questions. It has been said of Marxists that even apostates spend their lives struggling with the questions Marx addressed. The same can probably be said of Christianity. It leaves people with a set of questions they cannot escape, especially when these questions face them from their earliest years. I doubt whether there are many practicing academics who have been without religion, found themselves searching for answers to life's questions, and then converted as mature adults to Christianity—although I am aware of course that C. S. Lewis claimed to have followed such a path, as have some of my personal acquaintances. In Lewis's case, it is perhaps worth noting, one does see a person attempting through curious tricks of logic to prove that various answers supplied by Christianity can satisfy the logical, rational mind. But, despite the fact that Lewis holds some attraction for many educated Christians, I have not found his life pattern nor his rationalistic style at all typical. More common is that someone learns the basic stories of Christianity as a child, becomes a scholar sometime later, and yet continues to be influenced by the questions those stories asked, even though his or her rational arguments, theological outlook, and philosophy of life may have undergone much change.

Bible Stories

Let me illustrate my point by referring briefly to some of those stories. To begin at the beginning, take the story of Adam and Eve. To be sure, one can derive theological propositions from this story. But the most memorable aspects of the story itself are probably the questions it raises— questions about gender roles of course, as Elaine Pagels and others have recently argued, but more important questions about the nature and limits of human knowledge.[11] Christian scholars I have known take a variety of positions on epistemology, but I would venture the generalization that their interest in epistemological questions is at least relatively acute.

Or take the story of Samuel, of the people of Israel wanting a king, of Samuel anointing David, and of the conflict between David and Saul. I was recently at a little church in the Midwest where the adult Sunday School lesson for the day focused on this story. After viewing a well-presented retelling of the story on videotape, the class at the prompting of its leader considered the question of why the Israelites wanted a king. One person suggested it was a matter of keeping up with the Joneses because the surrounding tribes had kings; another, that as a society becomes larger it may be helpful to have a centralized source of authority; still another, that people who personally feel insecure may find vicarious esteem by identifying with a king. The leader did not select one answer as the correct one; that was not the point. The point was that the question is worth thinking about because it prompts reflection on the human condition. That seemed to me to be rather the same way a group of academics might have understood the task.

Or consider the parable of the Good Samaritan. Like virtually all of Jesus' parables, it ends with a question: which of these was neighbor to the man? In the story the answer may be obvious. But a parable is also a mirror in which to observe real life, and in real life it is still the question of neighbor that animates much discussion, not only in theological circles but in wider scholarly settings such as the social sciences. A Christian sociologist might argue that it is being neighborly to the countries in Latin America to send financial aid; another might argue that it is more neighborly to promote economic self-sufficiency; it is the importance of the question on which they agree.

Motivation

Robert Merton borrowed from the classical work of Max Weber in developing his argument about Puritanism and science. Weber thought religion figured into human behavior as a motivator.[12] The image he used was of a switchman. Different religions switch the behavior of their adherents onto different tracks. Having certain questions in one's mind can be a switchman of this kind. The effect of a particular religious upbringing may be to motivate one to pursue a certain kind of question in one's research. Or, more likely, as Weber would have argued, it provides motivation of a broad sort—not the kind of motivation that says study this instead of that, but the motivation it takes to get up in the morning and get to work because life has meaning.

I am not suggesting that people actually have the questions they learned from Bible stories as children buzzing around in their heads, consciously or subconsciously telling them what is important about the world. It used to be popular to think of motives that way—to imagine that someone might embark on a study of social justice in South Africa because the story of Moses and Pharaoh had always made a troubling impression on him. But motives are more complex than that. They are not univocal, but multivocal. They speak to us with many voices. And they do not often, it seems, speak to us in clear, rational voices.

Rather, they come to us piecemeal, as the bits and pieces from which a story about why we do what we do can be constructed. Listen to what French philosopher Bertrand Very says about them: "subjective motives are not rationally, but semantically built." There are two phases, he says, in the semantic construction of motives. First: "An objective fact, a casual event, a commonplace situation is loaded with meaning. Its crude exteriority disappears. It becomes a motive for a subjectivity." And then second: "This motive joins an affective frame, not as a cause mechanically awaiting its effect, but as a sign expected to be connected with other signs to determine a decision. Entangled—as in a musical score—with other motives, its meaning gains more weight and it leads the situation towards a certain outcome."[13]

Religion figures into both phases of this process. In the first phase certain objective facts or events take on subjective meaning for us—why?—in part at least because of the framework that our religious experiences give us. We are able somehow to see the importance of things because we have a story to tell ourselves about them. Perhaps it is a story that has special importance for us because it is about God. Perhaps it is a personal story about a time of being cared for or a crisis in one's life. Then in the second phase, as motives become more complex and compel action, our stories become the musical scores, the web of interconnected signs that allow us to make sense of what we do. These are the stories in which we construct ourselves as actors. They make sense of our biographies, allowing us to integrate our lives, and see the importance of what we are presently doing, both to ourselves and to some larger body of relevant others. It is in this sense that the divine word becomes powerful as we appropriate it and make it part of our own story, an idea of course that is entirely consistent with the Christian view of redemption.

What does it mean, then, to say "living the question"? It means pursuing the intellectual life because the questions are inherently important, not because one hopes primarily to advance his or her career or even because one necessarily expects to discover a definitive answer. For the first person on my journey this meant questioning continually the value of what he was working on, even the value of the intellectual life itself. For the second person it meant thinking hard about the church's future in Germany. For the group passing around Coke and crackers it meant thinking about the joy in life and the need to understand celebration. And for the friend at the Christian college it meant taking a responsible but critical stance toward his institution and his church.

The particular questions themselves are likely to vary. What Christianity does is add seriousness to the enterprise: it says, in effect, these are serious questions that people have raised in one way or another from the beginning of time; do your part to keep them alive. The message is what Madeleine L'Engle (a writer who readily identifies herself as a Christian but who disdains the term Christian writer) has likened to the task of pouring water into a lake. The scholar's contribution is like a cupful of water: it does not perceptibly alter the lake at all, but it and thousands of others like it replenish the lake and keep the cycle of nature flowing on perpetually.[14]

Putting it differently, we might say that Christianity *sacralizes*—makes sacred—the intellectual life. It gives the questions we struggle with in our work and in our lives a larger significance. Living the question becomes possible because our questions are animated. They have life breathed into them, not literally of course but by becoming part of the stories, the webs of significance, in which we locate ourselves. Any religion, any worldview does this, and does it not just to our intellectual questions but to the questions and tasks that confront us in every part of life. And yet to say that all religions work this way does nothing to diminish the particular way in which it happens for the Christian. The questions that take on significance in the Christian's intellectual work may be, as I have argued, quite diverse. But the reason they have significance is that they are part of a particular story, embedded as it were in a particular religious tradition, and in a particular person's biography within that tradition.

Epilogue

I said at the outset that social scientists are seldom any better at forecasting the future than anyone else. Readers who have come with me to this point may be fully convinced of the truth of that assertion. But I also suggested that the point of thinking about the future is less to predict it than to give ourselves a conceptual space in which to think about the present: Where are we? Where are we headed? Where do we want to go?

The challenges facing Christianity in the United States in the twenty-first century are to a considerable degree the challenges that already face it at the end of the twentieth century. For those who think of Christianity in institutional terms, asking questions about churches and their programs and leaders, it is already evident that resources are stretched thin at the same time that the need for expanded resources has never been greater. Optimistic appraisals flow in from some quarters about rising levels of financial giving and the great extent to which religious organizations are able to enlist volunteer time and energy. On the middle-class fringes of cities in the Midwest and South, new churches seem to have sprung up in every neighborhood. And yet the pastors of these churches probably feel they have inadequate resources for the programs they would like to initiate. In declining neighborhoods and in inner cities, churches are having to close their doors in large numbers. Mission and relief efforts scarcely keep up with the demand. Specialized denominational agencies concerned with economic justice, the environment, or racial relations have for the most part been scaled back considerably. And resources are scarcely available at all for new crises and needs that may emerge in the years ahead.

Religious leaders are themselves keenly aware of the importance of resources for the future of their organizations. It is, however, with misgivings that many of them approach this topic with their constituencies. American culture is deeply dualistic in its separation of the spiritual from the material. An overwhelming majority of the public wants the churches to be more involved in helping the needy. And yet there is widespread resistance to hearing religious leaders talking about money or trying to raise support for church programs. To do so is somehow to sully what it means to be spiritual. Clearly, then, this is a challenge that requires greater study, greater understanding, and more thoughtful attention. Even if churches were able to promote the worshipful, caring sense of community to which they aspire, they would still have to concern themselves actively with the mundane work of financial solicitation and planning.

But the quest for community is, as I have argued, itself problematic. And, perhaps curiously, it is especially problematic for churches. The reason is that Christianity has always championed community—its very theology encourages believers to be a people, concerned about the needs and welfare of one another. But the church, as it has evolved in the twentieth century, is in many ways ill suited to provide community. It brings people together once a week, drawing them from broad geographic areas, and expects them to forge some intimate bond when they probably will not see each other again for seven days. It adds people to its membership rolls—the more the better—until most of them have no idea who their fellow members are. It places a speaker up front and expects everyone else to sit in rows facing that speaker, much as they would at a concert or athletic event. If interaction happens before or after the service, it does so informally, *despite* everything else that has gone on. In short, the church is an administrative convenience, created unwittingly by a combination of its history and the programs planned by its leaders. If community is going to take place there at all, it must occur against high odds.

For many people, the odds against it happening at church are sufficiently high that they have given up entirely. Were they in desperate straits, they might turn to the church. But, frankly, they are not that desperate. They have friends at work, they can call relatives on the phone, and they can join a bowling league if they need to get out. For many other people, the church actually does provide community. But what they mean is not really the church, but some group that happens to meet at the church. A prayer group, Bible study, or twelve-step meeting is where they find caring and support.

To date, the churches have been enormously successful in starting small groups, providing them with planning and materials, and retaining members because of the support these groups have to offer. But it is not inconceivable that the churches, as administrative conveniences, will have less and less to do with such groups. Sooner or later, people will discover they can hold these groups just as well in their living rooms, at work, or in the town hall. Religious leaders may then need to rethink what they mean by the church, doing so in a way that may radically challenge present conceptions.

The quest for community will also be increasingly difficult in the coming years because of the diversity and fluidity of American society. In some ways, of course, unsettled lives may be easier to mold into caring communities than ones lived in staid, familiar complacency. But Christianity in the future will be faced with much more than the task of bridging denominational, ethnic, or regional lines. Racial divisions continue to be important, despite a generation or more of efforts by religious leaders to heal these tensions, in large part because American society has come increasingly to be divided between the "haves" and the "have nots" and because this division often corresponds to racial and geographic lines of separation. If American Christianity has come some distance toward improving its relations with Judaism, there is still much to be done on that front. And new relations must increasingly be forged with Muslims and with members of other world religions. Hispanic and Asian populations bring added diversity, as do alternative life-styles and sexual orientations.

But one of the lessons from observing the past half century must be that the major lines of division within American religion are seldom static or easily discernible. Just when it appeared that denominational boundaries were beginning to erode, for example, new tensions appeared between religious liberals and religious conservatives. In the future, ideological battles are likely to be waged on numerous fronts, challenging religious leaders to be responsibly involved in these battles, but also to be ministers of reconciliation. Moreover, attention must always be given to the smaller, or less vocal traditions whose importance may be overshadowed by such battles. White American Christians have much to learn from black American Christians. Members of old-line denominations have much to learn from the smaller denominations and sects. Protestants and Catholics continue to have much to learn from each other. And the Anglo majority has much to learn from Hispanics, Asians, and other ethnic minorities.

Although community is always important in its own right, Christians in the coming decades must also be concerned about what they—their communities—stand for. Do they stand for exclusivity or an attitude of acceptance? Do they embody an ethic of service and caring? Do they bring a moral dimension to public life? Do they represent justice and mercy? Do they promote a deeper relationship to God? Do they reflect anything more than cultural Americanism? Do they encourage economic and environmental responsibility?

I have not tried to identify particular issues and suggest specific stands that Christians should take on these issues. Christianity in the future will continue to be pluralistic, but will also remain committed to the assumption that some perspectives come closer to representing divine truth than others. The role that a social scientist can play is to identify some of the social forces that may make it harder to identify the truth, or for particular groups to advocate what they regard to be the truth.

One of the greatest challenges of all is how Christianity can perpetuate its varied conceptions of the truth at a time when family life is more unstable than ever before and at a time when the intergenerational transmission of values is weaker than ever before. The problem is especially severe for the millions of children now living in poverty and being raised by unmarried or single parents. But it is also serious for the millions of children who grow up in conventional middle-class homes. Although most parents tell pollsters they are confident about how they are raising their children, they also admit that their children seem to be guided by other values, and many parents candidly express uncertainties about what should be transmitted at all. Statistics on child abuse, incest, addictions, and emotional battering all testify to the pressures under which the family is currently operating.

Under such conditions, it becomes more doubtful, as I have suggested, that young people will learn how to be Good Samaritans simply from the warmth and love they experience from their parents. It also becomes more unlikely that they will stay in the churches of their parents long enough to develop a mature conception of faith. Fears about sexually transmitted diseases and diminishing expectations in the world of work may result in cynicism and shortsightedness that the churches are especially unprepared to confront. Clearly, Christianity must be passed on to the coming generation if it is to survive at all. Just as clearly, the task of doing so must be a top priority among religious leaders. Churches may be able to do more than they are currently doing. Campus ministries and parachurch groups may need to play an increasing role. Colleges and universities must also be challenged to do their part in promoting open inquiry and in providing training about religion, morality, ethics, and human values.

The other condition that any consideration of American society must include is the growing secularization of public life itself. Although some observers deny being able to find any evidence of secularization at all, basing their arguments chiefly on public opinion polls, other notions of what secularization means continue to apply widely to American society. The trends may not be evident in opinion surveys conducted in the past twenty years, and they may not become significantly more pronounced in the next twenty years. But they are part of the longer-term processes in modern societies that can be seen clearly with the advantage of historical hindsight. In many parts of the world, governments make it increasingly difficult for religious groups to function as they would like. More complex societies look even to democratic governments to solve more and more of their problems. Economic commitments cease to be understood in religious terms and bottom-line thinking pervades more and more of personal and public life.

The challenge here is not only to ponder carefully the relationships between church and state, or to guard First Amendment freedoms, but to consider more fundamentally what it means for Christianity to be part of the public life of our nation. Should it function chiefly by informing the beliefs and values of individual citizens? Should it attempt to influence public debate through the formation of special interest groups? Should preachers become more actively involved in politics? And should religious values be excluded from, or actively promoted, in the economic sphere?

Public debate of these questions themselves has been deeply polarized in recent decades. Liberals and conservatives have occupied different ends of the spectrum. But the spectrum itself has not always been clearly defined. Nor is it clear that the debate has gotten very far. The specter of a twenty-first century in which liberals and conservatives continue to be at loggerheads with each other over such issues points vividly to the need to move beyond the present impasse.

Efforts on the part of religious groups themselves to find middle ground, to heal the breach, and to think creatively about how better to get along with each other may of course be valuable. But such efforts often strike outsiders as being mildly amusing, if not actually irrelevant to the real business of public life. It may be more difficult, and yet in the long run more rewarding, for Christianity to influence public life by effecting coalitions with secular groups and by working quietly with neighborhood groups, civic organizations, and nonprofit associations. The danger is always that the distinctive identity and values of Christianity are then compromised. But the danger of insularity that comes from not forging such coalitions may be even more serious.

If these are some of the challenges facing Christianity in the coming years, where do they leave us at present? Is it reasonable to be optimistic about the future of Christianity in the United States? Or does a pessimistic assessment make more sense?

Clearly the challenges ahead argue for caution, a sober assessment of the future, and perhaps even some level of pessimism. But in my view, taking Christianity seriously argues even more strongly for an optimistic appraisal of the future. Christianity is well institutionalized in the United States. It has vast resources at its disposal. It commands loyalty in some degree from large numbers of the population. It has well-trained and dedicated leaders. Perhaps its greatest resource, though, is the orientation it poses toward the future itself. Christianity has always included a central message of hope. As the United States embarks on a new century, that message will clearly be needed as never before.

Notes

Introduction

1. For a compelling argument about the importance of institutions, see Robert N. Bellah, Richard Madsen, William M. Sullivan, Ann Swidler, and Steven M. Tipton, *The Good Society* (New York: Knopf, 1991), pp. 3–18.

2. Karl Rahner, *Theological Investigations,* Vol. XXII (New York: Crossroad, 1991), p. 123.

3. These questions are also raised as frames of references for a consideration of the Roman Catholic tradition in John A. Grindel, *Whither the U.S. Church? Context, Gospel, Planning* (Maryknoll, N.Y.: Orbis Books, 1991).

4. American Christianity will also be faced with increasing diversity in the wider culture as a result of growth in other religious traditions; on Islam, for example, see Sameer Y. Abraham and Nabeel Abraham, eds., *Arabs in the New World: Studies on Arab American Communities* (Detroit: Wayne State University Press, 1983); Earle Waugh, ed., *The Muslim Community in North America* (Edmonton: University of Alberta Press, 1983); and Yvonne Yazbeck Haddad and Adair T. Lummis, *Islamic Values in the United States: A Comparative Study* (New York: Oxford University Press, 1987).

5. These challenges have been little studied, but see the excellent discussions of challenges facing black, Hispanic, native American, and Asian Presbyterians in Milton J. Coalter, John M. Mulder, and Louis B. Weeks, eds., *The Diversity of Discipleship: The Presbyterians and Twentieth-Century Christian Witness* (Louisville: Westminster/John Knox, 1991).

6. I do not wish to imply that secularization will be unimportant for understanding religion in the next century; it will be, but in ways that must be assessed with models other than the linear decline of religion in mind. This rethinking of

secularization theory has been much emphasized in the recent sociological litera-ture—see, for example, Phillip E. Hammond, ed., *The Sacred in a Secular Age* (Berkeley: University of California Press, 1985); Mary Douglas and Steven M. Tipton, eds., *Religion and America: Spirituality in a Secular Age* (Boston: Beacon, 1983); Bryan Wilson, *Religion in Sociological Perspective* (Oxford: Oxford University Press, 1982), and James A. Beckford, *Religion and Advanced Industrial Society* (London: Unwin Hyman, 1989).

7. The notion of discursive space employed here is indebted chiefly to the discussion of "grids of specification" in Michel Foucault, *The Archeology of Knowledge* (New York: Harper & Row, 1973).

8. Recent textbooks in sociology of religion that pay particular attention to the U.S. context and that also include excellent bibliographies include Meredith B. McGuire, *Religion: The Social Context,* 3d ed. (Belmont, Calif.: Wadsworth, 1992); and Ronald L. Johnstone, *Religion in Society: A Sociology of Religion,* 4th ed. (Englewood Cliffs, N.J.: Prentice-Hall, 1992).

Chapter 1

1. An earlier version of this chapter was originally presented at a conference on the church held at Southern Baptist Theological Seminary in Louisville, Kentucky, in 1990.

2. Emile Durkheim, *The Elementary Forms of the Religious Life* (New York: Free Press, 1965; originally published 1915).

3. Max Weber, *The Protestant Ethic and the Spirit of Capitalism* (New York: Charles Scribner's Sons, 1958; originally published 1904–5).

4. Max Weber, *The Sociology of Religion* (Boston: Beacon, 1963; originally published 1922).

5. Durkheim, *Elementary Forms,* p. 62.

6. The congregation is also being rediscovered as an important topic for research investigations; for a guide to some of this recent work, see Carl S. Dudley, Jackson W. Carroll, and James P. Wind, eds., *Carriers of Faith: Lessons from Congregational Studies* (Louisville: Westminster/John Knox, 1991). For a particularly rich ethnographic study of change in one Presbyterian congregation that also provides a perspective on wider cultural influences, see R. Stephen Warner, *New Wine in Old Wineskins: Evangelicals and Liberals in a Small-town Church* (Berkeley: University of California Press, 1988). On Roman Catholic parishes, see the historical perspectives provided in Jay P. Dolan, ed., *The American Catholic Parish: A History from 1850 to the Present,* 2 vols. (Mahwah, N.J.: Paulist Press, 1987), and the contemporary research summarized in David C. Leege, *Notre Dame Study of Catholic Parish Life* (Notre Dame: University of Notre Dame Press, 1984–1989), Reports 1–20.

7. Robert Wuthnow, *The Restructuring of American Religion: Society and Faith Since World War II* (Princeton: Princeton University Press, 1988), p. 22.

8. The study of sacred places, sacred space, and the geographic dimension of religion has attracted increased attention in recent years; see, for example, Jamie Scott and Paul Simpson-Housley, eds., *Sacred Places and Profane Spaces: Essays in the Geographics of Judaism, Christianity, and Islam* (New York: Greenwood, 1991); and Belden C. Lane, *Landscapes of the Sacred: Geography and Narrative in American Spirituality* (New York: Paulist Press, 1988).

9. For a provocative sociological discussion on the links between stories and religious communities, see Andrew M. Greeley, *Religion: A Secular Theory* (New York: Free Press, 1982).

10. Dietrich Bonhoeffer, *Life Together* (New York: Harper & Row, 1954), p. 19.

11. Communities of memory are discussed in Robert N. Bellah, Richard Madsen, William M. Sullivan, Ann Swidler, and Steven M. Tipton, *Habits of the Heart: Individualism and Commitment in American Life* (Berkeley: University of California Press, 1985), esp. pp. 152–157. I discuss communities of memory in greater detail in chapter 3.

12. A particularly vivid argument about the relationship between geography and community is presented in Kai T. Erikson, *Everything in Its Path: Destruction of Community in the Buffalo Creek Flood* (New York: Simon & Schuster, 1976).

13. For an overview of the Southern Baptist Convention, see Nancy Tatom Ammerman, *Baptist Battles: Social Change and Religious Conflict in the Southern Baptist Convention* (New Brunswick, N.J.: Rutgers University Press, 1991).

14. Black churches are described in C. Eric Lincoln and Lawrence Mamiya, *The Black Church in the African-American Experience* (Durham, N.C.: Duke University Press, 1990).

15. On the denominational character of American religion, see especially Andrew M. Greeley, *The Denominational Society: A Sociological Approach to Religion in America* (Glenview, Ill.: Scott Foresman, 1972), and Wade Clark Roof and William McKinney, *American Mainline Religion: Its Changing Shape and Future* (New Brunswick, N.J.: Rutgers University Press, 1987).

16. H. Richard Niebuhr, *The Social Sources of Denominationalism* (New York: Meridian Books, 1959; originally published 1929).

17. I have discussed the declining significance of denominationalism in my book *Restructuring of American Religion,* pp. 71–99.

18. This observation is based on the research of one of my doctoral students, Marsha Witten, who has been examining sermons by Presbyterian and Southern Baptist preachers.

19. Peter L. Berger, "A Market Model for the Analysis of Ecumenicity," *Social Research* 30 (1963), 70–79.

20. Garrison Kiellor, *Lake Wobegon Days* (New York: Viking, 1985), p. 112.

21. The point here about isomorphic symbols draws primarily on John W. Meyer and Brian Rowan, "Institutional Organizations: Formal Structure as Myth and Ceremony," *American Journal of Sociology* 83 (1977), 340–363.

22. On the conflict between liberals and conservatives, see my book *The Struggle for America's Soul: Evangelicals, Liberals, and Secularism* (Grand Rapids, Mich.: Eerdmans, 1989). See also chapter 9 for a discussion of this conflict.

23. Wayne A. Meeks, *The First Urban Christians: The Social World of the Apostle Paul* (New Haven: Yale University Press, 1983).

24. One of the most valuable typologies for thinking about the relationship between congregational size and congregational styles is that of Arlin J. Rothauge, *Sizing Up a Congregation for New Member Ministry* (New York: Episcopal Church Center, 1983). Rothauge distinguishes four types of congregation: the family church (0–50 members), the pastoral church (50–150 members), the program church (150–350 members), and the corporation church (350–500+ members).

Chapter 2

1. Two highly readable surveys of the history of the church are A. M. Renwick and A. M. Harman, *The Story of the Church,* 2d ed. (Grand Rapids, Mich.: Eerdmans, 1985); and Justo L. Gonzalez, *The Story of Christianity,* 2 vols. (New York: Harper & Row, 1985).

2. For overviews of community and the medieval church, see Francis Oakley, *The Western Church in the Later Middle Ages* (Ithaca: Cornell University Press, 1979); John Bossy, "Blood and Baptism: Kinship, Community, and Christianity in Western Europe from the Fourteenth to the Seventeenth Centuries," in *Sanctity and Secularity: The Church and the World,* ed. Derek Baker (Oxford: Basil Blackwell, 1973), pp. 129–46; and R. W. Southern, *Western Society and the Church in the Middle Ages* (London: Penguin, 1970).

3. Standard sources on the Protestant Reformation include Roland H. Bainton, *The Age of the Reformation* (Princeton: D. Van Nostrand, 1956); Owen Chadwick, *The Reformation* (London: Penguin, 1972); Lewis W. Spitz, *The Protestant Reformation, 1517–1559* (New York: Harper & Row, 1985); and Steven E. Ozment, *The Reformation in the Cities: The Appeal of Protestantism to Sixteenth-Century Germany and Switzerland* (New Haven: Yale University Press, 1985).

4. For the history of the church in the United States, see Sydney E. Ahlstrom, *A Religious History of the American People* (New Haven: Yale University Press, 1972); Edwin Scott Gaustad, *A Religious History of America* (New York: Harper & Row, 1974); and Mark A. Noll, Nathan O. Hatch, George M. Marsden, David F. Wells, and John D. Woodbridge, eds., *Eerdmans' Handbook to Christianity in America* (Grand Rapids, Mich.: Eerdmans, 1983).

5. From a nationally representative survey of 2,110 adults in the United States, which I conducted in May 1989; these and other results from the same study are reported in my book *Acts of Compassion: Caring for Others and Helping Ourselves* (Princeton: Princeton University Press, 1991).

6. Rodney Stark and Charles Y. Glock, *American Piety: The Nature of Religious Commitment* (Berkeley: University of California Press, 1968), p. 166.

7. For a brief summary of these findings, see "Charitable Giving," *Emerging Trends* 12 (January 1990), 4.

8. *The Connecticut Mutual Life Report on American Values: The Impact of Belief* (New York: Research and Forecasts, 1981).

9. "Charitable Giving," p. 4.

10. See note 5.

11. Virginia A. Hodgkinson, Murray S. Weitzman, and Arthur D. Kirsch, "From Commitment to Action: An Exploration of the Relationship between Individual Giving and the Activities of Congregations," in *Faith and Philanthropy in America: Exploring the Role of Religion in America's Voluntary Sector,* ed. Robert Wuthnow and Virginia A. Hodgkinson (San Francisco: Jossey-Bass, 1990), pp. 93–114.

12. Bellah et al., *Habits of the Heart.*

13. On the varieties of individualism, see Steven Lukes, *Individualism* (New York: Harper & Row, 1973).

14. Weber, *The Protestant Ethic and the Spirit of Capitalism.*

15. Reinhold Niebuhr, *Christ and Culture* (New York: Harper & Row, 1951).

16. Still a powerful critique of the changes in contemporary religion is Thomas

Luckmann, *The Invisible Religion: The Transformation of Symbols in Industrial Society* (New York: Macmillan, 1967).

17. For Roman Catholics, see Andrew M. Greeley and Mary G. Durkin, *Angry Catholic Women* (Chicago: Thomas More Press, 1984); for Protestants, see Wuthnow, *Restructuring of American Religion,* esp. chap. 9.

18. Roof and McKinney, *American Mainline Religion.*

19. Wuthnow, *Restructuring of American Religion,* chap. 4.

20. *Presbyterian Panel Report* (March 1989).

Chapter 3

1. On the broader characteristics of modern societies that generate questions about individual identity, see especially the empirical work presented in Alex Inkeles and David H. Smith, *Becoming Modern: Individual Change in Six Developing Countries* (Cambridge, Mass.: Harvard University Press, 1974); and Alex Inkeles, *Exploring Individual Modernity* (New York: Columbia University Press, 1983). For a provocative set of essays on these issues by scholars in a variety of disciplines, see Thomas C. Heller, Morton Sosna, and David E. Wellbery, eds., *Reconstructing Individualism: Autonomy, Individuality, and the Self in Western Thought* (Stanford: Stanford University Press, 1986). I consider these broader questions of personal identity in chapter 13.

2. The idea of institutions conferring identities on individuals has been a particularly prominent theme in the work of John W. Meyer and his associates at Stanford University; see, for example, George M. Thomas, John W. Meyer, Francisco O. Ramirez, and John Boli, *Institutional Structure: Constituting State, Society and the Individual* (Beverly Hills, Calif.: Sage, 1987); George M. Thomas, *Christianity and Culture in the 19th-Century United States: The Dynamics of Evangelical Revivalism, Nation-Building, and the Market* (Chicago: University of Chicago Press, 1988); and John Boli, *New Citizens for a New Society* (New York: Pergamon, 1989); and for a related argument, see Mary Douglas, *How Institutions Think* (Syracuse: Syracuse University Press, 1986).

3. For examples, see Roof and McKinney, *American Mainline Religion,* chap. 3; and Wuthnow, *Acts of Compassion,* chap. 5.

4. Bellah et al., *Habits of the Heart,* p. 153.

5. I discuss the role of stories in chapter 4.

6. Alasdair MacIntyre, *After Virtue: A Study in Moral Theory,* 2d (Notre Dame: University of Notre Dame Press, 1984), p. 222.

7. The church as storyteller is emphasized with vivid observational evidence in James F. Hopewell, *Congregation: Stories and Structures,* ed. Barbara G. Wheeler (Philadelphia: Fortress Press, 1987).

8. Stanley Hauerwas, "Casuistry as Narrative Art," *Interpretation* 37 (1983), 388.

9. Some readers of my work have mistakenly assumed that I believe denominationalism is a thing of the past—a "dinosaur," as one reader suggested. I have never said this and do not say it here. My argument is that denominationalism has declined in significance *relative* to other cultural divisions and modes of religious identification. Denominations as organizations remain vital and influential to the ways in which church business is conducted and the ways in which resources are distributed. A number of valuable studies of particular denominations

have appeared in recent years, including Ellen M. Rosenberg, *The Southern Baptists: A Subculture in Transition* (Knoxville: University of Tennessee Press, 1989), and D. Newell Williams, ed., *A Case Study of Mainstream Protestantism: The Disciples' Relation to American Culture, 1880–1989* (Grand Rapids, Mich.: Eerdmans, 1991). John Mulder at Louisville Presbyterian Theological Seminary is conducting an ongoing research project on Presbyterianism, as is Jay P. Dolan at the University of Notre Dame on the Roman Catholic church in the United States.

10. See especially William Kornhauser, *The Politics of Mass Society* (New York: Free Press, 1959). Tocqueville, of course, had worried about the rise of mass society more than a century earlier; see Alexis de Tocqueville, *Democracy in America* (New York: Vintage, 1945; originally published 1835), vol. II, esp. p. 12.

11. See the essays in Wade Clark Roof, ed., *World Order and Religion* (Albany: State University of New York Press, 1991).

12. The shift from local to global consciousness has been emphasized more in the sociological literature; see, for example, Peter L. Berger, Brigitte Berger, and Hansfried Kellner, *The Homeless Mind: Modernization and Consciousness* (New York: Vintage, 1973), and Peter L. Berger, *Pyramids of Sacrifice: Political Ethics and Social Change* (Garden City, N.Y.: Doubleday, 1976). On the importance of local identities for religious commitment, however, see Wade Clark Roof, *Community and Commitment* (New York: Elesevier, 1979).

13. A similar point is made in regard to American Judaism in Samuel C. Heilman and Steven M. Cohen, *Cosmopolitans and Parochials: Modern Orthodox Jews in America* (Chicago: University of Chicago Press, 1989).

14. This statement is based on information obtained in personal conversations with James Davison Hunter at the University of Viriginia about a research project he is conducting on religion and power in three advanced industrial societies. For a gripping personal account, see William E. Diehl, *The Monday Connection: A Spirituality of Competence, Affirmation, and Support in the Workplace* (San Francisco: Harper, 1991).

15. Robert Bly, *Iron John: A Book about Men* (New York: Morrow, 1990).

16. Robert Wuthnow, *Small Groups—Key to Spiritual Renewal? A National Symposium and an Exploratory Survey* (Princeton: George H. Gallup International Institute, 1990).

17. *Ibid.*

Chapter 4

1. MacKinlay Kantor, "A Girl Named Frankie," *Reader's Digest* (May 1966), 86–90.

2. Russell Hardin, *Morality within the Limits of Reason* (Chicago: University of Chicago Press, 1988).

3. On Habermas, see my discussion in Robert Wuthnow, James Davison Hunter, and Edith Kurzweil, *Cultural Analysis* (London: Routledge, 1984).

4. Hauerwas, "Casuistry as a Narrative Art," p. 380.

5. For overviews, see Kirin Narayan, *Storytellers, Saints, and Scoundrels* (Philadelphia: University of Pennsylvania Press, 1989), and John C. Hoffman, *Law, Freedom, and Story: The Role of Narrative in Therapy, Society, and Faith* (Waterloo, Ontario: Wilfrid Laurier University Press, 1986).

6. The accounts presented in the following sections are from in-depth per-

sonal interviews conducted in several different parts of the country as part of a study of individualism and altruism in the United States; all the names and other identifying information has been falsified. For a description of the research methodology and more detail on many of the characters discussed here, see my book *Acts of Compassion.*

7. See for example S. P. Oliner and P. M. Oliner, *The Altruistic Personality* (New York: Free Press, 1988).

8. These results are from my own analyses of the data from a 1982 Gallup survey of the American public. Respondents whose fathers or mothers were no longer living were instructed not to answer the question. Support for using these questions was provided by my in-depth interviews in which respondents who described their parents as caring also tended to manifest feelings of closeness to them. Of the twelve relationships examined (between six measures of charitable activity and closeness to each parent), only two were statistically significant at or beyond the .05 level. Both of the significant relationships were with the question about mothers. Inspection of percentage variations across the four categories of closeness for each parent showed small and inconsistent variations on all the questions. An examination of the joint effects of closeness to father and mother also showed no significant patterns.

9. In a three-way table involving the relationships between charitable involvement, current happiness (very versus fairly or not very), and happiness while growing up (very versus fairly or not very), both of the partial gammas for current happiness were significant at or beyond the .05 level of probability, but neither of the partial gammas for childhood happiness was significant. These results are based on a national sample of 2,110 respondents interviewed in 1989; see Wuthnow, *Acts of Compassion,* for details.

10. The strength of the various relationships between those who had experienced a personal crisis sometime in their lives and engaging in various kinds of caring activities within the past year, as measured by the gamma statistic, were: loaned money (.205), donated time to a volunteer organization (.181), helped someone with car trouble (.103), cared for someone who was sick (.244), given money to a beggar (.104), contributed money (.200), tried to stop someone from using alcohol or drugs (.355), visited someone in the hospital (.205), helped someone through a crisis (.339), taken care of an elderly relative (.149). These relations were statistically significant and of similar magnitudes for men and women. These findings are also from the national survey I conducted in 1989.

11. Gamma statistics summarizing the strength of the relations between having experienced a personal crisis and each of the other items were: agreeing that helping others causes you to discover things about yourself (.204), saying that becoming a stronger person is a major reason to be kind and caring (.125), feeling good as a major reason to be caring (.168), and receiving a great deal of fulfillment from doing things for others (.155). The relation between having experienced a personal crisis and seeing caring as a way of becoming stronger was significant for men but not for women, while the relation between having had a crisis and gaining fulfillment from helping was significant for women but not for men.

12. For example, see Roger C. Shank, *Tell Me a Story: A New Look at Real and Artificial Memory* (New York: Charles Scribner's Sons, 1990).

13. Jerome Bruner, "Life as Narrative," *Social Research* 54 (1987),

14. *Ibid.,* 31.

Chapter 5

1. Gallup Report (January–February, 1987) nos. 256–57, pp. 2–7. Apart from some survey evidence, little attention has been paid by social scientists to the character and function of public heroes. William J. Goode, *The Celebration of Heroes: Prestige as a Control System* (Berkeley: University of California Press, 1978), p. 344, suggests that heroes are often people who help others at risk to their own life, but does not pursue this line of reasoning.

2. These figures are from my study of American values; for a full report of the methodology and sample, see Wuthnow, *Acts of Compassion.*

3. No difference was present between the two groups either in the proportions who thought selfishness was an extremely serious problem in our society.

4. The gamma statistic for the relation between identifying an example of compassion and saying people are becoming more interested in helping the needy was .235.

5. The relationship between being able to think of someone who demonstrates what it means to be compassionate and feeling that one could depend on the following if one or a member of one's family were seriously ill as measured by the gamma statistic are as follows: neighbors (.146), people at work (.250), close friends (.216), community volunteers (.265), social welfare agencies (.146).

Chapter 6

1. Some ethicists suggest that heroic acts of "going beyond the call of duty" be given a special name (such as "superogation") to set them apart. See, for example, Allen Buchanan, "Justice and Charity," *Ethics* 97 (1987), 559.

2. Paul Ricoeur, *The Symbolism of Evil,* trans. E. Buchanan (Boston: Beacon, 1967).

3. Although ethics has typically fallen outside the domain of interest to sociologists, recent work in the discipline is paying increasing attention to normative issues and is reviving the interest that Durkheim, Weber, and other founding theorists showed in questions of ethics. See, for example, Alan Wolfe, *Whose Keeper? Social Science and Moral Obligation* (Berkeley: University of California Press, 1989).

4. It is also arguable that some of the ambivalence expressed toward figures such as Mother Teresa can be traced to childhood projections of feelings about one's own mother. See, for example, James J. Preston, ed., *Mother Worship: Theme and Variations* (Chapel Hill: University of North Carolina Press, 1982); Judith Ochshorn, *The Female Experience and the Nature of the Divine* (Bloomington: Indiana University Press, 1981); and Nancy Chodorow, *The Reproduction of Mothering: Psychoanalysis and the Sociology of Gender* (Berkeley: University of California Press, 1978).

5. For a philosophical defense of the same view, see Allan Gibbard, *Wise Choices, Apt Feelings* (Cambridge, Mass.: Harvard University Press, 1990).

6. Paul Ricoeur, "The Symbol Gives Rise to Thought," in *Ways of Understanding Religion,* ed. Walter H. Capps (New York: Macmillan, 1972), pp. 309–17.

Chapter 7

1. This chapter is a revision of a short essay on religious orientations that appeared in the *Encyclopedia of Sociology,* vol. 3, ed. Edgar F. Borgatta and Marie L. Borgatta (New York: Macmillan, 1992), pp. 1651–56.

2. Robert N. Bellah, *Beyond Belief: Essays on Religion in a Post-Traditional World* (New York: Harper & Row, 1970), p. 16; Clifford Geertz, *The Interpretation of Cultures* (New York: Harper & Row, 1973), pp. 90–125.

3. Much of this research is summarized in Peter Farb, *Word Play* (New York: Bantam, 1973).

4. Susanne K. Langer, *Philosophy in a New Key* (New York: Mentor, 1951).

5. Greeley, *Religion: A Secular Theory,* pp. 53–70.

6. Peter L. Berger, *The Sacred Canopy* (Garden City, N.Y.: Doubleday, 1967), p. 45.

7. Roof, *Community and Commitment.*

8. Stark and Glock, *American Piety,* p. 77.

9. Charles Y. Glock and Rodney Stark, *Religion and Society in Tension* (Chicago: Rand McNally, 1965), pp. 3–17.

10. A useful overview of this literature is found in Bernard Spilka, Ralph W. Hood, Jr., and Richard L. Gorsuch, *The Psychology of Religion: An Empirical Approach* (Englewood Cliffs, N.J.: Prentice-Hall, 1985).

11. Philip Rieff, *The Triumph of the Therapeutic: Uses of Faith after Freud* (New York: Harper & Row, 1966); Peter Clecak, *America's Quest for the Ideal Self* (New York: Oxford University Press, 1983); Christopher Lasch, *The Culture of Narcissism: American Life in an Age of Diminishing Expectations* (New York: W. W. Norton, 1978).

12. Steven M. Tipton, *Getting Saved from the Sixties: Moral Meaning in Conversion and Cultural Change* (Berkeley: University of California Press, 1982).

13. See especially Guy E. Swanson, *The Birth of the Gods: The Origin of Primitive Beliefs* (Ann Arbor: University of Michigan Press, 1960); and Guy E. Swanson, *Religion and Regime: A Sociological Account of the Reformation* (Ann Arbor: University of Michigan Press, 1967).

14. One of the more penetrating discussions of religious pluralism to appear is recent years is Mark Silk, *Spiritual Politics: Religion and America since World War II* (New York: Simon & Schuster, 1988).

15. Empirical evidence supporting this view is presented in Kevin J. Christiano, *Religious Diversity and Social Change: American Cities, 1890–1906* (Cambridge: Cambridge University Press, 1987).

16. The concept of culture as "tool kit" is developed in Ann Swidler, "Culture in Action: Symbols and Strategies," *American Sociological Review* 51 (1987), 273–86.

Chapter 8

1. An expanded version of this chapter appears as Robert Wuthnow and Matthew P. Lawson, "Social Sources of Christian Fundamentalism in the United States," in *Fundamentalisms Explained,* ed. Martin Marty and Scott Appleby (Chicago: University of Chicago Press, 1993), chap. 6.

2. The framework employed in this chapter is adapted from one previously

developed as a means of specifying the relations between social structure and major episodes of cultural change; see Robert Wuthnow, *Communities of Discourse: Ideology and Social Structure in the Reformation, the Enlightenment, and European Socialism* (Cambridge, Mass.: Harvard University Press, 1989).

3. On the defining characteristics of fundamentalism in the United States, see Nancy Tatom Ammerman, "North American Protestant Fundamentalism" in *Fundamentalisms Observed,* ed. Martin Marty and R. Scott Appleby (Chicago: University of Chicago Press, 1990), chap. 1; for historical background, see George M. Marsden, *Fundamentalism and American Culture* (Oxford: Oxford University Press, 1980); and George M. Marsden, *Understanding Fundamentalism and Evangelicalism* (Grand Rapids, Mich.: Eerdmans, 1991). For a useful discussion of how fundamentalism has been conceptualized in the sociological literature, see Frank Lechner, "Fundamentalism Revisited: A Sociological Analysis," in *In Gods We Trust,* 2d ed., ed. Thomas Robbins and Rick Anthony (New Brunswick, N.J.: Transaction, 1990), pp. 77–97.

4. The foregoing analysis draws conceptually from the general framework of church and state relations presented in David Martin, *A General Theory of Secularization* (New York: Harper & Row, 1975).

5. Mary Fulbrook, *Piety and Politics* (Cambridge: Cambridge University Press, 1985).

6. On the effects of state growth and market expansion in advanced industrial societies, see Robert Wuthnow, ed., *Between States and Markets: The Voluntary Sector in Comparative Perspective* (Princeton: Princeton University Press, 1991).

7. Following in the line of Max Weber and James Luther Adams, this argument is developed in Max L. Stackhouse, "The Space for Voluntary Associations," in *Faith and Philanthropy in America: Exploring the Role of Religion in America's Voluntary Sector,* ed. Robert Wuthnow and Virginia A. Hodgkinson (San Francisco: Jossey-Bass, 1990), chap. 2.

8. Immanuel Wallerstein, *Geopolitics and Geoculture: Essays on the Changing World-System* (Cambridge: Cambridge University Press, 1991).

9. Jerome L. Himmelstein, *To the Right: The Transformation of American Conservatism* (Berkeley: University of California Press, 1990).

10. Michael T. Hannan and John Freeman, "The Population Ecology of Organizations," *American Journal of Sociology* 82 (1977), 929–64; and Howard E. Aldrich, *Organizations and Environments* (Englewood Cliffs, N.J.: Prentice-Hall, 1979).

11. Clifford Geertz, *Local Knowledges* (New York: Viking, 1975).

12. See Lynn Davidman, *Tradition in a Rootless World: Women Turn to Orthodox Judaism* (Berkeley: University of California Press, 1991), for a study that emphasizes themes similar to those in the present chapter—the impact of modernity, the presence of diverse social niches, and the continuing quest for meaning—for Orthodox Judaism.

13. For example, a direct-mail solicitation from Ron Robison, dated October 1990, calling for the ouster of a female professor at the University of Massachusetts.

14. For examples from fundamentalist sermons, see Robert Wuthnow, "Religious Discourse as Public Rhetoric," *Communication Research* 15 (June 1988), 318–38; see also Wuthnow, *Rediscovering the Sacred: Perspectives on Religion in Contemporary Society* (Grand Rapids, Mich.: Eerdmans, 1992), chap. 3.

Chapter 9

1. Kristin Luker, *Abortion and the Politics of Motherhood* (Berkeley: University of California Press, 1984).

2. Christopher Lasch, *The True and Only Heaven* (New York: W. W. Norton, 1991).

3. Nancy Tatom Ammerman, *Bible Believers* (New Brunswick, N.J.: Rutgers University Press, 1987), p. 8.

4. Susan Harding, unpublished paper presented at a conference on fundamentalism at the University of Chicago, November 1990.

5. See especially M. M. Bakhtin, *The Dialogic Imagination,* trans. Caryl Emerson and Michael Holquist (Austin: University of Texas Press, 1981); Katerina Clark and Michael Holquist, *Mikhail Bakhtin* (Cambridge, Mass.: Harvard University Press, 1984); Gary Saul Morson and Caryl Emerson, eds., *Rethinking Bakhtin: Extensions and Challenges* (Evanston, Ill.: Northwestern University Press, 1989); David Patterson, "Bakhtin on Word and Spirit: The Religiosity of Responsibility," *Cross Currents* 41 (Spring 1991), 33–51; Frederic Jameson, *The Political Unconscious: Narrative as a Socially Symbolic Act* (Ithaca: Cornell University Press, 1981); William C. Dowling, *Jameson, Althusser, Marx: An Introduction to the Political Unconscious* (Austin: University of Texas Press, 1981).

6. Quoting Pasternak, Bakhtin writes, "The image of the world appears miraculously in the word"; M. M. Bakhtin, *Speech Genres and Other Late Essays,* trans. Vern W. McGee (Austin: University of Texas Press, 1986), p. 159.

7. Elaine Pagels, "The Social History of Satan, the 'Intimate Enemy': A Preliminary Sketch," unpublished paper presented to the Religion and Culture Workshop at Princeton University, April 1991.

8. The complex engagement of fundamentalists and evangelicals with historical criticism is chronicled in Mark A. Noll, *Between Faith and Criticism: Evangelicals, Scholarship, and the Bible in America,* 2d ed. (Grand Rapids, Mich.: Baker, 1991).

9. John Shelby Spong, *Rescuing the Bible from Fundamentalism: A Bishop Rethinks the Meaning of Scripture* (San Francisco: Harper, 1991), pp. 5, 10.

10. Diogenes Allen, *Christian Belief in a Postmodern World* (Louisville: Westminster/John Knox, 1989); David Ray Griffin and Huston Smith, *Primordial Truth and Postmodern Theology* (Albany: State University of New York Press, 1989); Edgar V. McKnight, *Post-Modern Use of the Bible: The Emergence of Reader-Oriented Criticism* (Nashville: Abingdon, 1988).

11. William Richard Stegner, *Narrative Theology in Early Jewish Christianity* (Louisville: Westminster/John Knox, 1989); Ronald F. Thiemann, *Constructing a Public Theology: The Church in a Pluralistic Culture* (Louisville: Westminster/John Knox, 1991), chap. 7; Don M. Wardlaw, ed., *Preaching Biblically* (Philadelphia: Westminster, 1983); Ernest Edward Hunt III, *Sermon Struggles: Four Methods of Sermon Preparation* (New York: Seabury, 1982).

Chapter 10

1. For a useful overview of the term public religion, see John F. Wilson, *Public Religion in American Culture* (Philadelphia: Temple University Press, 1979).

2. See especially Walther von Loewenich, *Martin Luther: The Man and His Work* (Minneapolis: Augsburg, 1982).

3. These summary references to the views of public and private found in Luther and Rousseau are based on a more extended examination in Wuthnow, *Communities of Discourse.*

4. See chapter 7.

5. For a recent overview, see Thiemann, *Constructing a Public Theology,* chap. 1.

6. Wuthnow, *Restructuring of American Religion;* Wuthnow, *The Struggle for America's Soul.* See also Steve Bruce, *A House Divided: Protestantism, Schism, and Secularization* (London: Routledge, 1990), and James Davison Hunter, *Culture Wars: The Struggle to Define America* (New York: Basic Books, 1991).

7. Among surveys indicating this division between religious liberals and conservatives is one I conducted for my study, *Acts of Compassion.*

8. *Ibid.,* esp. chap. 5.

9. Wuthnow, *Restructuring of American Religion,* esp. chap. 9.

10. On the fundamentalist-modernist controversy and its immediate aftermath, see David Harrington Watt, *A Transforming Faith: Explorations of Twentieth-Century American Evangelicalism* (New Brunswick, N.J.: Rutgers University Press, 1991), esp. chap. 2.

11. *Ibid.,* chap. 7.

12. See R. Stephen Warner, *Communities of Faith* (New York: Basic Books, forthcoming).

13. Bellah, *Beyond Belief,* p. 179.

14. Among other overviews of civil religion, see especially Gail Gehrig, *American Civil Religion: An Assessment* (Storrs, Conn.: Society for the Scientific Study of Religion Monographs, 1979).

15. Background is provided in Wuthnow, *Communities of Discourse.*

16. Wuthnow, *Acts of Compassion,* chap. 9.

Chapter 11

1. A version of this chapter was originally presented at the Center for Ethics and Public Policy in Washington, D.C., in 1991.

2. Robert C. Liebman and Robert Wuthnow, "Introduction," in *The New Christian Right: Mobilization and Legitimation,* ed. Robert C. Liebman and Robert Wuthnow (New York: Aldine, 1983), p. 1.

3. Although the phrase "New Christian Right" remains accurate as a label for the movement that emerged in the late 1970s, I shall refer mostly to the "religious Right," partly because it is no longer "new" and partly because I want to suggest ways in which the broader movement may change in the years ahead. I am, therefore, not concerned with specific organizations (such as Moral Majority or Christian Voice) but with the loosely organized movement consisting largely of conservative Christians (primarily Protestants) who are actively engaged in conservative politics.

4. The factors discussed here address the conditions I identified as having given rise to the religious Right in my *Restructuring of American Religion* and, more briefly, *The Struggle for America's Soul,* chap. 2. In those works I was attempting to account for the emergence of various conditions in American religion that came into prominence in the 1970s and 1980s, particularly the division

between religious conservatives and religious liberals. Thus, my focus here is different, both in looking more toward the future, and in dealing specifically with the religious Right. The conditions that contributed to polarization were not always the ones that nurtured the religious Right. I am, therefore, interested in how well these broader conditions help us understand the present trajectory of the religious Right.

5. The "this-worldly" orientation in American religion, I have argued, was not so much rooted in the kind of abstract theodicy that Weber identified but was framed within a discourse of "promise and peril" that became prominent in the United States after World War II and legitimated an exceptional level of religious activism; see Wuthnow, *Restructuring of American Religion*, pp. 35–53.

6. Premillennialism is often included in the very definition of fundamentalism; see, for example, Ammerman, "North American Protestant Fundamentalism," in Marty and Appleby, *Fundamentalisms Observed*, chap. 1; for historical background on the emergence and varieties of American fundamentalism, see Marsden, *Fundamentalism and American Culture*.

7. For a broader discussion of the social conditions encouraging (or discouraging) millennial orientations, see Robert Wuthnow, *Meaning and Moral Order: Explorations in Cultural Analysis* (Berkeley: University of California Press, 1987), chap. 5.

8. Wuthnow, *Restructuring of American Religion*, pp. 54–70.

9. For a brief statistical survey, see Wuthnow, *Restructuring of American Religion*, pp. 17–29.

10. Some interesting comparative evidence to this effect is presented in John Boli, "Sweden: Is There a Viable Third Sector?" in *Between States and Markets: The Voluntary Sector in Comparative Perspective*, ed. Robert Wuthnow (Princeton: Princeton University Press, 1991), chap. 4.

11. George Gallup, Jr., *Religion in America: 1990* (Princeton: Princeton Religion Research Center, 1990), complete report.

12. Wuthnow, *Restructuring of American Religion*, pp. 71–99; evidence on the weakening of denominational boundaries is also presented in Roof and McKinney, *American Mainline Religion*.

13. This cooperation should not be overemphasized; but see A. James Reichley, "Pietist Politics," in *The Fundamentalist Phenomenon*, ed. Norman J. Cohen (Grand Rapids, Mich.: Eerdmans, 1990), p. 98, for a similar argument.

14. On the Southern Baptist Convention, see Ammerman, *Baptist Battles*.

15. The concept of special purpose groups and some evidence on their growing importance in American religion is developed in Wuthnow, *Restructuring of American Religion*, pp. 100–31. See Barbara M. Yarnold, ed., *The Role of Religious Organizations in Social Movements* (Westport, Conn.: Greenwood, 1991), for some empirical evidence on the role of these organizations in the New Right and in other recent religious movements.

16. See Robert C. Liebman, "Mobilizing the Moral Majority," in Liebman and Wuthnow, *New Christian Right*, pp. 50–74, for the best discussion of these clergy networks.

17. Wuthnow, *Restructuring of American Religion*, pp. 168–72.

18. Wuthnow, *Acts of Compassion*, chap. 5; this conclusion is drawn from discriminant and multiple regression analyses of the factors distinguishing self-identified religious liberals from religious conservatives in a national survey I conducted in 1989 as part of a project on altruism and individualism in American

culture; the question and analysis were identical to the ones I used earlier in examining the 1984 data.

19. On the importance of differences in social status, see John H. Simpson, "Moral Issues and Status Politics," in Liebman and Wuthnow, *New Christian Right,* chap. 10.

20. On government growth and its consequences for religious participation, see Wuthnow, *The Struggle for America's Soul,* chap. 5.

21. See chapter 12.

22. For more detail, see Wuthnow, *The Struggle for America's Soul,* chap. 6.

23. A candid admission of this misconception is found in Kevin Phillips, "The Rise of the Religious Right," *New York Times* (March 1, 1988), p. A23.

24. Research currently in progress by James Davison Hunter at the University of Virginia suggests a relatively high level of anticlericalism in the United States generally. It is, therefore, interesting to observe a "trend" of sorts in the national leadership of the religious Right away from the parish clergy: from Jerry Falwell as a congregational pastor, to Pat Robertson as a pastor without a parish, to prominent laity such as Tim LaHaye, Beverly LaHaye, Charles Colson, and James Dobson.

25. Among the numerous studies of religious television, see especially Jeffrey K. Hadden, "Religious Broadcasting and the Mobilization of the New Christian Right," *Journal for the Scientific Study of Religion* 26 (1987), 1–24.

26. For more detail, see Wuthnow, *The Struggle for America's Soul,* chap. 6.

27. For a supportive argument that fundamentalism does not constitute a threat to basic democratic ideals in American society, see Richard John Neuhaus, "Fundamentalism and the American Polity," in Cohen, *The Fundamentalist Phenomenon,* chap. 7.

28. Wuthnow, *Restructuring of American Religion,* chap. 9.

29. For a brief commentary on the conflict between Jerry Falwell's variety of fundamentalism and that of Jim and Tammy Bakker's PTL Club, see George M. Marsden, "Defining American Fundamentalism," in Cohen, *The Fundamentalist Phenomenon,* p. 27.

30. Hodding Carter III, "Like It or Not, Religion Has a Place in Politics," *Wall Street Journal* (February 15, 1990), p. A15.

31. For evidence that this shift is already under way, see D. Shribman, "Going Mainstream: Religious Right Drops High-Profile Tactics, Works on Local Level," *Wall Street Journal* (September 26, 1989), p. 1.

Chapter 12

1. An earlier version of this chapter was presented at a conference at Baylor University held in 1991 and published in the proceedings of that conference: *Religion in the Making of Public Policy,* ed. James E. Wood, Jr. and Derek Davis (Waco, Tex.: J. M. Dawson Institute of Church-State Studies, 1991), pp. 81–99.

2. See for example Steven Bruce, *The Rise and Fall of the New Christian Right* (Oxford: Clarendon Press, 1988); James L. Guth, Ted Jelen, Lyman Kellstedt, Corwin Smidt, and Kenneth Wald, "The Politics of Religion in America: Issues for Investigation," *American Politics Quarterly* 116 (1988), 118–59; Clyde Wilcox, "America's Radical Right Revisited: A Comparison of Activists of the Christian Right in Two Decades," *Sociological Analysis* 48 (1987), 46–57; and Matthew Scully,

"Right Wing and a Prayer—Still Alive and Kicking," *Washington Times* (November 8, 1989), p. E2.

3. The term "public sphere" is usefully developed in Jürgen Habermas, *Structural Transformation of the Public Sphere* (Cambridge, Mass.: MIT Press, 1989).

4. On the limited political gains of the religious Right, see Rob Gurwitt, "The Christian Right Has Gained Political Power: Now What Does It Do?" *Governing* (October 1989), 52–58.

5. Unpublished remarks presented at a conference on the future of the religious Right sponsored by the Ethics and Public Policy Center, Washington, D.C., in November 1990.

6. Kenneth Wald, *Religion and Politics in the United States* (New York: St. Martins Press, 1987), p. 205.

7. Robert Booth Fowler, "The Failure of the New Christian Right," unpublished paper, Univesity of Wisconsin, Madison, 1990.

8. On the recent record of religious lobbies in general, a valuable source is Allen D. Hertzke, *Representing God in Washington: The Role of Religious Lobbies in the American Polity* (Knoxville: University of Tennessee Press, 1988).

9. Thiemann, *Constructing a Public Theology,* p. 32, expresses a similar point in his description of "religion's rhetorical power and political impotence."

10. E. P. Thompson, *The Making of the English Working Class* (Oxford: Oxford University Press, 1968).

11. Will Herberg, *Protestant–Catholic–Jew* (Garden City, N.Y.: Anchor, 1955).

12. On religious belief and belonging, see Gallup, *Religion in America.*

13. For a different perspective from which the same conclusion can be inferred, see Charles Colson, "From a Moral Majority to a Persecuted Minority," *Christianity Today* (May 14, 1990), 80.

14. These declines are documented in Roof and McKinney, *American Mainline Religion.*

15. Bellah et al., *Habits of the Heart.*

16. Wuthnow, *Acts of Compassion,* esp. chap. 9.

17. For a detailed look at the role of these resources in one community, see N. J. Demerath III and Rhys H. Williams, *A Bridging of Faiths: Religion and Politics in a New England City* (Princeton: Princeton University Press, 1992).

18. On these groups, see the forthcoming book by Warner, *Communities of Faith.*

19. For one classic example, see Neil J. Smelser, *Theory of Collective Behavior* (New York: Free Press, 1962).

Chapter 13

1. This chapter is an adaptation of an essay that originally appeared as "The Precarious Quest for Identity," *Religion and American Culture* 4 (1991), 3–8.

2. Psychologist Abraham Maslow once described marching in the counterpart ceremony at Harvard as one of his most intense peak experiences.

3. Robert Wuthnow, *The Consciousness Reformation* (Berkeley: University of California Press, 1976), p. 260.

4. *Self-Esteem Survey* (Princeton: Gallup Organization, 1982). I was the principal consultant on this study.

5. Wuthnow, *Acts of Compassion,* chap. 1.

6. The discussion of five examples in Mary Catherine Bateson, *Composing a Life* (New York: Atlantic Monthly Press, 1989), provides a vivid illustration.

7. For a useful assessment of the broader implications of this shift, see Anthony Giddens, *Modernity and Self-Identity: Self and Society in the Late Modern Age* (Stanford: Stanford University Press, 1991).

8. Among other discussions, see Talcott Parsons, *The Social System* (New York: Free Press, 1952), chap. 3.

9. On the changing philosophical dimensions of self identity, see Charles Taylor, *Sources of the Self: The Making of the Modern Identity* (Cambridge, Mass.: Harvard University Press, 1989).

10. Herberg, *Protestant–Catholic–Jew.*

11. An exceptionally fine study of the ways in which social and cultural changes in the United States in the period since Herberg have influenced the self-identities and religious practices of American Jews is Steven M. Cohen, *American Modernity and Jewish Identity* (New York: Tavistock, 1983).

12. Roland Robertson, *Meaning and Change: Explorations in the Cultural Sociology of Modern Societies* (New York: New York University Press, 1978), esp. chap. 5.

13. See chapter 2.

14. Bellah et al., *Habits of the Heart.*

Chapter 14

1. Milan Kundera, *The Book of Laughter and Forgetting* (New York: Penguin, 1981), p. 37.

2. U.S. Bureau of the Census, *Historical Statistics* (Washington, D.C.: Government Printing Office, 1975), part 1.

3. Everett Ladd, "Americans at Work," *Public Opinion* (August–September 1981), 21.

4. The names are fictional, but the people and the comments quoted are real, taken from interviews conducted in 1991 as part of a project on religion and economic life under a grant from the Lilly Endowment.

5. "Leisure," *Index to International Public Opinion* (1985–1986), 446.

6. *Ibid.*

7. "Time at Premium for Many Americans; Younger People Feel the Pressures Most," *Gallup Poll* (November 4, 1990).

8. Susan E. Shank, "Women and the Labor Market: The Link Grows Stronger," *Monthly Labor Review* III (1988), 3–8.

9. For evidence, see Arlie Hochschild, *The Second Shift* (New York: Viking, 1990).

10. My own analysis of data collected for my book, *Acts of Compassion.*

11. Indeed, the survey showed that people who thought of money as a problem were *more likely* to consider it essential for themselves than were people who did not regard it as a problem. The proportions who considered making a lot of money absolutely essential declined from 11 percent among those who thought emphasizing money is an extremely serious problem in our society, to only 5 percent among those who did not think of it as a problem.

12. Susan Chance, "My Generation," *Seventeen* (October 1989), 99–106.

13. Annual surveys conducted in the United States among college freshmen have documented an upward trend in the proportions who list being very well

off financially among their top values: from 39 percent who did so in 1970 to 71 percent in 1985; see Cooperative Institutional Research Program, *The American Freshman: Twenty Year Trends, 1966–1985* (Los Angeles: Higher Education Research Institute, 1987), p. 97.

14. National Center for Health Statistics, *Health Promotion and Disease Prevention: United States, 1985* (Washington, D.C.: U.S. Department of Health and Human Services), series 10, no. 163, p. 30.

15. Anetta Miller, "Stress on the Job," *Newsweek* (April 25, 1988), 40–45; Emily T. Smith, "Stress: The Test Americans Are Failing," *Business Week* (April 18, 1988), 74–76.

16. Robert Teitelman, "Does Prosperity Kill?" *Forbes* (August 26, 1985), 127–128.

17. Horace Bushnell, *Work and Play* (London: Alexander Strahan, 1864), pp. 21–22.

Chapter 15

1. This chapter is a revision of an article published in *Cross Currents* 5 (1990), 17–30.

2. Tanya Gazdik, "Some Colleges Warn Students That Cult-Like Methods Are Being Used by Christian Fundamentalist Groups," *Chronicle of Higher Education* (November 15, 1989), 1. Although this article is perhaps distinctive in its bias against religion on campus, the more general climate of distrust toward religion fostered by the modern university has been a subject of much commentary in recent years. For example, see Page Smith, *Killing the Spirit* (New York: Viking, 1990), and Ronald H. Nash, *The Closing of the American Heart* (Lexington: Probe Books, 1990).

3. Richard Hofstadter, *Anti-Intellectualism in American Life* (New York: Vintage, 1962).

4. For a summary of these studies, see Wuthnow, *Restructuring of American Religion,* esp. chap. 7.

5. One view of this process is presented in James Tunstead Burtchaell, "The Decline and Fall of the Christian College," *First Things* (April 1991), 16–29, and (May 1991), 30–38. For other assessments, see William J. Byron, "Identity and Purpose in Church Related Higher Education," *Susquehanna University Studies* 12 (1984), 21–29, and Robert R. Parsonage, ed., *Church-Related Higher Education* (Valley Forge, Penn.: Judson Press, 1978).

6. For interesting material on the relationship between evangelicalism and higher education, both among students and in the wider society, I refer the reader to the following works by James Davison Hunter: "The New Class and the Young Evangelicals," *Review of Religious Research* 22 (1980), 155–69; *American Evangelicalism: Conservative Religion and the Quandary of Modernity* (New Brunswick, N.J.: Rutgers University Press, 1983); and *Evangelicalism: The Coming Generation* (Chicago: University of Chicago Press, 1987).

7. Wuthnow, *Restructuring of American Religion,* chap. 7.

8. Results from a national survey of the American population I conducted in 1989; see Wuthnow, *Acts of Compassion,* chap. 5.

9. Robert K. Merton, *Science, Technology and Society in Seventeenth-Century England* (New York: Harper & Row, 1970; originally published 1938).

10. Wuthnow, *Meaning and Moral Order,* chap. 8.

11. Elaine Pagels, *Adam, Eve, and the Serpent* (New York: Random House, 1988).

12. Weber, *The Sociology of Religion*.

13. Bertrand Very, "Milan Kundera or the Hazards of Subjectivity," *Review of Contemporary Fiction* 9 (Summer 1989), 81.

14. Madeleine L'Engle, *Walking on Water* (New York: Farrar, Straus, and Giroux, 1981), chap. 3.

Selected
Bibliography

Abraham, Sameer Y., and Nabeel Abraham, eds. *Arabs in the New World: Studies on Arab American Communities*. Detroit: Wayne State University Press, 1983.

Ahlstrom, Sydney A. *A Religious History of the American People*. New Haven: Yale University Press, 1972.

Allen, Diogenes. *Christian Belief in a Postmodern World*. Louisville: Westminster/John Knox, 1989.

Ammerman, Nancy Tatom. *Bible Believers*. New Brunswick, N.J.: Rutgers University Press, 1987.

———. *Baptist Battles: Social Change and Religious Conflict in the Southern Baptist Convention*. New Brunswick, N.J.: Rutgers University Press, 1991.

Bainton, Roland H. *The Age of the Reformation*. Princeton: D. Van Nostrand, 1956.

Bakhtin, M. M. *The Dialogic Imagination*. Translated by Caryl Emerson and Michael Holquist. Austin: University of Texas Press, 1981.

Beckford, James A. *Religion and Advanced Industrial Society*. London: Unwin Hyman, 1989.

Bellah, Robert N. *Beyond Belief: Essays on Religion in a Post-Traditional World*. New York: Harper & Row, 1970.

Bellah, Robert N., Richard Madsen, William M. Sullivan, Ann Swidler, and Steven M. Tipton. *Habits of the Heart: Individualism and Commitment in American Life*. Berkeley: University of California Press, 1985.

———. *The Good Society*. New York: Knopf, 1991.

Berger, Peter L. "A Market Model for the Analysis of Ecumenicity." *Social Research* 30 (1963), 70–79.

————. *Pyramids of Sacrifice: Political Ethics and Social Change*. Garden City, N.Y.: Doubleday, 1976.

————. *The Sacred Canopy*. Garden City, N.Y.: Doubleday, 1967.

Berger, Peter L., Brigitte Berger, and Hansfried Kellner. *The Homeless Mind: Modernization and Consciousness*. New York: Vintage, 1973.

Boli, John. *New Citizens for a New Society*. New York: Pergamon, 1989.

Bonhoeffer, Dietrich. *Life Together*. New York: Harper & Row, 1954.

Bossy, John. "Blood and Baptism: Kinship, Community, and Christianity in Western Europe from the Fourteenth to the Seventeenth Centuries." In *Sanctity and Secularity: The Church and the World,* edited by Derek Baker, pp. 129–46. Oxford: Basil Blackwell, 1973.

Bruce, Steve. *The Rise and Fall of the New Christian Right*. Oxford: Clarendon Press, 1988.

————. *A House Divided: Protestantism, Schism, and Secularization*. London: Routledge, 1990.

Burtchaell, James Tunstead. "The Decline and Fall of the Christian College." *First Things* (April 1991), 16–29, and (May 1991), 30–38.

Byron, William J. "Identity and Purpose in Church Related Higher Education." *Susquehanna University Studies* 12 (1984), 21–29.

Chadwick, Owen. *The Reformation*. London: Penguin, 1972.

Chodorow, Nancy. *The Reproduction of Mothering: Psychoanalysis and the Sociology of Gender*. Berkeley: University of California Press, 1978.

Christiano, Kevin J. *Religious Diversity and Social Change: American Cities, 1890–1906*. Cambridge: Cambridge University Press, 1987.

Clark, Katerina, and Michael Holquist. *Mikhail Bakhtin*. Cambridge, Mass.: Harvard University Press, 1984.

Clecak, Peter. *America's Quest for the Ideal Self*. New York: Oxford University Press, 1983.

Coalter, Milton J., John M. Mulder, and Louis B. Weeks, eds. *The Diversity of Discipleship: The Presbyterians and Twentieth-Century Christian Witness*. Louisville: Westminster/John Knox, 1991.

Cohen, Norman J., ed. *The Fundamentalist Phenomenon*. Grand Rapids, Mich.: Eerdmans, 1990.

Cohen, Steven M. *American Modernity and Jewish Identity*. New York: Tavistock, 1983.

Davidman, Lynn. *Tradition in a Rootless World: Women Turn to Orthodox Judaism*. Berkeley: University of California Press, 1991.

Demerath, N. J., III and Rhys H. Williams. *A Bridging of Faiths: Religion and Politics in a New England City*. Princeton: Princeton University Press, 1992.

Dolan, Jay P., ed. *The American Catholic Parish: A History from 1850 to the Present*. 2 vols. New York: Paulist Press, 1987.

Douglas, Mary. *How Institutions Think*. Syracuse: Syracuse University Press, 1986.

Douglas, Mary, and Steven M. Tipton, eds. *Religion and America: Spirituality in a Secular Age*. Boston: Beacon, 1983.

Dowling, William C. *Jameson, Althusser, Marx: An Introduction to the Political Unconscious*. Austin: University of Texas Press, 1981.

Dudley, Carl S., Jackson W. Carroll, and James P. Wind, eds. *Carriers of Faith: Lessons from Congregational Studies*. Louisville: Westminster/John Knox, 1991.

Durkheim, Emile. *The Elementary Forms of the Religious Life*. New York: Free Press, 1965. Originally published 1915.

Erikson, Kai T. *Everything in Its Path: Destruction of Community in the Buffalo Creek Flood*. New York: Simon & Schuster, 1976.

Farb, Peter. *Word Play*. New York: Bantam, 1973.

Foucault, Michel. *The Archeology of Knowledge*. New York: Harper & Row, 1973.

Fulbrook, Mary. *Piety and Politics*. Cambridge: Cambridge University Press, 1985.

Gallup, George, Jr. *Religion in America: 1990*. Princeton: Princeton Religion Research Center, 1990.

Gaustad, Edwin Scott. *A Religious History of America*. New York: Harper & Row, 1974.

Geertz, Clifford. *The Interpretation of Cultures*. New York: Harper & Row, 1973.

———. *Local Knowledges*. New York: Viking, 1975.

Gehrig, Gail. *American Civil Religion: An Assessment*. Storrs, Conn.: Society for the Scientific Study of Religion Monographs, 1979.

Giddens, Anthony. *Modernity and Self-Identity: Self and Society in the Late Modern Age*. Stanford: Stanford University Press, 1991.

Glock, Charles Y., and Rodney Stark. *Religion and Society in Tension*, Chicago: Rand McNally, 1965.

Gonzalez, Justo L. *The Story of Christianity*. 2 vols. New York: Harper & Row, 1985.

Goode, William J. *The Celebration of Heroes: Prestige as a Control System*. Berkeley: University of California Press, 1978.

Greeley, Andrew M. *The Denominational Society: A Sociological Approach to Religion in America*. Glenview, Ill.: Scott Foresman, 1972.

———. *Religion: A Secular Theory*. New York: Free Press, 1982.

Greeley, Andrew M., and Mary G. Durkin, *Angry Catholic Women*. Chicago: Thomas More Press, 1984.

Griffin, David Ray, and Huston Smith. *Primordial Truth and Postmodern Theology*. Albany: State University of New York Press, 1989.

Grindel, John A. *Whither the U.S. Church? Context, Gospel, Planning*. Maryknoll, N.Y.: Orbis Books, 1991.

Guth, James L., Ted Jelen, Lyman Kellstedt, Corwin Smidt, and Kenneth Wald. "The Politics of Religion in America: Issues for Investigation." *American Politics Quarterly* 116 (1988), 118–59.

Habermas, Jürgen. *Structural Transformation of the Public Sphere*. Cambridge, Mass.: MIT Press, 1989.

Haddad, Yvonne Yazbeck, and Adair T. Lummis. *Islamic Values in the United States: A Comparative Study*. New York: Oxford University Press, 1987.

Hammond, Phillip E., ed. *The Sacred in a Secular Age*. Berkeley: University of California Press, 1985.

Heilman, Samuel C., and Steven M. Cohen. *Cosmopolitans and Parochials: Modern Orthodox Jews in America*. Chicago: University of Chicago Press, 1989.

Heller, Thomas C., Morton Sosna, and David E. Wellbery, eds. *Reconstructing Individualism: Autonomy, Individuality, and the Self in Western Thought*. Stanford: Stanford University Press, 1986.

Herberg, Will. *Protestant–Catholic–Jew*. Garden City, N.Y.: Anchor, 1955.

Hertzke, Allen D. *Representing God in Washington: The Role of Religious Lobbies in the American Polity*. Knoxville: University of Tennessee Press, 1988.

Himmelstein, Jerome L. *To the Right: The Transformation of American Conservatism*. Berkeley: University of California Press, 1990.

Hofstadter, Richard. *Anti-Intellectualism in American Life*. New York: Vintage, 1962.

Hopewell, James F. *Congregation: Stories and Structures*. Edited by Barbara G. Wheeler. Philadelphia: Fortress Press, 1987.

Hunt, Earnest Edward, III. *Sermon Struggles: Four Methods of Sermon Preparation*. New York: Seabury, 1982.

Hunter, James Davison. "The New Class and the Young Evangelicals." *Review of Religious Research* 22 (1980), 155–69.

———. *American Evangelicalism: Conservative Religion and the Quandary of Modernity*. New Brunswick, N.J.: Rutgers University Press, 1983.

———. *Evangelicalism: The Coming Generation*. Chicago: University of Chicago Press, 1987.

———. *Culture Wars: The Struggle to Define America*. New York: Basic Books, 1991.

Inkeles, Alex. *Exploring Individual Modernity*. New York: Columbia University Press, 1983.

Inkeles, Alex, and David H. Smith. *Becoming Modern: Individual Change in Six Developing Countries*. Cambridge, Mass.: Harvard University Press, 1974).

Jameson, Frederic. *The Political Unconscious: Narrative as a Socially Symbolic Act*. Ithaca: Cornell University Press, 1981.

Johnstone, Ronald L. *Religion in Society: A Sociology of Religion*. 4th ed. Englewood Cliffs, N.J.: Prentice-Hall, 1992.

Kornhauser, William. *The Politics of Mass Society*. New York: Free Press, 1959.

Lane, Belden C. *Landscapes of the Sacred: Geography and Narrative in American Spirituality*. New York: Paulist Press, 1988.

Langer, Susanne K. *Philosophy in a New Key*. New York: Mentor, 1951.

Lasch, Christopher. *The Culture of Narcissism: American Life in an Age of Diminishing Expectations*. New York: W. W. Norton, 1978.

———. *The True and Only Heaven*. New York: W. W. Norton, 1991.

Leege, David C. *Notre Dame Study of Catholic Parish Life*. Notre Dame: University of Notre Dame, 1984–1989, Reports 1–20.

L'Engle, Madeleine. *Walking on Water*. New York: Farrar, Straus, and Giroux, 1981.

Liebman, Robert C., and Robert Wuthnow, eds. *The New Christian Right: Mobilization and Legitimation*. New York: Aldine, 1983.

Lincoln, C. Eric, and Lawrence Mamiya. *The Black Church in the African-American Experience*. Durham, N.C.: Duke University Press, 1990.

Loewenich, Walther von. *Martin Luther: The Man and His Work*. Minneapolis: Augsburg, 1982.

Luckmann, Thomas. *The Invisible Religion: The Transformation of Symbols in Industrial Society*. New York: Macmillan, 1967.

Luker, Kristin. *Abortion and the Politics of Motherhood*. Berkeley: University of California Press, 1984.

Lukes, Steven. *Individualism*. New York: Harper & Row, 1973.

Marsden, George M. *Fundamentalism and American Culture*. Oxford: Oxford University Press, 1980.

———. *Understanding Fundamentalism and Evangelicalism*. Grand Rapids, Mich.: Eerdmans, 1991.

Marty, Martin E., and Scott Appleby, eds. *Fundamentalisms Explained*. Chicago: University of Chicago Press, 1993.

McGuire, Meredith B. *Religion: The Social Context*. 3d ed. Belmont, Calif.: Wadsworth, 1992.

McKnight, Edgar V. *Post-Modern Use of the Bible: The Emergence of Reader-Oriented Criticism*. Nashville: Abingdon, 1988.

Meeks, Wayne A. *The First Urban Christians: The Social World of the Apostle Paul*. New Haven: Yale University Press, 1983.

Merton, Robert K. *Science, Technology and Society in Seventeenth-Century England*. New York: Harper & Row, 1970. Originally pubilshed 1938.

Meyer, John W., and Brian Rowan. "Institutional Organizations: Formal Structure as Myth and Ceremony." *American Journal of Sociology* 83 (1977), 340–63.

Morson, Gary Saul, and Caryl Emerson, eds. *Rethinking Bakhtin: Extensions and Challenges*. Evanston, Ill.: Northwestern University Press, 1989.

Nash, Ronald H. *The Closing of the American Heart*. Lexington: Probe Books, 1990.

Niebuhr, H. Richard. *The Social Sources of Denominationalism*. New York: Meridian Books, 1959. Originally published 1929.

———. *Christ and Culture*. New York: Harper & Row, 1951.

Noll, Mark A. *Between Faith and Criticism: Evangelicals, Scholarship, and the Bible in America*. 2d ed. Grand Rapids, Mich.: Baker, 1991.

Noll, Mark A., Nathan O. Hatch, George M. Marsden, David F. Wells, and John D. Woodbridge, eds. *Eerdmans' Handbook to Christianity in America*. Grand Rapids, Mich.: Eerdmans, 1983.

Oakley, Francis. *The Western Church in the Later Middle Ages*. Ithaca: Cornell University Press, 1979.

Ochshorn, Judith. *The Female Experience and the Nature of the Divine*. Bloomington: Indiana University Press, 1981.

Oliner, S. P., and P. M. Oliner. *The Altruistic Personality*. New York: Free Press, 1988.

Ozment, Steven E. *The Reformation in the Cities: The Appeal of Protestantism to Sixteenth-Century Germany and Switzerland*. New Haven: Yale University Press, 1985.

Pagels, Elaine. *Adam, Eve, and the Serpent*. New York: Random House, 1988.

Parsonage, Robert R., ed. *Church-Related Higher Education*. Valley Forge, Penn.: Judson Press, 1978.

Patterson, David. "Bakhtin on Word and Spirit: The Religiosity of Responsibility." *Cross Currents* 41 (Spring 1991), 33–51.

Preston, James J., ed. *Mother Worship: Theme and Variations*. Chapel Hill: University of North Carolina Press, 1982.

Rahner, Karl. *Theological Investigations*. Vol. XXII. New York: Crossroad, 1991.

Renwick, A. M., and A. M. Harman. *The Story of the Church*. 2d ed. Grand Rapids, Mich.: Eerdmans, 1985.

Ricoeur, Paul. *The Symbolism of Evil*. Translated by E. Buchanan. Boston: Beacon, 1967.

———. "The Symbol Gives Rise to Thought." In *Ways of Understanding Religion*, edited by Walter H. Capps. pp. 309–17. New York: Macmillan, 1972.

Rieff, Philip. *The Triumph of the Therapeutic: Uses of Faith after Freud*. New York: Harper & Row, 1966.

Robertson, Roland. *Meaning and Change: Explorations in the Cultural Sociology of Modern Societies*. New York: New York University Press, 1978.

Roof, Wade Clark. *Community and Commitment*. New York: Elesevier, 1979.

———, ed. *World Order and Religion*. Albany: State University of New York Press, 1991.

Roof, Wade Clark, and William McKinney. *American Mainline Religion: Its Changing Shape and Future*. New Brunswick, N.J.: Rutgers University Press, 1987.

Rosenberg, Ellen M. *The Southern Baptists: A Subculture in Transition*. Knoxville: University of Tennessee Press, 1989.

Rothauge, Arlin J. *Sizing Up a Congregation for New Member Ministry*. New York: Episcopal Church Center, 1983.

Scott, Jamie, and Paul Simpson-Housley, eds. *Sacred Places and Profane Spaces: Essays in the Geographics of Judaism, Christianity, and Islam*. New York: Greenwood, 1991.

Silk, Mark. *Spiritual Politics: Religion and America since World War II*. New York: Simon & Schuster, 1988.

Smith, Page. *Killing the Spirit*. New York: Viking, 1990.

Southern, R. W. *Western Society and the Church in the Middle Ages*. London: Penguin, 1970.

Spilka, Bernard, Ralph W. Hood, Jr., and Richard L. Gorsuch. *The Psychology of Religion: An Empirical Approach*. Englewood Cliffs, N.J.: Prentice-Hall, 1985.

Spitz, Lewis W. *The Protestant Reformation, 1517–1559*. New York: Harper & Row, 1985.

Spong, John Shelby. *Rescuing the Bible from Fundamentalism: A Bishop Rethinks the Meaning of Scripture*. San Francisco: Harper, 1991.

Stark, Rodney, and Charles Y. Glock, *American Piety: The Nature of Religious Commitment*. Berkeley: University of California Press, 1968.

Stegner, William Richard. *Narrative Theology in Early Jewish Christianity*. Louisville: Westminster/John Knox, 1989.

Swanson, Guy E. *The Birth of the Gods: The Origin of Primitive Beliefs*. Ann Arbor: University of Michigan Press, 1960.

———. *Religion and Regime: A Sociological Account of the Reformation*. Ann Arbor: University of Michigan Press, 1967.

Swidler, Ann. "Culture in Action: Symbols and Strategies." *American Sociological Review* 51 (1987), 273–86.

Taylor, Charles. *Sources of the Self: The Making of the Modern Identity*. Cambridge, Mass.: Harvard University Press, 1989.

Thiemann, Ronald F. *Constructing a Public Theology: The Church in a Pluralistic Culture*. Louisville: Westminster/John Knox, 1991.

Thomas, George M. *Christianity and Culture in the 19th-Century United States: The Dynamics of Evangelical Revivalism, Nation-Building, and the Market*. Chicago: University of Chicago Press, 1988.

Thomas, George M., John W. Meyer, Francisco O. Ramirez, and John Boli. *Institutional Structure: Constituting State, Society and the Individual*. Beverly Hills, Calif.: Sage, 1987.

Thompson, E. P. *The Making of the English Working Class*. Oxford: Oxford University Press, 1968.

Tipton, Steven M. *Getting Saved from the Sixties: Moral Meaning in Conversion and Cultural Change*. Berkeley: University of California Press, 1982.

Tocqueville, Alexis de. *Democracy in America*. 2 vols. New York: Vintage, 1945; Orginally published 1835.

Wald, Kenneth. *Religion and Politics in the United States*. New York: St. Martins Press, 1987.

Wallerstein, Immanuel. *Geopolitics and Geoculture: Essays on the Changing World-System*. Cambridge: Cambridge University Press, 1991.

Wardlaw, Don M., ed. *Preaching Biblically*. Philadelphia: Westminster, 1983.

Warner, R. Stephen. *New Wine in Old Wineskins: Evangelicals and Liberals in a Small-town Church*. Berkeley: University of California Press, 1988.

————. *Communities of Faith*. New York: Basic Books, forthcoming.

Watt, David Harrington. *A Transforming Faith: Explorations of Twentieth-Century American Evangelicalism*. New Brunswick, N.J.: Rutgers University Press, 1991.

Waugh, Earle, ed. *The Muslim Community in North America*. Edmonton: University of Alberta Press, 1983.

Weber, Max. *The Protestant Ethic and the Spirit of Capitalism*. New York: Charles Scribner's Sons, 1958. Originally published 1904–1905.

————. *The Sociology of Religion*. Boston: Beacon, 1963. Originally published 1922.

Wilcox, Clyde. "America's Radical Right Revisited: A Comparison of Activists of the Christian Right in Two Decades." *Sociological Analysis* 48 (1987), 46–57.

Williams, D. Newell, ed. *A Case Study of Mainstream Protestantism: The Disciples' Relation to American Culture, 1880–1989*. Grand Rapids, Mich.: Eerdmans, 1991.

Wilson, Bryan. *Religion in Sociological Perspective*. Oxford: Oxford University Press, 1982.

Wilson, John F. *Public Religion in American Culture*. Philadelphia: Temple University Press, 1979.

Wolfe, Alan. *Whose Keeper? Social Science and Moral Obligation*. Berkeley: University of California Press, 1989.

Wuthnow, Robert. *The Restructuring of American Religion: Society and Faith Since World War II*. Princeton: Princeton University Press, 1988.

————. *The Struggle for America's Soul: Evangelicals, Liberals, and Secularism*. Grand Rapids, Mich.: Eerdmans, 1989.

————. *Acts of Compassion: Caring for Others and Helping Ourselves*. Princeton: Princeton University Press, 1991.

————. *Rediscovering the Sacred: Perspectives on Religion in Contemporary Society*. Grand Rapids, Mich.: Eerdmans, 1992.

————. ed. *Between States and Markets: The Voluntary Sector in Comparative Perspective*. Princeton: Princeton University Press, 1991.

Wuthnow, Robert, and Virginia A. Hodgkinson, eds. *Faith and Philanthropy in America: Exploring the Role of Religion in America's Voluntary Sector*. San Francisco: Jossey-Bass, 1990.

Yarnold, Barbara M., ed. *The Role of Religious Organizations in Social Movements*. Westport, Conn.: Greenwood, 1991.

Index